THE

ANATOMY

OF A

DISH

THE

ANATOMY

OF A

DISH

DIANE FORLEY

with

CATHERINE YOUNG

PHOTOGRAPHS BY VICTOR SCHRAGER

DESIGN BY DOYLE PARTNERS

ARTISAN
NEW YORK

Published by Artisan
A Division of Workman Publishing Company, Inc.
708 Broadway
New York, New York 10003
www.artisanbooks.com

Library of Congress Cataloging-in-Publication Data

Forley, Diane.
  The anatomy of a dish / by Diane Forley with Catherine
Young; photographs by Victor Schrager.
      p. cm.
Includes index.
  ISBN 1-57965-189-5
  1. Cookery. I. Young, Catherine. II. Title.
  TX651 .F624   2002
  641.5—dc21   2002074580

Printed in Italy

10 9 8 7 6 5 4 3 2 1

First printing

Book design by Doyle Partners

To my husband,
Michael,
and our daughter,
Olivia

contents

**Lemon Verbena—
the restaurant's
namesake**

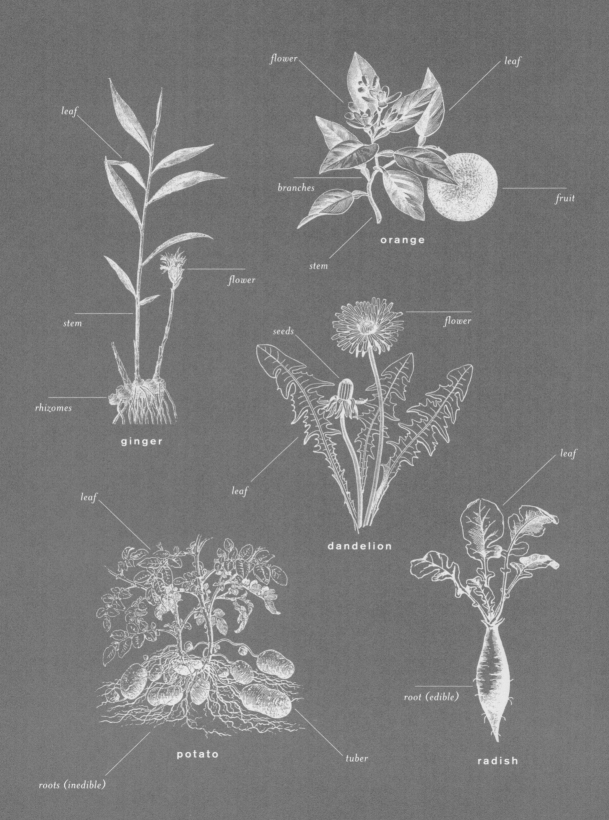

flower

leaf

branches

fruit

stem

orange

leaf

flower

stem

rhizomes

ginger

seeds

flower

leaf

dandelion

leaf

leaf

root (edible)

tuber

potato

roots (inedible)

radish

why
botanical study

As a chef, I was drawn to the possibilities of better understanding the culinary world through a study of botanical classification—a system that identifies physical relationships among plants. It is a complex and evolving system, and authorities in the field don't always agree on the finer points. However, the general relationships that it provides prompted me to ask myself, why not explore culinary relationships from this perspective? I came to realize that exploring the connections between flavor and structure, and bridging the gap between the culinary and botanical languages, were key to retrieving a sense of the interrelatedness of the natural world. Shared anatomical characteristics identified in the botanical world offered a way of understanding how to cook.

Each part of a plant that we eat and enjoy has a designated role in nature that perpetuates the life cycle of the plant. Our awareness of the complex relationships among the plants we eat gets lost in the cooking categories of fruits, vegetables, and grains. The word *vegetable*, for example, is not a botanical term. It is, rather, a nonscientific grouping of edible plant parts. Fruits and seeds are distinguished from vegetables in their popularly accepted definition despite the common understanding that some vegetables (tomatoes, squash) are actually fruit. Beans and grains are, in fact, all seeds.

The search for the connection between the botanical and the culinary worlds has provided a way to join my interests in various cultural and ethnic traditions while allowing intuitive and experimental possibilities. I do this not to make cooking substitutions or flavor combinations foolproof or formulaic, but to reestablish a connection to the natural world and to gain a broader understanding of how and what we eat. This study is a work in progress. I enter into it as an accomplished cook and an eager student of botany. My hope is that this book will encourage interpretive, creative liberties with the recipes and provide the means for the invention and discovery that make cooking so satisfying.

my garden and my kitchen

I had been looking at restaurant sites for months. Then in the fall of 1993, my brother and I stepped into a junk-filled empty lot behind a low-ceilinged tavern space on New York's Irving Place and discovered what would become my restaurant's garden. At that time, I knew very little about gardening, but I found magical the chance for a bit of green under blue sky. I knew immediately that I wanted to surround people with the herbs and leaves that excite me as a cook. I named the restaurant Verbena to keep this vision constantly in my mind as my early hopes met daily challenges.

I worked on the restaurant, designing, cooking, and hiring, and began to educate myself about planting and growing.

My garden grew, developing its own personality. Tarragon, lamb's lettuce, nasturtium, rosemary, and (of course) verbena shared the soil with tomatoes, cucumbers, and sweet peas. Transparent panels guarding pressed leaves separated garden tables, and an oak leaf hydrangea finally matured into a shady prima donna.

My food evolved too. The Union Square farmers' market three blocks away allowed me to join locally grown produce with my own herbs. Trips to the market filled my baskets with produce and, increasingly, my head with wonder at the intricacies of planting, growing, and harvesting. The year, once divided into four seasons, became broken into shorter increments identified not by date but by the availability of the first spring asparagus, early-summer strawberries, August corn, and late-summer heirloom tomatoes.

The first four years, I was content with my novice efforts at growing vegetables and flowers as I turned Verbena's courtyard into a cottage garden. But that changed one morning in 1999. I was tidying in the walk-in refrigerator, replacing jumbled crates and discarding vegetables past their prime, when I spotted a bunch of salsify that had sprouted. I was about to throw it out when I noticed that the new leaves atop the stalks looked like endive.

Verbena's
courtyard garden

All the plants in the Solanaceae family share a structurally similar flower. The tubular flowers resemble bells.

tomato

potato

chile pepper

I walked out of the refrigerator, still holding the salsify, and bumped into a farmer delivering potatoes. He was not at all surprised by the similarity and explained that endive and salsify are members of the same plant family. Botanists (unlike cooks) classify plants, edible and not, by looking at structural similarities, paying special attention to the shape of the flower the plant produces. For example, a flower with petals that tightly surround a circular center characterizes the Compositae family. Daisies and sunflowers, endive and salsify are all in this family.

Potatoes, he explained, indicating the crate at his feet, are members of the Solanaceae family, as are tomatoes. The five-petaled flowers that they share is the reason that Europeans were initially reluctant to eat these native American fruits and vegetables. In Europe, the flower was an indicator of an inedible species—highly toxic belladonna is in the Solanaceae family.

I was fascinated. My fifteen years in professional kitchens had prepared me to group vegetables by plant part (leaf, root, and so on), and by seasonal availability. This was an entirely different system. I was thrilled and curious about what implications, if any, this alternative way of categorizing vegetables might have for my cooking. The next day, I raided the gardening section of the local bookstore, looking not for books on growing plants, but for books on scientifically classifying them.

Poring over vegetal family trees, I began to realize that there were culinary connections I had never considered but that reverberated throughout my kitchen. The Liliaceae family, for example, contains garlic, chives, and leeks. It also contains asparagus. Although I had always thought of asparagus as part of the vaguely defined group of spring vegetables—artichokes, morels, and fava beans—I had to acknowledge a certain likeness with its botanical kin. Asparagus has a delicate but strong and penetrating flavor. Thinking back over my menus, I realized that asparagus and leeks are a favorite pairing of mine. I remembered leek chowder with asparagus

Botanists look for structural similarities when they classify plants. Cooks, on the other hand, group plants based upon what parts you eat, when you eat them, and culinary similarities.

petunia

belladonna

tobacco

The Solanaceae family is also referred to as nightshade and contains many poisonous plants. Whether bearing culinary stars or the stuff of poison potions, the flowers look alike.

and pea shoots and fricassee of asparagus, leeks, and snow peas served with lemon porridge. My cooking, it seems, was one step ahead of my learning.

Botanical family groupings trace legacies of flavor and nutrition that I needed to understand more fully. I went through my recipe files and noted the plant family of each vegetable in every dish. Also I began to pay more attention to what part of the plants I was using—shoots, stalks, flowers, leaves, roots, and/or bulbs. It was like a crossword puzzle, with each discovery lending clues and authority to the next. I had begun learning a new language and was starting to bridge the gap between the botanical and culinary worlds.

This foray into the plant world has extended my ability to comprehend my culinary choices and consider them from another point of view. I look with new eyes at dishes that pair formerly unrecognized botanical relatives and appreciate great dishes that involve no such combinations from a freshly knowl-

edgeable vantage. It has made me think harder about taste and culinary compatibility and about the relationship between plant anatomy and seasonal availability. I am able to pay greater attention to what I cook, when, how, and why.

My approach to cooking has always been rigorous and multifaceted. It is engaged but not necessarily apparently systematic. Each dish I create is an exercise in bringing together information and skills. I seek to understand traditional approaches so that I can integrate them in a way that makes sense to me. I struggle to master chemistry so that I can control the transformations foods undergo through the application of heat. And now I study the botanical relationships of plants in order to reinvigorate old culinary associations and tempt me to new ones. This book is an invitation to share my experience and knowledge through practice and reflection.

about this book

For me, vegetables, fruits, and grains define flavor, texture, and sensibility in cooking. Meats, fish, and poultry play supporting roles. The progression of recipes in this book reflects this attitude. I begin with preparations that focus on individual vegetables, move to vegetable combinations, including salads, stews, soups, and savory pastries, then on to compositions that feature fish, meat, and poultry, and end with desserts. Charts, photographs, and drawings throughout illustrate my intersecting viewpoints as a practiced chef and eager student of botany.

The unfolding of the recipes also mirrors the way I use ingredients to build dishes and menus. The first part of the book offers recipes, which I view as technique studies or building blocks. These form a foundation for the rest of the book. Arranged by defining ingredient, this admittedly incomplete gathering of recipes is intended to focus attention on individual vegetables and cooking methods. Notes suggest other vegetables that might be similarly handled and complementary preparations found later in the book.

From single vegetables, I move to the vegetable combinations in the next section, which are a little more complicated. The salads, soups and stews, pastas, tarts, savory pastries, and breads found here work as main courses, though I tend to serve them as first courses or light meals, or as side dishes in more elaborate menus. Again, the notes with these recipes suggest links with others in the book.

In the next section the focus shifts from individual dishes to meals. I begin here to work with fish, meat, and poultry. These dishes can be cooked as they are, but many of them can also be viewed as components to be broken apart and reshuffled. I note menu alternatives, some tried and some considered.

Desserts are the focus of part three. These recipes are intended both as complements to the savory dishes that precede them and as stand-alone treats.

I have charted the flavor spectrum found in each botanical family, illustrated the association between seasonal availability and the culinary plant part (fruit, leaf, root, and so on), and singled out certain culinarily important vegetables (mushrooms, lettuces) to compare in the light of their botanical relationships. In addition, I have diagrammed the scientific hierarchy used by botanists to discuss plants—all in order to provide a framework for the recipes I have developed over the years.

plum

Rosaceae

The rose family
contains many
flowering and
fruiting trees and
shrubs; many
are ornamental.

CHERRY, APRICOT
PEACH, PLUM
APPLE, PEAR
QUINCE
STRAWBERRY
BLACKBERRY
RASPBERRY

carrot

Umbelliferae

All have flowers
in umbels, or flat
or round-topped
clusters whose
original flower stems
originate from a
single point. Many
are vegetables or
aromatic herbs.

PARSNIP, CARROT
FENNEL, CELERY
CELERIAC
PARSLEY ROOT
PARSLEY
CARAWAY, DILL
ANISE, CORIANDER

cress

Cruciferae

These plants have a
four-petaled flower that
resembles a cross.

KALE, COLLARDS
CABBAGE, BROCCOLI
BRUSSELS SPROUT
KOHLRABI
HORSERADISH
RUTABAGA, RADISH
TURNIP, GARDEN CRESS
WATERCRESS

dandelion

Compositae

The sunflower or
daisy family, one
of the largest
plant families, is
characterized
by tight, circular
flower clusters
and ray petals.

ENDIVE, CHICKORY
ARTICHOKE
RADICCHIO
DANDELION, SALSIFY
LETTUCE (ROMAINE
BIBB, ICEBERG)
CHAMOMILE
TARRAGON

beet

Chenopodiaceae

The goosefoot family has
inconspicuous flowers
and a weedy or
shrublike nature.

SPINACH
SWISS CHARD, BEET
QUINOA

cucumber

Cucurbitaceae

The gourd family
consists of vines
with yellow or white
flowers and large,
fleshy, typically
seedy fruits.

MELON
CUCUMBER
PUMPKIN
SQUASH

leek

Liliaceae

The lily family grows
mainly from bulbs,
corms, and rhizomes.
Flowers are showy
with six equal
segments.

ASPARAGUS
CHIVE, LEEK
GARLIC, ONION
SHALLOT

millet

Gramineae

The grass family
comprises most
grain crops,
the seed being the
edible plant part.

CORN, BARLEY
WHEAT, RICE
MOST GRAINS

sage

Labiatae

Considered
members of the
mint family, these
are easily
recognized by the
square stem, leaves
in opposite pairs,
and spikelike flowers.
Many of the group
are aromatic with
attractive foliage.

OREGANO
MARJORAM
LAVENDER, BASIL
MINT, ROSEMARY
SAGE, THYME

potato

Solanaceae

Most bear flowers
that are star- or
saucer-shaped and
five-petaled.
Fruits are berries
or capsules.
Although plants are
frequently rank
smelling and stems
and leaves poisonous,
the fruit of many
varieties is important
culinarily.

PEPPER
POTATO, EGGPLANT
TOMATO
TOMATILLO
GOOSEBERRY

sweet pea

Leguminosae

This family has
a variety of flower
formations;
most common
are flowers
shaped like
butterflies. All bear
seeds in pods
called legumes.

PEANUT
SWEET PEA, BEAN
LENTIL

orange

Rutaceae

The family includes
many shrubs and
trees, particularly the
citrus variety. Most
have oil glands in
leaves or other parts
and are aromatic.

LEMON, LIME
KUMQUAT
GRAPEFRUIT
ORANGE

the plant kingdom

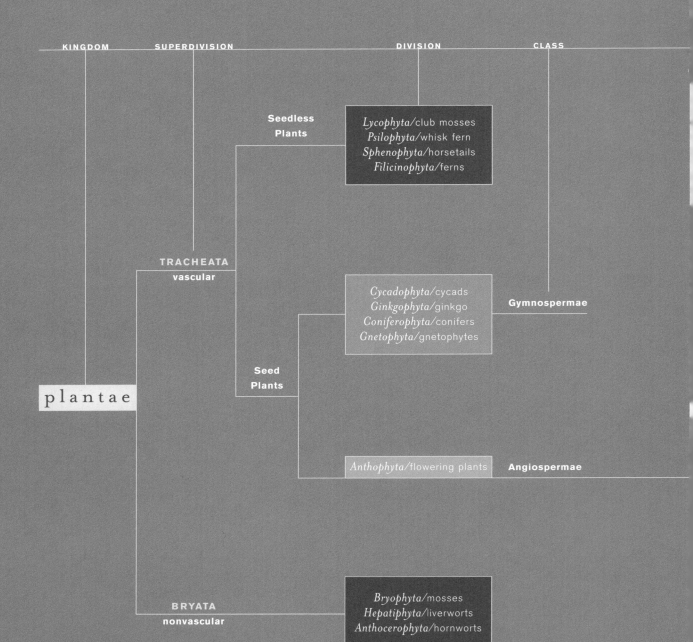

KINGDOM	SUPERDIVISION	DIVISION	CLASS

Seedless Plants

Lycophyta/club mosses
Psilophyta/whisk fern
Sphenophyta/horsetails
Filicinophyta/ferns

TRACHEATA
vascular

Cycadophyta/cycads
Ginkgophyta/ginkgo
Coniferophyta/conifers
Gnetophyta/gnetophytes

Gymnospermae

Seed Plants

plantae

Anthophyta/flowering plants   **Angiospermae**

BRYATA
nonvascular

Bryophyta/mosses
Hepatiphyta/liverworts
Anthocerophyta/hornworts

Carl Linnaeus (1707–1778) was the early botanist who created the two-part
Latin naming system (known as the binomial system) used to classify genus and
species for plants. He based his system on observation of similarities in flower
structure (a plant's reproductive organ). Likenesses in overall anatomy are now
also considered. Current technology using gene sequence studies has taken
classification to more complex levels but still relies on Linnaeus's naming system.

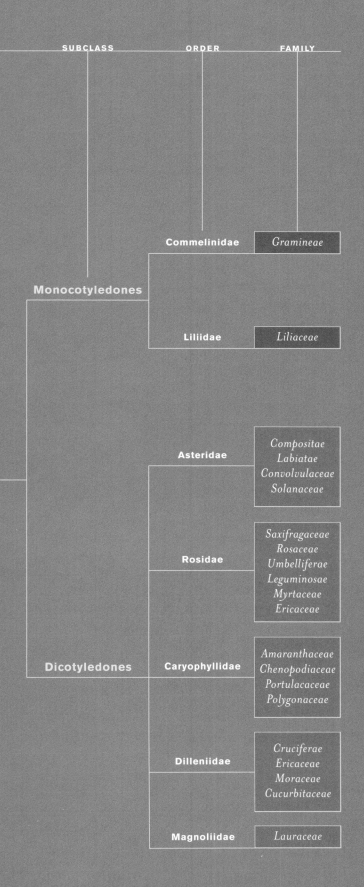

SUBCLASS	ORDER	FAMILY

Monocotyledones

Commelinidae · *Gramineae*

Liliidae · *Liliaceae*

Dicotyledones

Asteridae · *Compositae*
Labiatae
Convolvulaceae
Solanaceae

Rosidae · *Saxifragaceae*
Rosaceae
Umbelliferae
Leguminosae
Myrtaceae
Ericaceae

Caryophyllidae · *Amaranthaceae*
Chenopodiaceae
Portulacaceae
Polygonaceae

Dilleniidae · *Cruciferae*
Ericaceae
Moraceae
Cucurbitaceae

Magnoliidae · *Lauraceae*

flower study

CHENOPODIACEAE

goosefoot

beet

oak of jerusalem

spinach

sea orach

COMPOSITAE

chicory

daisy

artichoke

marigold

dandelion

sunflower

CRUCIFERAE

cress

wallflower

mustard

aubretia

kohlrabi

CUCURBITACEAE

cucumber

gourd

squash

red berried bryony

waterspout gourd

GRAMINEAE

barley

spelt

rye

tall cottongrass

millet

LABIATAE

cedronella

mint

lavender

rosemary

coleus

sage

Plants, both edible and inedible, within botanical families tend to share flower characteristics.

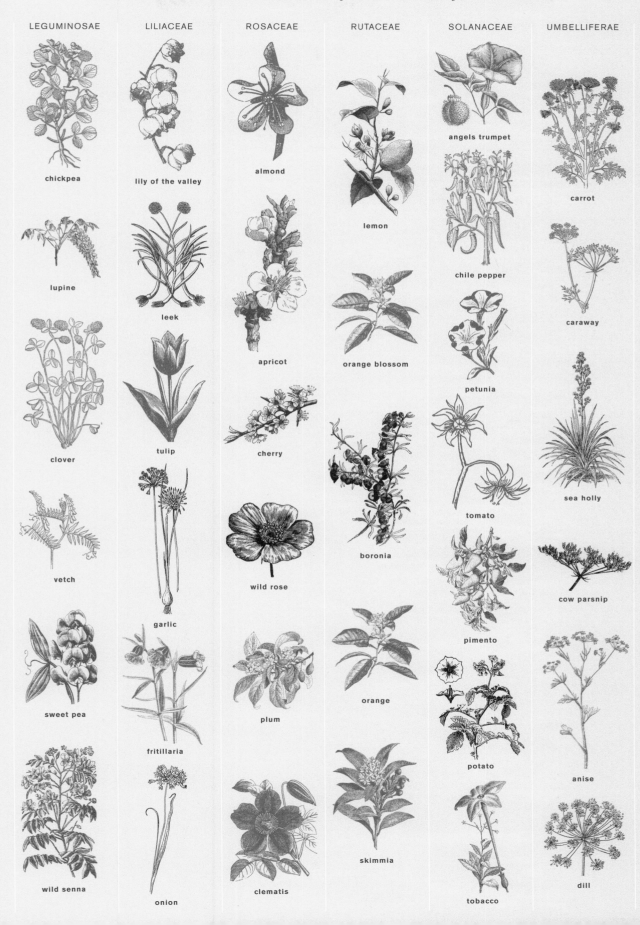

| LEGUMINOSAE | LILIACEAE | ROSACEAE | RUTACEAE | SOLANACEAE | UMBELLIFERAE |

chickpea

lily of the valley

almond

lemon

angels trumpet

carrot

lupine

leek

apricot

orange blossom

chile pepper

caraway

clover

tulip

cherry

petunia

sea holly

vetch

garlic

wild rose

boronia

tomato

cow parsnip

sweet pea

fritillaria

plum

orange

pimento

anise

wild senna

onion

clematis

skimmia

potato

dill

tobacco

parts of the plant
and when we eat them

This chart indicates seasonal availability in most of the United States.
It is arranged by plant part. Note the relationship between the time
of year when a vegetable ripens and what part of the plant is eaten
(leaf, bulb, root, flower, or seed).

Leaves

*The season for
leaf vegetables
begins in the
spring and
extends through
the fall until the
first frost.*

SEASON	PLANT	FAMILY
April–August	LAMB'S LETTUCE/MÂCHE	Valerianaceae
April–October	CHICORY	Compositae
April–October	SORREL	Polygonaceae
May–August	VERBENA	Verbenaceae
May–September	CRESS	Cruciferae
May–September	DANDELION	Compositae
May–September	LETTUCE	Compositae
May–September	PARSLEY	Umbelliferae
May–October	ARUGULA	Cruciferae
May–November	COLLARD	Cruciferae
May–November	SPINACH	Chenopodiaceae
June–August	PURSLANE	Portulacaceae
June–October	ESCAROLE	Compositae
June–November	BEET	Chenopodiaceae
July–October	KOHLRABI	Cruciferae
July–October	RADICCHIO	Compositae
August–October	KALE	Cruciferae
August–October	SWISS CHARD	Chenopodiaceae
August–November	RED CABBAGE	Cruciferae
September–November	BRUSSELS SPROUT	Cruciferae
September–November	CABBAGE	Cruciferae
September–May	ENDIVE	Compositae

Stalks

SEASON	PLANT	FAMILY
April–June	**ASPARAGUS**	Liliaceae
April–June	**RHUBARB**	Polygonaceae
July–October	**FENNEL**	Umbelliferae
August–October	**CELERY**	Umbelliferae

Stalk vegetables tend to mature in the spring and summer.

Bulbs

SEASON	PLANT	FAMILY
April–June; September–November	**LEEK**	Liliaceae
May–September	**SCALLION**	Liliaceae
June–October	**GARLIC**	Liliaceae
August–November	**SHALLOT**	Liliaceae
August–November	**ONION**	Liliaceae

Bulb vegetables are most commonly gathered in the spring and fall; like flower bulbs, they must be planted in the fall before the first frost.

Roots

SEASON	PLANT	FAMILY
May–October	**RADISH**	Cruciferae
June–February	**SALSIFY**	Compositae
June–November	**BEET**	Chenopodiaceae
June–November	**CARROT**	Umbelliferae
June–November	**HORSERADISH**	Cruciferae
July–October	**TURNIP**	Cruciferae
September–April	**CELERY ROOT**	Umbelliferae
September–December	**RUTABAGA**	Cruciferae
September–January	**PARSNIP**	Umbelliferae

Root vegetables are generally ready for harvest in the fall, but because they can be successfully stored for long periods, they are perceived as year-round vegetables, particularly popular in the fall and winter.

Fruit

Fruits, both sweet and savory, begin to become available in the spring, but some varieties don't ripen until just before the first frost.

SEASON	PLANT	FAMILY
January–March	**KUMQUAT**	Rutaceae
January–April	**AVOCADO**	Lauraceae
April–September	**CAPE GOOSEBERRY**	Solanaceae
April–September	**TOMATILLO**	Solanaceae
May–July	**STRAWBERRY**	Rosaceae
May–August	**BLACKBERRY**	Rosaceae
May–September	**CUCUMBER**	Cucurbitaceae
June	**RED CURRANT**	Saxifragaceae
June	**BLACK CURRANT**	Saxifragaceae
June–July	**BLUEBERRY**	Ericaceae
June–July	**CHERRY**	Rosaceae
July	**APRICOT**	Rosaceae
July–August	**NECTARINE**	Rosaceae
July–September	**RASPBERRY**	Rosaceae
July–September	**PEACH**	Rosaceae
July–September	**SUMMER SQUASH**	Cucurbitaceae
July–September	**TOMATO**	Solanaceae
July–October	**GREEN BEAN**	Leguminosae
July–October	**YELLOW BEAN**	Leguminosae
July–November	**EGGPLANT**	Solanaceae
July–December	**APPLE**	Rosaceae
August–October	**PLUM**	Rosaceae
August–October	**SWEET PEPPER**	Solanaceae
August–October	**HOT PEPPER**	Solanaceae
August–November	**PEAR**	Rosaceae
September–October	**GRAPE**	Vitaceae
September–October	**WATERMELON**	Cucurbitaceae
September–October	**BUTTERNUT SQUASH**	Cucurbitaceae
September–November	**PUMPKIN**	Cucurbitaceae
October–December	**QUINCE**	Rosaceae
November	**CRANBERRY**	Ericaceae

parts of the plant and when we eat them

SEASON	PLANT	FAMILY
December–March	GRAPEFRUIT	Rutaceae
December–March	ORANGE	Rutaceae
December–March	LEMON	Rutaceae
December–March	LIME	Rutaceae

Flowers

SEASON	PLANT	FAMILY
January–October	BROCCOLI	Cruciferae
May–October	ARTICHOKE	Compositae
July–October	CAULIFLOWER	Cruciferae

Flower vegetables include thistles and buds of plants; they mature in late spring and summer.

Tubers

SEASON	PLANT	FAMILY
July–November	POTATO	Solanaceae
August–November	YELLOW POTATO	Solanaceae
September–November	SWEET POTATO	Convolvulaceae
October–March	SUNCHOKE	Compositae

Like root vegetables, tubers are available from late summer through the winter.

Seeds

SEASON	PLANT	FAMILY
April–May	PEAS	Leguminosae
July–September	SWEET CORN	Gramineae
September–October	FAVA BEAN	Leguminosae
October–November	SUNFLOWER SEED	Compositae

Seed vegetables include legumes and grains; they are generally available in the spring and fall, after the flower has bloomed and the fruits have formed.

PART I

building a dish

vegetable studies

The cooking techniques in this chapter draw on lessons I learned early in my cooking career in the vegetable-laden stations of "prep" and "garde manger." Some of the preparations such as Flame-Roasted Peppers are easy and familiar; others such as Artichoke Griddle Cakes are more involved and unusual. Most can be used as part of other recipes later in the book as well as on their own. All illustrate a specific vegetable cooking technique (blanching, roasting, braising, pickling, and so on), and all are essential to my culinary grammar.

This first group of recipes, arranged alphabetically by main ingredient, offers culinary techniques applied to various vegetables. The recipes are accompanied by notes that suggest other applications for the highlighted techniques and links to complementary dishes.

I have explained what needs to be done in each instance. The recipes have been tested and retested and can be trusted, but not blindly. When you cook, you should enter the kitchen fully aware. Consider the equipment and the weather. Be aware that cooking times can differ depending on the age and condition of ingredients and that stoves are quirky. Cooking is, or should be, an engaging pursuit. A good cook is always mindful of what is happening in the pan and views recipes not as formulas, but as trails to intermediate and final goals.

For most of us, this sort of focus and understanding does not come naturally. Awareness is a kitchen technique, and, like any other, must be practiced. Working with the recipes in this somewhat quirky assembly of my favorite vegetable and fruit cooking techniques can be a good place to start.

Cabbage and radish are members of the Cruciferae family; endive and artichoke, the Compositae

braised artichokes

MAKES 8

Braised artichokes are delicious served warm or cold dressed simply with some of the braising liquid mixed with extra virgin olive oil. Use them to make Artichoke Bruschetta (page 31), Artichoke Gratin (page 32), and Couscous with Artichokes and Gigante Beans (page 89). Slice them into salads or onto sandwiches. I fry the leaves as garnish (see page 32) and use the braising liquid as a base for soups, sauces, and vinaigrettes.

2 lemons, halved
8 artichokes
2 tablespoons extra virgin olive oil
1 small onion, peeled and diced
1 small carrot, peeled and diced
1 stalk celery, diced
Kosher salt and freshly ground
  black pepper
Sachet filled with:
  ½ head garlic
  1 teaspoon fennel seeds
  1 tablespoon coriander seeds
  1 tablespoon black peppercorns
  5 cloves
  stems from 1 bunch parsley
  a handful of basil sprigs
  4 sprigs thyme
½ cup dry white wine
½ cup rice wine vinegar

My inspiration for this recipe is the classic French aromatic olive-oil-and-wine-flavored braise known as a *barigoule*. I have lightened this version to allow for a clearer artichoke taste.

Trimming the artichokes.
Squeeze the juice of the lemons into a large bowl. Add about 8 cups of water and the lemon rinds. Pull off enough of the tough outer leaves of the artichokes so that you can see the bend in the remaining leaves. Using a serrated knife, cut off the tip of the leaves at the indentation. Discard the leaf tops. Pull off any remaining dark green leaves. Cut off the stems (alternatively, trim and then peel them) and place the artichokes in enough lemon water to cover them.

Preparing the braising liquid.
Heat the oil in a large pot over medium heat. Add the onion, carrot, celery, and salt and pepper to taste and cook until the oil begins to sizzle and the vegetables soften slightly, about 5 minutes. Add ½ cup water and the sachet and cook, stirring occasionally, until the vegetables are tender, about 15 minutes more.

Add the wine, increase the heat to medium-high, and simmer until the liquid is reduced by half, about 10 minutes. Add the vinegar.

Braising the artichokes.
Drain the artichokes and add them to the pot. Cover with water (about 6 cups) and season with salt and pepper. Lay a paper towel over the artichokes to keep them submerged, cover the pan with a lid, and gently simmer over medium heat until the artichokes can be easily pierced with a sharp knife, about 30 minutes. Remove from the heat and allow the artichokes to cool in the braising liquid.

Once they are cool, remove the artichokes from the liquid (set the pan aside). Pull away and reserve the pale green leaves from each artichoke. Discard the purple-tinged innermost leaves, which are bitter, and the hairy choke (it pulls out easily once the artichoke is cooked). Return the hearts to the cooking broth. Store the artichokes in the broth and the leaves separately. Covered and refrigerated, they will keep for at least a week.

steamed artichokes

MAKES 4

4 artichokes
1 lemon, halved
2 tablespoons extra virgin olive oil
2 cloves garlic, peeled
1 bay leaf
A handful of mixed fresh herbs,
    such as flat-leaf parsley, mint,
    basil, thyme, and tarragon
Kosher salt

This is an extremely easy way to cook artichokes.
It is not as flavorful as braising them in aromatic broth
(see page 30), but it is less work.

Trimming the artichokes.
Pull off the tough outer leaves. Cut off the leaves
where they bend, then cut off the stems. Rub the tops
and bottoms with half the lemon. Place the artichokes
in a single layer in a large pot. Add the olive oil.

Slice the remaining lemon half. Add the lemon slices
to the pot along with the garlic, bay leaf, herbs,
and enough water to come halfway up the artichokes.
Season with salt, cover, and simmer until the artichokes can be easily pierced with a sharp knife, about
40 minutes. Serve warm or chilled with or without
further cleaning. Reserve the pale inner leaves (not
the bitter purple ones) for other recipes (see the
sidebar, page 30).

artichoke bruschetta

SERVES 4 AS AN HORS D'OEUVRE

4 slices country bread (or 8 slices
    baguette)
About ¾ cup extra virgin olive oil
Kosher salt and freshly ground
    black pepper
4 braised or steamed artichoke
    hearts (see page 30 or above),
    chopped
2 cloves garlic, peeled and
    chopped
1½ tablespoons chopped tarragon
½ cup olive oil or to taste
Juice of 2 lemons

Artichoke puree, here used to top bruschetta, is also
good spooned over fish or stirred into pesto. The word
bruschetta is derived from the Italian *bruscare*—to
coal-roast—a reference to the toasted or grilled bread
that is the common denominator of all bruschetta.

Making the croutons.
Preheat the oven to 375°F.

Place the bread in a single layer on a baking sheet.
Brush or sprinkle the bread with about 2 tablespoons
of olive oil, season with salt and pepper, and toast in
the oven, turning each piece once, until golden and
crunchy, about 25 minutes.

Assembling the bruschetta.
Combine the artichoke hearts, garlic, and tarragon in
a small bowl. Using a fork, blend in olive oil to taste,
about ½ cup plus 2 tablespoons. Season with the
lemon juice and salt and pepper. Serve spooned onto
the croutons.

*Vegetable purees
combined with olive
oil and seasoned with
garlic, herbs, and
lemon make tasty
bruschetta toppings.
Bean or bell pepper
purees and Roasted
Eggplant Puree
(page 41) and Kale
Pesto (page 44) are
also good toppings.*

artichoke gratin

SERVES 4 TO 6

A gratin dish is a shallow baking vessel. Its shape is critical to the preparation of a marvelous genre of crisp-topped but creamy vegetable dishes. I make many different types of gratins. Braised fennel, celery, celery root, and chard stems all are nice topped either with bread crumbs or cheese or both. Sautéed Mushrooms (page 48) are also good this way.

Hearts and pale green inner leaves of 6 braised or steamed artichokes (see page 30 or 31)
7 ounces robiola cheese
1 cup heavy cream
2 tablespoons chopped flat-leaf parsley
2 tablespoons chopped tarragon
2 tablespoons chopped mint
Kosher salt and freshly ground black pepper
2 tablespoons butter (plus additional for greasing the dish), softened
1 cup Homemade Bread Crumbs (page 127)

This gratin, like most, can be made ahead and frozen; reheat it in a preheated 350°F oven for about 45 minutes. It makes a simple but lovely supper served with an herb omelet and an arugula salad.

Preheat the oven to 400°F.

Slice the artichoke hearts. Separate the leaves. Place the hearts and leaves in a bowl, add the cheese, cream, parsley, tarragon, and mint, and mix well. Season with salt and pepper and mix well.

Grease a medium gratin dish or a baking dish (an 8-inch square will work well). Dust the dish with about ¼ cup of the bread crumbs, then spoon in the artichoke mixture, spreading it in an even layer. Mix the butter with the remaining bread crumbs and spread the mixture over the artichokes.

Bake the gratin until it is golden and bubbly, about 45 minutes. Serve warm.

fried artichoke leaves

MAKES ABOUT 2 CUPS

Fried foods, like salads, are best seasoned with sea salt. Serve these as a snack, toss them in salads, or use them to garnish Artichoke Bruschetta (page 31).

Pale green leaves from 8 braised or steamed artichokes (see page 30 or 31)
Olive oil (blended or extra virgin)
Fine sea salt

These crunchy chips have a sweet taste if you remove them from the oil when they are golden; if they get too dark, they become bitter. Season the leaves with sea salt when they are still warm.

Dry the leaves on paper towels. Heat about ½ inch oil in a large saucepan over medium heat until hot; a thermometer should indicate a temperature of about 340°F and a leaf dropped into the oil should sizzle. Fry the leaves in small batches, stirring occasionally, until they are crisp, golden, and somewhat translucent (like potato chips), about 3 minutes per batch. Remove the leaves from the oil with a slotted spoon and drain on paper towels; sprinkle with salt while still warm. Serve warm or at room temperature.

artichoke griddle cakes

MAKES FOUR 8-INCH PANCAKES

⅔ cup all-purpose flour
¼ cup potato starch
⅓ teaspoon baking powder
Kosher salt and freshly ground
   black pepper
¼ cup milk
2 eggs
6 tablespoons butter, melted and
   cooled
8 braised or steamed artichoke
   hearts and their leaves
   (see page 30 or 31)
2 tablespoons extra virgin olive oil
4 shallots, peeled and thinly sliced
2 tablespoons chopped tarragon

This is a favorite recipe of mine. Be sure to follow the instructions precisely when making the batter, which will not work well if it is over- or underbeaten.

Making the batter.
Combine the flour, starch, baking powder, and a pinch each of salt and pepper in a bowl.

Combine the milk and eggs in a medium bowl. Using an electric mixer, beat on medium-high speed for 2 minutes, or until the mixture is thick and frothy. Add the butter, then reduce the speed to low and add the dry ingredients.

Making the griddle cakes.
Preheat the oven to 250°F.

Thinly slice the artichoke hearts. Separate the leaves. Heat a very thin film of oil in an 8-inch skillet, preferably nonstick, over medium heat. Add the shallots and cook, stirring occasionally, until they begin to soften and brown, about 5 minutes. Increase the heat to medium-high and add the artichoke hearts and leaves. Cook until they begin to brown, about 3 minutes more. Add the tarragon and cook for 1 minute.

Transfer all but a quarter of the artichoke mixture to a bowl. Return the pan to the heat and add a quarter of the batter (about ½ cup). Season with salt and pepper and cook until the cake is set and the bottom golden, about 5 minutes. Flip the griddle cake (this is most easily done by inverting the cake onto a plate, then sliding it back into the pan) and cook until the second side is golden, about 3 minutes more. Keep the cake warm in the oven while you cook the remaining cakes, wiping out the skillet after each one and adding a little more oil. Serve warm.

Serve artichoke griddle cakes with poached eggs for brunch. Topped with an herb salad and accompanied by a confit of shrimp (page 138), artichoke griddle cakes become an elegant appetizer.

asparagus

poached eggs in asparagus nests

SERVES 2

1 pound jumbo asparagus, ends
  trimmed
Kosher salt
¼ cup extra virgin olive oil
Freshly ground black pepper
4 eggs
1 tablespoon chopped flat-leaf
  parsley

In this recipe you braise the shaved asparagus in a mixture of oil and water, and then poach the eggs in the emulsified asparagus broth. Serve the eggs on the asparagus, as if the thin shavings were noodles. Add a drizzle of Asparagus Vinaigrette (page 35) to reinforce and vary the asparagus flavor.

Preparing the asparagus.
Using a vegetable peeler, shave the asparagus stems into thin strips; trim the tips. Reserve the shavings and tips separately.

Blanch the asparagus tips in boiling salted water just until they are tender, about 3 minutes, then refresh in ice water, drain, and set aside.

Braising the asparagus.
Divide the asparagus shavings between two small skillets (alternatively, use one large skillet—the presentation just won't be as tidy). Add 2 tablespoons of the olive oil and ¼ cup water to each. Season with salt and pepper. Bring to a simmer over medium-high heat, reduce the heat to medium-low, and cook until the asparagus shavings are just tender, 3 minutes or so. (If the asparagus is beginning to look dry, add a tablespoon of water).

Poaching the eggs.
Crack 2 eggs into each skillet and season with salt and pepper. Reduce the heat and simmer very gently, uncovered, until the egg whites are set, about 7 minutes. Slide the asparagus and eggs onto plates and serve garnished with the asparagus tips and parsley.

the anatomy of a dish

asparagus vinaigrette

MAKES ABOUT 1 CUP

Kosher salt
Trimmed stalks and peelings from
   ½ pound asparagus (use the tips
   for another purpose)
1 small shallot, peeled
1½ tablespoons tarragon leaves
1½ tablespoons flat-leaf parsley
   leaves
Juice of ½ lemon
2 tablespoons grapeseed oil
2 tablespoons extra virgin olive oil

Serve this vinaigrette over blanched and chilled asparagus or seafood. Or warm slightly over very low heat (don't let it simmer, or it will discolor) and serve it with Asparagus Crepes (page 110) or Rolled Soufflé (page 108).

Bring a medium pot of salted water to a boil. Add the asparagus stalks and shallot and boil until the stalks are almost tender, about 7 minutes. Add the tarragon and parsley and continue cooking just until the herbs are bright green, about 1 minute. Drain.

Place the herbs and vegetables in a blender or food processor, add 2 ice cubes and ¼ cup water, and puree until smooth. Add the lemon juice and a pinch of salt, then, with the motor running, add the grapeseed and olive oils. Adjust the seasoning if necessary, then strain through a fine sieve and serve.

Vegetable and fruit purees are a great starting point for vinaigrettes—see Spicy Green Salad with Strawberry Vinaigrette (page 62) and Peppercress Salad with Yellow Pepper Vinaigrette (page 64).

beans and legumes

chickpeas

MAKES ABOUT 4 CUPS

1 cup dried chickpeas, soaked
   overnight in water to cover by
   several inches
1 small stalk celery
1 small carrot, peeled
1 small onion, peeled and stuck
   with 5 cloves
4 sprigs thyme
1 bay leaf
¼ cup extra virgin olive oil
Kosher salt and freshly ground
   black pepper

Chickpeas (also known as garbanzo beans) must be presoaked and cooked slowly. The exact amount of time required for a particular batch to reach tenderness is a consequence of the age of the beans you are cooking.

Drain the chickpeas and place them in a medium pot. Add the celery, carrot, onion, thyme, bay leaf, olive oil, and water to cover by about 1 inch. Bring the chickpeas to a very gentle simmer over medium heat. Cook the chickpeas, stirring once or twice, until tender, about 1½ hours.

Season the chickpeas liberally with salt and pepper, then allow them to cool in their cooking liquid. Remove the vegetables and herbs. Store the chickpeas in their liquid in the refrigerator for up to 5 days.

VARIATION

gigante beans

Substitute I cup dried gigante beans for the chickpeas and proceed as directed. (Makes about 2 cups.)

Chickpeas are an ingredient in the Roasted Winter Vegetable Stew (page 91). On a simpler note, they are also good pureed with olive oil and Garlic Confit (page 41) and seasoned with lemon juice.

lentils

MAKES ABOUT 3 CUPS

Serve lentils warm, dressed with their cooking juices and a little more olive oil, or cold with Lemon–Mustard Vinaigrette (page 72). Salad possibilities abound. They are good mixed with shredded Duck Confit (page 163) and diced roasted sunchokes.

1 cup French green lentils, rinsed
¼ cup extra virgin olive oil
1 small carrot, peeled and halved
½ small onion, peeled and studded with 2 to 3 cloves
1 stalk celery, halved
2 sprigs thyme
2 sprigs rosemary
Kosher salt

Lentils contain more protein than any other vegetable except soybeans. They are also an excellent source of folic acid and iron. The small green lentils used in this recipe, lentilles de Puy, are delicate and hearty. They hold their shape better when cooked than most other varieties—so long as you are careful never to boil them.

Combine the lentils, olive oil, carrot, onion, celery, thyme, and rosemary in a medium pot. Add enough water to just cover the lentils, about 1 cup, and bring to a simmer over medium-high heat. Reduce the heat to medium-low and gently simmer until two-thirds of the water has been absorbed, about 30 minutes.

Add salt to taste and continue to cook gently until the lentils are tender and the pan is almost but not quite dry, about 20 minutes more. Discard the carrot, onion, celery, and herb sprigs, adjust the seasoning, and serve.

white lentils

MAKES 3 CUPS

White lentils, sometimes labeled urad dahl, *are available at Indian and Pakistani markets. They are also available by mail order from Kalustyan's (123 Lexington Avenue, New York, NY 10016; tel. 212-685-3451).*

Adding cinnamon gives the lentils an aromatic, meaty flavor I think goes particularly nicely with Roasted Monkfish with Curried Kumquats (page 154).

1½ cups white lentils
2 tablespoons butter
1½ cups Chicken Stock (page 170)
Kosher salt
¼ teaspoon ground cinnamon (optional)

These uncommon lentils look like rice, a fact I like to take advantage of. I simmer them just long enough so they are tender, but not so long that they lose their shape.

Rinse the lentils three times. Combine them with the butter, stock, and 1 cup water in a pot. Add salt and bring to a boil. Cover and reduce the heat to medium-low. Simmer until the lentils are tender and the liquid has been absorbed, about 25 minutes (if the liquid evaporates too quickly, add another ¼ cup water). Add cinnamon if using. Let the lentils stand for 5 minutes, then serve warm.

split peas
with sausage

SERVES 4

5 tablespoons extra virgin olive oil
½ pound (about 4 medium links) merguez or other spicy sausage, sliced
1 onion, peeled and diced
1 teaspoon turmeric
Kosher salt and freshly ground black pepper
2 cups green split peas, rinsed
Pinch of cayenne pepper

Merguez, spicy lamb sausage, lends a slightly unexpected note to this familiar pairing. Served as a side dish, it would be particularly good with leg of lamb, Slow-Roasted Tomatoes (page 55), and Naan (page 124).

Heat 1 tablespoon of the oil in a large pot over medium heat. Add the sausage and cook, stirring occasionally, until browned, about 10 minutes. Remove the sausage with a slotted spoon and reserve.

Pour off all but 2 tablespoons of fat from the pot and add the onion, turmeric, salt, and pepper to taste. Cook, stirring occasionally, until the onion is soft, about 15 minutes. Add the split peas, the remaining ¼ cup olive oil, and 4 cups water and bring to a simmer. Cook gently until the peas are tender, about 35 minutes.

Stir in the reserved sausage, then remove the pot from the heat, cover, and allow to steam for 10 minutes. Adjust the seasoning with salt and cayenne and serve.

pickled beets

MAKES ABOUT 2 CUPS

½ cup dry red wine
½ cup red wine vinegar
6 tablespoons sugar
1 shallot, peeled and thinly sliced
Sachet filled with:
  1 sprig thyme
  1 bay leaf
  ½ teaspoon black peppercorns
  1 clove
  ½ cinnamon stick
¼ pound beets (2 to 3 small),
  scrubbed and trimmed

The shallots used to flavor the liquid are, once pickled, themselves a wonderful addition to salads. Any leftover pickling liquid makes a nice vinaigrette combined with equal measures of extra virgin olive and grapeseed oils. Beet vinaigrette is very nice warm over pan–roasted wild striped bass or drizzled over Sautéed Greens (page 43).

Preparing beets can be a messy business. In this recipe, you avoid much of the untidiness by scrubbing the skins and leaving them on. The beets are sliced very thin and then braised in pickling liquid; prepared this way, the skins are neither tough nor bitter and the sliced beets can be cooked to perfect crisp tenderness. I use beets prepared this way in Pickled Beet Salad with Oranges and Taleggio Cheese (page 71). When whole or diced beets are the order of the day, they must be peeled before braising in the pickling liquid. See Roasted Beets (below) for another approach.

Combine the wine, vinegar, sugar, shallot, and sachet in a medium saucepan. Slice the beets as thin as possible (a mandoline is helpful), and add to the wine mixture, along with ½ cup water. Bring to a simmer over medium heat. Reduce the heat, partially cover, and simmer gently until the beets are tender, about 1 hour. Remove the pan from the heat and allow the beets to cool in the liquid.

Remove the sachet and store the beets in their liquid in the refrigerator. They will keep for several weeks.

roasted beets

SERVES 4 TO 8

1 to 1½ pounds small beets
  (8 to 12), scrubbed and trimmed
2 tablespoons extra virgin olive oil

I like roasted beets warm, dressed with extra virgin olive oil and seasoned with sea salt. They are also good pickled. See Ruby Risotto with Winter Greens (page 104) and Borscht (page 79).

I never boil beets in water, much preferring to roast them whole. Roasting beets concentrates their flavor and sweetness and preserves their sensational color. It also circumvents the need to peel raw beets. The skins slip off easily once the beets are cool.

Preheat the oven to 400°F.

Place the beets in a small roasting pan. Add the olive oil and ¼ cup water. Turn the beets in the liquid, then cover the pan with aluminum foil. Roast until the beets can be pierced easily with a knife, about 1½ hours.

Let the beets cool slightly, then peel away the skin, using a paring knife. Serve warm or let cool.

celery root
celery root mash

SERVES 4

3 pounds celery root (2 medium knobs), peeled and coarsely chopped
Kosher salt
¾ cup heavy cream
Freshly ground black pepper

Celery root is not the root of garden celery but rather a specially cultivated variety. I like this knobby globe julienned raw in salads, thinly sliced and seared (see Seared Celery Root and Smoked Trout Salad, page 142), or, as here, boiled and mashed with a little cream. Because celery root is less starchy than potatoes, it can be pureed in a food processor without becoming gluey. The creamy tang of this mash makes it a nice complement to roasted and braised meats, in particular, Beer-Braised Short Ribs (page 169).

Place the celery root in a medium pot, cover with water, add salt, and bring to a boil. Reduce the heat and simmer until the celery root is tender, about 30 minutes. Drain.

Mash the celery root with the cream, season to taste with salt and pepper, and serve.

Other ideas for vegetable mashes: pureed carrots with turnips; potatoes with rutabagas. Parsley root, when it is available, is also delicious mashed. Try adding toasted nuts, croutons, or legumes such as chickpeas to mashes; see Parsnip Puree (page 51) and Sunchoke and Potato Puree (page 54).

corn
posole

SERVES 4

2 cups posole
1 small onion, peeled and halved
1 carrot, peeled
1 stalk celery
1 turnip, peeled
Sachet filled with:
  1 bay leaf
  1½ teaspoons black peppercorns
  1½ teaspoons coriander seeds
  2 cloves
  ½ bunch flat-leaf parsley
  ½ bunch thyme
4 cups Chicken Stock (page 170)
Kosher salt

Posole, dried corn, is a delicious full-flavored grain. It is good mixed with rice and black beans or served with chicken. Be aware that the cooking time can range from 2 to 4 hours.

Combine the posole, onion, carrot, celery, turnip, and sachet in a large pot. Add the stock and 4 cups water, bring to a simmer over medium heat, and simmer until the posole is soft, at least 2 hours, adding more water if necessary. Season with salt, cover, and set aside the posole for 10 minutes. Remove the vegetables and sachet and serve.

Try combining the posole, sachet, and stock in a pot as directed in the recipe. Season with salt and pepper. Cook for 1 hour, then add a chicken cut into 8 pieces. Simmer about 20 minutes, then add the vegetables, all neatly diced. Cook until the chicken is done and the vegetables are tender.

cucumbers **pickles**

3 English cucumbers, washed and
   sliced ¼ inch thick
½ cup kosher salt
½ cup coriander seeds
¼ cup mustard seeds
2 tablespoons white peppercorns
1 bay leaf
1 sprig thyme
2 teaspoons turmeric
½ cup sugar
4 cups Champagne vinegar

This pickling recipe works with many different vegetables.
Instead of cucumbers, try pickling peppers, eggplant,
cauliflower, okra, green beans, carrots, scallions—
the list goes on.

Place the cucumbers in a bowl. Add the salt, about
2 trays of ice cubes, and water to cover. Refrigerate
the cucumbers overnight (this helps them to crisp).

Combine the coriander seeds, mustard seeds, peppercorns, bay leaf, thyme, turmeric, sugar, and vinegar
in a saucepan and bring to a simmer over medium-
high heat. Remove the pan from the heat and allow
the pickling liquid to cool.

Drain the cucumbers and place them in a container
with a lid. Pour the pickling liquid over them, cover,
and refrigerate for at least 24 hours. Stored in the
refrigerator, these pickles will keep for at least 1 month.

eggplant

roasted eggplant puree

MAKES ABOUT 3 CUPS

6 Japanese eggplants, halved
   lengthwise
¼ cup extra virgin olive oil
Kosher salt

Eggplants, like tomatoes, are a fruit, not a vegetable, and members of the Solanaceae family. For many years after their introduction to Italy from the East in the fourteenth century, eating eggplants was thought to lead to madness. Perhaps the European fear was linked to the eggplant's familial relationship to poisonous plants such as belladonna, or perhaps it was because early eggplants were bitter. Cross-breeding has sweetened modern eggplants, but bitterness is still a concern. I prefer Japanese eggplants. They are the most consistently mellow tasting. I avoid baby eggplants; they can be especially astringent.

Preheat the oven to 375°F.

Place the eggplants cut side up on a baking sheet. Score the flesh by making crosshatch incisions through it, stopping short of the skin (this helps the eggplants to cook evenly). Drizzle the eggplants with the olive oil, and season with salt. Roast until soft, about 40 minutes.

Scoop the flesh out of the skins into a bowl. Beat until smooth. Season with salt and pepper and serve warm or at room temperature or refrigerate up to 3 days.

This recipe is the starting point for Eggplant and Garlic Stew with Merguez Sausage (page 90). The puree is also good seasoned and served as a dip or spread: Just mix in olive oil, parsley, and Garlic Confit (below), which is also an ingredient in the eggplant and garlic stew.

garlic

garlic confit

MAKES ABOUT 18 GARLIC CLOVES AND 1 CUP OIL

2 heads garlic, cloves separated
   and peeled
1 cup extra virgin olive oil
½ teaspoon kosher salt
1 bunch thyme
1 bay leaf

Garlic is a bulb planted in the fall and harvested in the spring and summer. It has a long shelf life, but its flavor dissipates over time. Garlic confit, garlic cloves stewed in oil, has a sweeter, rounder taste than fresh. I prefer its subtlety in most instances. The garlic oil is a delicious byproduct. Store garlic confit covered in oil in the refrigerator. Any garlic or oil that has been left out should be discarded.

Combine the garlic, oil, salt, thyme, and bay leaf in a saucepan. Add ¼ cup water, bring to just below a simmer over low heat, and cook (the oil should steam but only bubble occasionally) until the garlic is soft and white, about 45 minutes. Use or refrigerate.

Garlic confit can be used to flavor mashed potatoes and mayonnaise. It is nice in salads, particularly those made with bitter greens. Use it in any soup, stew, or sauce calling for fresh garlic, over pasta, steak, or chicken, to make garlic bread, or as a stronger-tasting alternative to plain olive oil in Shrimp Confit (page 138).

mixed grain pilaf

SERVES 4

¼ cup sunflower seeds
4 tablespoons butter
½ cup millet
½ cup quinoa
2 shallots, peeled and minced
¾ cup long-grain brown rice
Kosher salt
Finely grated zest of 1 lemon

*Try the pilaf as a side dish for roasted lamb (see Baby Lamb Chops with Roasted Eggplant Salad, page 171) or grilled fish or chicken.
To serve this pilaf as an entrée, add beans, lentils (page 36), or chickpeas (page 35) and Sautéed Greens (page 43).*

Nuts can be substituted for the seeds in this recipe. You can also add dried fruit—cranberries, cherries, or chopped apricots.

Preheat the oven to 350°F.

Spread the sunflower seeds in a single layer on a baking sheet and toast until fragrant, about 20 minutes.

Meanwhile, divide the butter between two medium saucepans and heat over medium-low heat. Add the millet and quinoa to one saucepan; add the shallots and the rice to the other. Stir to coat the grains with butter. Add 4 cups water and about ¼ teaspoon salt to the quinoa and millet mixture and bring to a boil. Add 3 cups water and ¼ teaspoon salt to the rice and bring to a boil. Reduce the heat under both pans to low, cover, and gently simmer until the grains are tender and the liquid absorbed, 15 to 20 minutes. Remove the pans from the heat and allow the grains to rest, covered, for 5 minutes.

Combine the quinoa and millet with the rice. Add the sunflower seeds and lemon zest, adjust the seasoning with salt, and serve.

wheat berries

MAKES ABOUT 4 CUPS

1½ cups wheat berries
1 sprig rosemary
1 bay leaf
1 small onion, peeled and studded
  with 4 cloves
Kosher salt and freshly ground
  black pepper
2 tablespoons butter (optional)

Use wheat berries in salads, add them to soups and stews, or serve in place of rice as a side dish.

Wheat berries are wheat in its most "untampered with" edible form: whole wheat grains simply rid of their tough outer coats. Cook wheat berries slowly in plenty of water.

Combine the wheat berries, rosemary, bay leaf, and onion in a large pot. Add 5 cups water, salt and pepper to taste, and the butter, if using, and bring to a boil. Reduce the heat to medium and gently simmer until the water has been absorbed and the wheat berries are tender, about 1 hour and 45 minutes. Serve warm or at room temperature.

greens

sautéed greens

SERVES 4 TO 6

2 tablespoons extra virgin olive oil, or more as desired
1 teaspoon Garlic Confit (page 41) or 1 clove garlic, sliced
16 cups chopped dark leafy greens, such as kale, chard, dandelion, collards, or beet (about 1 pound trimmed)
Fine sea salt and freshly ground black pepper

Water is added to the greens in this sauté so the olive oil and water emulsify, saucing the greens as they cook. Use garlic confit if you have it, rather than the fresh garlic, because it has a richer flavor. Fresh garlic is okay, but take care that it doesn't brown.

Heat the olive oil in a large skillet over medium heat. Add the garlic and cook just until fragrant, about 2 minutes. Add a large handful of the greens, season with a little salt and pepper, and cook, stirring, until the greens begin to wilt. Repeat, adding seasoning and more greens a little at a time. When all the greens are wilted, add ½ to 1 cup water (the amount will depend on how close to tender your greens are at this point) and cook until the liquid evaporates. Serve warm, as is or dressed with additional olive oil.

I eat sautéed greens as often as I can—plain, dressed with olive oil and seasoned with sea salt. I fold them into omelets, pile them on croutons, use them in pies, and stuff pasta with them.

horseradish

horseradish dumplings

MAKES ABOUT 24

2 tablespoons olive oil
2 eggs, lightly beaten
½ cup matzoh meal
1 teaspoon kosher salt
A 1-inch piece fresh horseradish, peeled and finely grated

Horseradish is a member of the Cruciferae family, which contains such strongly flavored vegetables as collards, kale, and broccoli. A pungent and peppery root, horseradish is at its most powerful when freshly peeled and grated.

Combine the olive oil, eggs, matzoh meal, salt, and horseradish in a bowl, and mix well. Add just enough water to hold the mixture together, about 2 tablespoons, and mix again.

Bring a large pot of salted water to a simmer. Working in batches, use a wet teaspoon to form dumplings, slip them into the water, and cook for 3 to 5 minutes after the dumplings float to the surface. Drain and serve.

For a stronger taste, substitute 1 tablespoon mustard oil for 1 tablespoon olive oil. Try these dumplings with Beer-Braised Short Ribs (page 169), warming them in the braising liquid for a minute or so before serving. They are also very good in chicken soup.

kale pesto

MAKES ABOUT 1 CUP

*Serve the pesto with
Sunchoke Ravioli
(page 105) or freshly
made fettuccine.
You can also use kale
pesto (without the
optional chicken
stock) as a spread
and a bruschetta
topping.*

½ cup plus 2 tablespoons extra
 virgin olive oil
½ pound kale, tough ribs removed
 and leaves chopped
Kosher salt and freshly ground
 black pepper
¼ cup pine nuts, toasted
¼ cup freshly grated Parmigiano-
 Reggiano
¼ cup Chicken Stock (page 170),
 warmed (optional)

This pesto can be made with virtually any assertive green. This recipe calls for kale, tamed slightly with a quick sauté before combining it with the familiar flavorings of pesto Genovese—olive oil, Parmigiano-Reggiano, and pine nuts.

Heat 2 tablespoons of the oil in a large skillet over medium heat. Add the chopped kale and salt and pepper to taste and stir to coat the kale with oil. Add about ⅓ cup water and cook until the kale is tender and the pan dry, about 5 minutes.

Transfer the kale to a blender. Add the pine nuts, cheese, and the remaining ½ cup oil. Blend until pureed. Adjust the seasoning with salt and pepper.

If the pesto is to be used as a sauce over pasta, add the warm stock or ½ cup warm water and blend well.

VARIATION

grilled vegetable pesto

Slice I small eggplant; I small fennel bulb, cored; I small zucchini; I small carrot, peeled; and I medium red onion, peeled. Brush the vegetables with extra virgin olive oil, season liberally with salt and freshly ground black pepper. Grill over a medium-hot flame until soft and slightly charred. Combine the vegetables in a food processor, add ¼ cup extra virgin olive oil, ½ cup unsalted sunflower seeds, and 2 cups cleaned arugula and pulse until coarsely ground. Season with the juice of I lemon, salt, and pepper and serve as a sandwich spread or dip. (Makes about 2 cups.)

kumquats

candied kumquats

MAKES ABOUT 2 CUPS

¼ cup red wine vinegar
¼ cup sugar
12 kumquats, stemmed, quartered, and seeded
Sachet filled with 1 tablespoon chamomile tea, or 1 teabag chamomile tea

Kumquats can be a little sour and their rinds tough. Cooking them in sugar syrup tenderizes and sweetens them. The sugar combines with the natural pectin in the fruit and thickens the poaching liquid to form a sweet syrup.

Combine the vinegar and sugar in a small saucepan and heat over medium-high heat, stirring to dissolve the sugar. Add ½ cup water, the kumquats, and chamomile and bring to a boil. Reduce the heat slightly and simmer until the kumquats are translucent and the liquid syrupy, about 45 minutes. Serve warm or at room temperature.

I serve candied kumquats with ice cream or cake and use the syrup to soak pound cake. Adding sautéed red onions, black pepper, and savory spices moves the kumquats from the sweet to the savory realm; serve like a chutney with game, pork, or poultry. See, too, Roasted Monkfish with Curried Kumquats (page 154).

leeks

braised leeks

SERVES 4

2 cups Chicken Stock (page 170)
1 teaspoon coriander seeds
1 bay leaf
1 sprig thyme
1 clove garlic, peeled
2 tablespoons extra virgin olive oil
½ teaspoon kosher salt
8 small leeks or 4 large leeks, split lengthwise and cut into ½-inch-wide slices

Leeks must be cleaned carefully and cooked fully. Cut off the fibrous dark green tops (save these for stock), then split the leeks lengthwise, stopping just short of the root end. Hold them under cold running water, separating the layers as you rinse. Braising leeks in chicken stock adds richness, but you could replace the stock with water for a leekier taste. Either way, I add a little olive oil, which flavors the leeks and rounds out their taste.

Combine the stock, coriander seeds, bay leaf, thyme, and garlic in a large saucepan. Add the olive oil and salt and bring to a simmer over medium-high heat. Add the leeks and cover them with a clean towel to keep them submerged. Reduce the heat, and gently simmer until the leeks are tender, about 20 minutes. Allow the leeks to cool in the braising liquid. Serve at room temperature or reheat.

Braised leeks served warm or at room temperature with Lemon–Mustard Vinaigrette (page 72) make a nice first-course salad. I also serve them warm as a side dish with roasted fish. Endive, celery, and fennel can all be braised in the same way. Simply adjust the quantity of liquid and cooking time according to your choice of vegetable.

leek and apple hash

Try topping the hash with pan-roasted foie gras and serving it as a first course. It also works as a side dish. You could substitute the hash for Pineapple Chutney and serve it with the Pan-Roasted Duck Breast (page 178). The combination of apples and leeks is good for breakfast, when you might add some diced potato and serve the hash with eggs.

2 tablespoons extra virgin olive oil
4 leeks, halved lengthwise and sliced about ½ inch thick
4 shallots, peeled and thinly sliced
Kosher salt and freshly ground black pepper
2 Granny Smith apples, peeled, cored, and diced
3 tablespoons butter
¼ cup apple cider vinegar
¼ cup rice wine vinegar
1 cup apple cider
2 teaspoons mustard seeds

A hash is a combination of diced or minced vegetables (and meat), which is flattened into a cake and then sautéed. Though hash can be made from leftovers, this should not be viewed as its primary utility. There are twenty-nine recipes for *hashis* (the French term for hash) in *Larousse Gastronomique,* made with everything from sweetbreads to lobster. This is a fruit and vegetable hash. I like to serve it as a side dish.

Heat the oil in a large skillet over medium heat. Add the leeks, shallots, and salt and pepper to taste and cook, stirring frequently, until the vegetables soften and begin to brown, about 10 minutes.

Add the apples and butter and cook until the apples begin to color, then add the cider and rice wine vinegars. Allow the vinegars to bubble away, then add the cider and mustard seeds. Season with salt and pepper, reduce the heat, and simmer gently until the apples are tender, about 10 minutes. Serve warm.

lemons

candied lemon peel

This recipe produces two useful products: the peel and the poaching syrup. I use the candied (but not sugared) peel in savory dishes, particularly fish mousses, and as a garnish for Sea Bass in Lemon Nage (page 152), and the chopped sugared peel in cakes and citrus desserts. I soak pound cake in the delicious syrup and spoon it over ice cream.

2 lemons, scrubbed
¼ cup sugar, plus extra for coating if desired

Meyer lemons are available in the winter months. Their rinds are less bitter and more tender than most other commonly available lemon varieties. Grapefruit, lime, and orange peel will work as well. Just remember to avoid the bitter pith.

Using a vegetable peeler, remove the peel from the lemons, taking as little white pith as possible. Reserve the lemons for another purpose. Cut the lemon peel into very thin slivers (julienne).

Blanch the peel in a small saucepan of boiling water for 2 minutes to remove the bitterness, then drain. Repeat.

Combine the sugar and ½ cup water in a small pot and bring to a simmer. Reduce the heat to medium, add the lemon peel, and cook until the peel is tender and translucent and the poaching liquid is syrupy, about 20 minutes.

Using a slotted spoon, lift the lemon peel out of the poaching syrup and place on a plate lined with parchment paper. (The syrup can be reused.) Let the candied peel dry for about 2 hours, until it is slightly tacky. Roll the peel in sugar to coat, if desired. Store in a sealed container.

lemons

quick preserved lemons

MAKES ABOUT 10 SLICES

1 lemon, scrubbed
1 tablespoon kosher salt
2 teaspoons sugar

Chopped preserved lemons enhance salads, roasts, and fish dishes. They are the flavor key to Lemon Nage (page 152).

Cut the lemon in half crosswise, then slice it as thin as possible. Cover a plate with plastic wrap. Shingle the lemon in a single overlapping layer on the plate. Mix the salt and sugar together and sprinkle over the lemon. Cover with plastic wrap and refrigerate overnight, then transfer to a sealed container. Before using, lightly rinse the salt-sugar cure from the lemon slices.

VARIATION

traditional preserved lemons

Quarter 1 scrubbed lemon and layer in a jar with 1 tablespoon kosher salt. Add the juice of 1½ lemons and cure in the refrigerator, turning occasionally, for 1 month. (Makes 4 quarters.)

Quick-preserved lemons do not have the depth of flavor of their long-cured counterparts, but they boast a nice fresh salty-sweet-sour taste. They will keep in the refrigerator for at least 2 weeks.

mushrooms sautéed mushrooms

SERVES 4

Sautéed mushrooms are an excellent simple side dish, particularly with Seared Sirloin with Mushroom Worcestershire (page 168). They are also great over pasta, incorporated into stuffing, stirred into scrambled eggs, or mixed with most grains.

2 to 4 tablespoons extra virgin olive oil
8 cups trimmed and sliced wild and/or cultivated mushrooms (about 2 pounds)
1 shallot, peeled and finely chopped
1 tablespoon chopped minced herbs, such as flat-leaf parsley, tarragon, chives, thyme, and chervil
Kosher salt and freshly ground black pepper

I recommend sautéing tender mushrooms with a relatively high moisture content, such as shiitake, button, cremini, and oyster. Drier, meatier mushrooms such as morels and hen-of-the-woods are better braised. With these, begin as on page 47, then add a little stock or water, lower the heat, cover, and cook until the mushrooms are tender. Save any remaining cooking liquid to stir into sauces, soups, and braises; reduced, it is a great vinaigrette base.

Heat a large skillet over medium-high heat. Add a film of oil and enough mushrooms to loosely cover the bottom of the pan (it is much better to add too few than too many). Cook the mushrooms until the first sides are golden, 2 to 3 minutes, then turn them and add a little of the shallot and herbs. Continue cooking just until the mushrooms are tender, about 1 minute more, then season with salt and pepper and transfer to a plate or bowl. Wipe out the pan and repeat with the remaining mushrooms. Once all the mushrooms are cooked, return them to the skillet just long enough to heat through, 1 to 3 minutes. Serve warm.

mushroom puree

MAKES ABOUT 1¾ CUPS

Mushroom puree is a versatile ingredient. It is the starting point for the Mushroom Torte (page 113). Also try it folded into a soufflé (see Rolled Soufflé, page 108) or combined with ricotta cheese and herbs and stuffed under the skin of chicken before roasting.

2 tablespoons extra virgin olive oil
1 small onion, peeled and chopped
1½ pounds mushrooms, chopped
1 tablespoon soy sauce
Kosher salt and freshly ground black pepper

Button mushrooms, cremini, and portobellos work well in this recipe. Use mushroom scraps or trimmings but avoid shiitake stems, which are a little too tough. The soy sauce reinforces the earthy flavor. Add dried mushrooms if you want greater intensity (but cook the puree a little longer).

Heat the oil in a large skillet over medium-low heat. Add the onion and cook, stirring occasionally, until it softens, about 10 minutes. Add the mushrooms and 2 tablespoons water, cover, and cook over low heat until the mushrooms are almost tender, about 10 minutes. Add the soy sauce and salt and pepper to taste, cover, and continue cooking until the mushrooms are very soft, about 15 minutes more (some types of mushrooms will take longer). Allow the mixture to cool slightly.

Puree the mushroom mixture in a food processor or blender. The puree can be stored in the refrigerator for up to 5 days and in the freezer for up to 3 months.

VARIATION

mushroom soup

I use the puree as a base for an easy mushroom soup—add vegetable or chicken stock and finish with cream. Another quick mushroom soup: Grind dried mushrooms, then combine ½ cup of the powder with 4 cups stock, heat, add cream to taste, and garnish with sautéed fresh mushrooms.

mushroom worcestershire sauce

MAKES ABOUT 1½ CUPS

1 pound cremini, portobello, or
   shiitake mushrooms, sliced
3 tablespoons kosher salt
1½ teaspoons black peppercorns
10 allspice berries
¾ cup red wine vinegar
1 shallot, peeled and sliced
2 cups Chicken Stock (page 170)

In my version of this famous sauce, you cure the mushrooms, then add spices and vinegar. The result is a strong but delicious mixture that's great with steak. This sauce is also the starting point for my turkey gravy (page 180). Be advised: This is wonderful sauce, but assertive—use a little at a time. It will keep in the refrigerator for weeks.

Curing the mushrooms.
Combine the mushrooms and salt in a bowl. Mix thoroughly, then cover and refrigerate overnight.

Making the Worcestershire.
Grind the pepper with the allspice berries in a spice grinder.

Transfer the cured mushrooms and their juices to a saucepan. Add the pepper mixture, vinegar, shallot, and chicken stock and bring to a boil, then reduce the heat to medium and simmer until the liquid is reduced by three-fourths, about 1½ hours. Let cool slightly.

Pulse the sauce in a food processor until it is a coarse puree. Refrigerate until ready to serve.

Worcestershire sauce, so the story goes, was invented through a happy accident: A barrel of spiced vinegar was forgotten and left to ferment. Lea and Perrins, a chemist's shop, had made the vinegar according to a recipe provided by a client, but the client never returned to pick it up. After several years, the shopkeepers, about to throw the whole thing out, decided to give it a taste. It was delicious, salty, and sour, so they decided to bottle and sell the sauce. The recipe remains a secret.

onions

smoked onion puree

MAKES ABOUT ¾ CUP

This is an easy home-smoking method, but make sure your kitchen is well ventilated or do it outside on the grill. (You can use the same method to smoke trout.) This puree is great stirred into sauces, mashed potatoes, or rice.

Serve with grilled or pan-roasted meat, chicken, or fish. This puree can also be made with sautéed onions.

1 cup rice (any type)
1 cup plus 1 tablespoon sugar
¼ cup Darjeeling tea leaves
1 medium onion, peeled and cut into wedges
2 to 4 tablespoons heavy cream

An onion is a bulb made up of layers of overlapping leaves. There are many types of onions. I divide them into two flavor categories: sweet and pungent. Vidalia onions are sweet, Spanish onions are pungent. Either sort will work in this recipe.

Line a large skillet with aluminum foil. Add the rice, 1 cup of the sugar, and the tea. Place a metal steamer basket in the skillet (or make your own by forming three or four aluminum foil "logs," then covering them with a sheet of foil just large enough to hold the onion wedges in a single layer).

Place the onions in the steamer, then tightly cover the pan with a lid or foil. Heat the skillet over high heat until it begins to smoke, then reduce the heat to medium-low and smoke the onions until brown and tender, about 1½ hours.

Discard the rice and transfer the onions to a blender or food processor. Add the cream and the remaining tablespoon sugar and puree until smooth.

VARIATION

smoked onion rice

Combine 2 cups jasmine rice and 2 cups water in a medium saucepan. Add 1 teaspoon salt and bring to a boil, then reduce the heat to low, cover, and simmer until the rice is tender and the water absorbed, about 10 minutes. Stir ½ cup of the smoked onion puree and 1½ tablespoons butter into the rice. Adjust the seasoning if necessary with salt and more onion puree. (Serves 4.)

the anatomy of a dish

parsnip and potato galette

SERVES 4

2 egg whites, beaten to a froth
2 medium parsnips, peeled
1 Idaho or other russet potato, peeled
½ red onion, peeled and very thinly sliced
Kosher salt and freshly ground black pepper
2 tablespoons extra virgin olive oil
2 tablespoons butter

Parsnips are sweetest when harvested after the first frost, so December is prime parsnip season in New York, making this a perfect alternative to traditional Hanukkah latkes. Shaving rather than slicing or grating the potato and parsnip gives the pancake a distinctive texture. The egg whites bind the ingredients and give a silky finish. Don't be afraid to use plenty of fat to prevent the galette from sticking and to add flavor.

Place the egg whites in a bowl. Using a vegetable peeler, shave the parsnips into the egg whites. Still using the peeler, shave the potato lengthwise into the bowl. Mix well. Add the onion and salt and pepper to taste and mix again.

Heat a large, well-seasoned cast-iron or nonstick skillet over medium-high heat. Add the oil and 1 tablespoon of the butter. When the butter froths, add the parsnip mixture, pressing it into the pan to form an even, compact pancake. Reduce the heat to medium and cook until the bottom of the galette is well browned, about 15 minutes.

Turn the galette over—this is most easily done by turning it out onto a plate, then sliding it back into the pan—adding the remaining butter before you return the galette to the pan. Press the galette down and continue cooking until the second side is well browned, about 15 minutes more. Serve warm.

I like to serve this, cut into wedges, with Leek and Apple Hash (page 46) and scrambled eggs for breakfast. It makes a good side dish at dinner, and could be substituted for the potato galette in the recipe on page 179.

parsnip puree

SERVES 4 TO 6

2 pounds parsnips, peeled and chopped
2½ cups milk
2½ cups heavy cream
Kosher salt and freshly ground black pepper
1 cup chopped toasted hazelnuts

Parsnips go particularly well with game and poultry. This puree is also good with a meaty fish such as monkfish.

Combine the parsnips, milk, and cream in a saucepan, season with salt and pepper, and bring to a simmer over medium heat. Simmer gently until the parsnips are tender (much of the milk will have been absorbed), about 30 minutes.

Mash or process the parsnips until smooth. Stir in the hazelnuts, adjust the seasoning, and serve.

Chopped toasted nuts add crunch to this puree. Bread cubes sautéed in butter would also be nice. Add nuts, seeds, or croutons to any vegetable puree; see Celery Root Mash (page 39) and Sunchoke and Potato Puree (page 54).

flame-roasted peppers

MAKES 6

6 red or yellow bell peppers

I serve roasted peppers simply dressed with extra virgin olive oil, Champagne vinegar, and sea salt. Once dressed, the peppers can be left to marinate in the refrigerator for up to 5 days.

Char the peppers over an open flame, turning occasionally, until all sides are blackened, about 10 minutes. Put the peppers in a bowl, cover with plastic wrap, and set aside to steam and cool for about 10 minutes.

Peel, core, and seed the peppers. Cut into any shape desired and serve.

Add roasted peppers to pastas, sandwiches, and salads. Puree them for sauces; see Spiced Tuna with Romesco Sauce (page 155) and Peppercress Salad with Yellow Pepper Vinaigrette (page 64). Or use the puree as a soup base—simply add chicken stock and thicken with a little potato puree or cream.

roasted whole pineapple

SERVES 8 TO 10

1 tablespoon black peppercorns
1½ teaspoons Szechuan peppercorns
1 teaspoon juniper berries
Pinch of ground cloves
1 pineapple, trimmed and peeled
3 tablespoons grapeseed oil

Roasted whole pineapple is soft and juicy, not chewy like the dried fruit. Because this is a spicy version, it works with both savory and sweet foods. You can pair it with seafood and game, combine it with other tropical fruits in salads, and slice it and serve it with cake or ice cream.

Preheat the oven to 375°F.

Grind the black pepper, Szechuan pepper, and juniper berries together in a mortar or spice grinder. Add the cloves. Coat the peeled pineapple with the spices.

Heat the oil in a large skillet over medium heat. Add the pineapple and cook, turning occasionally, until browned on all sides, about 5 minutes.

Transfer the pineapple to a deep baking dish, cover with foil, and roast until a thermometer inserted in the middle of the pineapple registers 170°F, about 40 minutes.

Remove the pineapple from the oven and allow to cool. Slice and serve.

For chewy pineapple, slice the raw fruit about ½ inch thick, lay it on a parchment-lined baking sheet, sprinkle it with black pepper, and bake at 325°F until the edges brown, about 45 minutes.

quinoa

MAKES ABOUT 4 CUPS

2 cups quinoa
Kosher salt and freshly ground
  black pepper

Corn, barley, wheat, and rice are members of the Gramineae, or grass family. Quinoa, known to the Incas as the "mother seed," is not. Quinoa is higher in protein and contains all the amino acids necessary for nutritional absorption. From the cook's viewpoint, quinoa has much in common with grains.

Combine the quinoa with 2 cups water in a medium saucepan. Season with salt and pepper and bring to a boil. Reduce the heat to low, cover the pan, and cook the quinoa until the water has been absorbed, about 10 minutes. Remove the pan from the heat and let the quinoa steam for 15 minutes more, then serve.

Use cooked quinoa to "bread" chicken (see page 176), add it to soups and stews instead of rice or pasta, and serve it as a side dish. It's particularly good cooked pilaf-style with fruits and nuts. Quinoa is sold at health food and gourmet stores as well as in some supermarkets.

braised salsify

SERVES 4

¼ cup Champagne vinegar
Juice of ½ lemon
1 teaspoon coriander seeds
1 teaspoon kosher salt
2 tablespoons all-purpose flour
1 pound salsify

Salsify is sometimes called the oyster plant—an allusion to its rich flavor and an invitation to cook it as you would the briny mollusks. It reminds me of white asparagus, although the two have little in common from a botanical point of view: Asparagus is a stalk and salsify a root; asparagus a member of the Liliaceae family and salsify the Compositae. Despite these differences, salsify is a good substitute for white asparagus, which has a short season.

Combine the vinegar, lemon, coriander, and salt in a large saucepan. Add 6 cups water and bring to a simmer.

Meanwhile, peel the salsify and trim the ends.

Sift the flour into the pan, whisking to combine. Add the salsify (cut the stalks in half if they are too long), reduce the heat to medium-low, and simmer very gently until the salsify is tender, about 30 minutes.

Drain the salsify and serve immediately, or lay the salsify stalks out on a plate to cool (the stalks will stay the shape they cool in, so it is important to lay them out straight). Before serving, cut the salsify into ¾-inch pieces on the bias, then warm in melted butter. Serve immediately.

Salsify stalks are covered with an inedible peel. Once this is removed, the cook's job is to keep the exposed white flesh from browning. Peeled salsify should be kept in acidulated water (lemon water), then cooked à blanc, a French term that refers to cooking in milk or a mixture of flour and water.

I like to warm salsify in a bit of crème fraîche and serve the saucy salsify with Mackerel with Paprika Sauce (page 153).

spinach

spinach and herb sauce

Serve this light sauce with steamed fish, scrambled eggs, or Rolled Soufflé (see page 108).

MAKES ABOUT 1½ CUPS

2 tablespoons butter
¾ pound spinach
Kosher salt and freshly ground black pepper
2 tablespoons 1-inch chive lengths
2 tablespoons tarragon leaves
½ cup flat-leaf parsley leaves

Almost any leafy green could be substituted for the spinach in this sauce. Sorrel, which seems to melt as it cooks, works particularly well.

Melt the butter in a large saucepan over medium heat. Add the spinach and salt and pepper to taste and cook, stirring occasionally, until the spinach is wilted, about 5 minutes. Add the chives, tarragon, and parsley, then add ½ cup water and bring to a simmer. Puree the sauce in a blender or food processor. Adjust the seasonings and serve warm.

sunchokes

sunchoke and potato puree

Use this puree to fill ravioli (see page 105) or serve it as a side dish with warm Short Rib Terrine (page 160). For more about vegetable purees, see Celery Root Mash (page 39) and Parsnip Puree (page 51).

SERVES 4

2 Idaho or other russet potatoes, peeled and cut into large pieces
16 medium sunchokes (Jerusalem artichokes), peeled and cut into pieces the same size as the potatoes
Kosher salt
6 tablespoons butter

Sunchokes are a tuber (root shoot) of a type of sunflower. Like endive, salsify, and artichokes, they belong to the Compositae family. They can be simply roasted and peeled or, as here, mashed.

Place the potatoes and sunchokes in a saucepan. Add about 1 teaspoon salt, 2 tablespoons of the butter, and water to cover. Bring to a boil and cook until the vegetables are tender, about 20 minutes.

Drain the vegetables, and return them to the pan. Add the remaining 4 tablespoons butter and mash until smooth. Season to taste with salt and serve.

slow-roasted tomatoes

MAKES 8

8 medium tomatoes, cored
2 cloves garlic, peeled and sliced
3 sprigs thyme
3 tablespoons extra virgin olive oil
Kosher salt and freshly ground
    black pepper

Roasting vegetables concentrates their flavor (see Roasted Beets, page 38). It is a great technique to keep in mind when the vegetables at hand need a little extra coaxing to share their essence.

Preheat the oven to 300°F.

Blanch the tomatoes in a large pot of boiling water just long enough to loosen their skins—generally about 30 seconds, but the time will vary depending upon the ripeness of the tomatoes. Peel the tomatoes. Cut them in half and remove the seeds, then place the tomatoes cut side down on a parchment-lined baking sheet. Scatter the garlic and thyme over the tomatoes, drizzle with the olive oil, and season generously with salt and pepper.

Roast the tomatoes until they have released most of their liquid and are soft and just beginning to brown, about 1¼ hours. Use immediately or refrigerate for up to 1 week.

Roasted tomatoes are always in my refrigerator in the late summer and fall. I serve them chopped and sautéed in a little olive oil over pasta (this recipe makes enough for about 1 pound), stirred into soups and stews, in sandwiches and salads. They are also an ingredient in Romesco Sauce (page 155).

puttanesca vinaigrette

MAKES ABOUT 2 CUPS

I serve Puttanesca Vinaigrette as a second sauce for chilled Braised Octopus (page 136). I also like it cold over hot pasta in the summertime, and as a sauce for seared tuna.

½ cup plus 2 tablespoons extra virgin olive oil
2 shallots, peeled and diced
1 small onion, peeled and diced
Kosher salt and freshly ground black pepper
3 cloves garlic, peeled and chopped
5 plum tomatoes, peeled (or canned, with their juices)
2 tablespoons capers, rinsed and chopped
4 anchovy fillets, rinsed and minced
¾ teaspoon sugar
2 tablespoons balsamic vinegar
1 tomato, peeled, halved, seeded, and chopped
½ cup flat-leaf parsley leaves

Puttanesca sauce is a classic pasta sauce with plenty of garlic, capers, anchovy, and pepper, reputedly quickly made and eaten by Italian "ladies of the night." To use these flavors in a vinaigrette, I reduced the tomato, increased the oil, and added balsamic vinegar. This spicy tomato vinaigrette is not quite as quick to cook as the original sauce, but it will keep longer, about a week in the refrigerator.

Heat 2 tablespoons of the oil in a medium saucepan over medium heat. Add the shallots and onion and season with salt and pepper. Cook, stirring occasionally, until the onion and shallots are soft and golden, about 15 minutes.

Add the garlic and cook until fragrant, about 5 minutes, then add the tomatoes, 1 tablespoon of the capers, the anchovies, and sugar. Bring to a simmer and cook until the oil rises to the surface, about 30 minutes.

Transfer the sauce to a blender or food processor and add the balsamic vinegar and the remaining ½ cup oil. Blend until the mixture emulsifies. Transfer to a bowl, adjust the seasoning with salt and pepper, stir in the remaining 1 tablespoon capers, the chopped tomato, and parsley, and serve.

vegetable stock

4 onions, peeled
2 tablespoons extra virgin olive oil
4 leeks, white parts only, chopped
4 medium turnips, peeled and
  chopped
3 carrots, peeled and chopped
3 fennel bulbs, cored and chopped
2 tomatoes, chopped
Kosher salt

This is a basic vegetable stock recipe. For a more acidic taste, add white wine. Use herbs and spices such as tarragon, parsley, thyme, coriander seeds, fennel seeds, or black pepper to move the stock from sweet to spicy and from fragrant to robust.

Preheat the broiler. Cut 1 onion in half and place it cut side up on a baking sheet. Cook the onion halves under the broiler until dark brown, about 15 minutes.

Meanwhile, chop the remaining 3 onions. Heat the oil in a large stockpot over medium heat. Add the chopped onions, leeks, turnips, carrots, and fennel. Cook, stirring occasionally, until the vegetables soften, about 20 minutes.

Add the browned onion, tomatoes, and water to cover (about 2 gallons). Bring to a boil, then reduce the heat and simmer until the stock is flavorful, about 2 hours. Season with salt.

Line a large fine sieve with four layers of cheesecloth and set the sieve over a bowl. Pour the stock through the sieve, then refrigerate overnight, letting it slowly drain. Refrigerate for up to 1 week or freeze for up to 2 months.

salads

This chapter contains both composed and green salads. Composed salads combine cooked and raw vegetables that are separately dressed, then artfully integrated to balance flavors, colors, and textures. They are a sophisticated way to start a multicourse meal and often my choice for the main event at lunch. Composed salads run the gamut from relatively simple (Tomato and Cucumber Salad with Avocado Cream, page 68) to quite complex (Carpaccio of Quince with Endive Salad and Pecan Vinaigrette, page 70). In truth, they all take

some time, but they are very forgiving. Any demanding and tedious work can be done ahead, leaving only the final dressing and presentation.

At my restaurant, the garde manger, or pantry cook, makes the composed salads. He or she is also responsible for the green salads. For most cooks, making the perfect green salad is the greater challenge. Green salads are easy to make, and easy to make poorly. Here, as elsewhere in cooking, the fewer the ingredients, the greater the need for skill.

When making a salad, I let the choice of greens dictate the choice of dressing. I always choose what is freshest, though I tend to look within categories: spicy, sweet, crunchy, or soft. All have their place, sometimes alone and sometimes mixed. On

page 61, you will find a chart of the varieties of greens I frequently use in simple salads.

Wash the greens immediately after you buy them. Separate the leaves, then submerge them in a large bowl of cold water (not the sink—it is never clean enough). Move the leaves around in the water, then lift them out and into a colander. Drain the water, wipe out the bowl, and repeat until there is no visible dirt in the water *and* a leaf tastes grit-free. Dry the greens, wrap them in paper towels, and store them in sealed plastic bags in the refrigerator until you are ready to use them—which should be later that day.

A vinaigrette is a sauce made by combining one part vinegar with a pinch of salt and three to four parts oil. Start by choosing the vinegar.

With this chapter the focus shifts from techniques that emphasize individual vegetables to recipes that combine vegetables into side dishes, light meals, and first courses. These recipes are loosely arranged according to seasonal suitability and are accompanied by notes that suggest building links.

Salad greens from different families: Compositae, Chenopodiaceae, Cruciferae— red-leaf lettuce, Swiss chard, arugula

I like to use Champagne vinegar rather than white wine vinegar because I think the quality is more dependable. When I want a touch of sweetness, I opt for sherry vinegar; when I want a smooth subtlety, I use rice wine vinegar. Balsamic vinegar adds a rich sweet-and-sour taste (you can reduce commercial balsamic to a syrup to replicate the remarkable flavor of artisanal varieties). White balsamic vinegar, which can be hard to find, is particularly delicious. Lemon juice, alone or combined with vinegar, is my choice when I want to brighten flavor.

Add salt (I use sea salt in salads and vinaigrettes—it has a more vibrant taste) to the vinegar, so it will dissolve, then add the oil. I often use extra virgin olive oil but am mindful of the wide range of taste and quality. I like Sciabica, an oil made by a small producer in California. Generally, softer, sweeter greens call for smoother, lighter oil. Some lettuces are simply too delicate to stand up to any olive oil. When I want neutral oil, I use grapeseed, alone or mixed with olive or nut oil.

Just before serving a salad, season it with a little more sea salt and freshly ground pepper. Add half the amount of dressing you think you need, then mix gently. Spoon a bit more dressing over the top and serve.

salad greens chart

Not all salad greens come from the same family, which is why selecting from the various groups when composing a salad can meld sweet, bitter, spicy, and peppery tastes in one bite. The chart is organized by botanical family and genus.

LEAF	FAMILY	GENUS/SPECIES	FLAVOR	TEXTURE
CHICORY	Compositae	*Cichorium intybus* (Foliosum)	very bitter	crunchy
ENDIVE	Compositae	*Cichorium endivia* (Foliosum)	mild/bitter	crunchy
RADICCHIO	Compositae	*Cichorium intybus* (Foliosum)	mild/bitter	crunchy
BIBB LETTUCE	Compositae	*Lactuca sativa* (Capitata)	sweet	light crunch/soft
RED LEAF	Compositae	*Lactuca sativa* (Crispa)	sweet	light crunch
ROMAINE LETTUCE	Compositae	*Lactuca sativa* (Longifolia)	sweet	crunchy
DANDELION	Compositae	*Taraxacum officinale*	very bitter	soft
CABBAGE	Cruciferae	*Brassica oleracea* (Capitata)	strong/pungent	crunchy
ARUGULA	Cruciferae	*Eruca vesicaria sativa*	hot/peppery	light crunch
GARDEN CRESS	Cruciferae	*Lapidium sativum*	hot/peppery	crunchy
WATERCRESS	Cruciferae	*Nasturtium officinale*	hot/peppery	crunchy
SPINACH	Chenopodiaceae	*Spinacia oleracea*	mild/sweet	soft
PURSLANE	Portulacaceae	*Portulaca oleracea*	mild/sour	crunchy
SORREL	Polygonaceae	*Rumex* spp.	sour	soft
LAMB'S LETTUCE/ MÂCHE	Valerianaceae	*Valerianella locusta*	mild/sweet	soft

spicy green salad with strawberry vinaigrette

I use the same flavor combination in desserts. Add a little sugar to the berry and vinegar mixture, omit the oil, and you have an excellent topping for strawberry shortcake (see Scones, page 120).

FOR THE VINAIGRETTE

¼ pound strawberries, stems removed and quartered
¼ cup balsamic vinegar
¼ teaspoon freshly ground black pepper, or more to taste
1 star anise
6 tablespoons grapeseed oil

FOR THE SALAD

2 endives
⅓ pound watercress, tough stems removed

Spicy greens, those with bitter or peppery flavors, come from two plant families. The bitter leaves—endive, frisée, chicory, radicchio, and dandelion—are in the Compositae family. The more peppery-tasting greens—arugula, watercress, peppercress, and mustard greens—are in the Cruciferae family. I like to use a mixture.

With spicy greens, my preference is for a vinaigrette that is sweet, sour, and sharp. Berries, vinegar, and pepper are an unusual but very good combination that works perfectly.

Making the vinaigrette.
Combine the strawberries, vinegar, pepper, and star anise in a small saucepan. Add 2 tablespoons water and bring to a simmer. Reduce the heat to low and cook until the strawberries are very tender, 15 to 20 minutes.

Remove the star anise and puree the strawberry mixture in a blender. Gradually blend in the grapeseed oil. Adjust the seasoning if necessary with pepper.

Making the salad.
Remove any torn outer leaves from the endives, then slice them in rounds, avoiding the core. Combine the endive and watercress in a salad bowl. Add salt and just enough dressing to coat the greens. Mix gently and serve.

bulgur wheat salad with fava beans

½ cup bulgur wheat (medium grind)
2 teaspoons freshly ground coriander seeds
1 teaspoon freshly ground cumin seeds
½ teaspoon freshly ground white pepper
Kosher salt
1 lemon
½ cup blanched peeled fava beans (see the sidebar)
3 scallions, minced
¼ cup slivered mint leaves
¼ cup roughly chopped flat-leaf parsley

Bulgur wheat is whole wheat grains with the bran removed that have been cracked, partially steamed, and dried. Cracked wheat is crushed grains of whole wheat (see Wheat Berries, page 42). I use bulgur in this recipe and rehydrate it by seasoning the wheat, then adding boiling water. This causes the spices to "bloom" as the wheat expands and softens. Cracked wheat could be substituted, but it must be cooked longer.

Cooking the wheat.
Bring 1¼ cups water to a boil.

Combine the wheat, coriander, cumin, pepper, and a generous pinch of salt in a large bowl. Pour the boiling water over the mixture, cover the bowl with plastic wrap, and set aside for 20 minutes.

Making the salad.
Zest the lemon and add the zest to the wheat. Add the favas, scallions, mint, and parsley. Halve the lemon and squeeze lemon juice to taste over the salad. Mix well and season with salt. Serve at room temperature or chilled.

How to handle a fava bean: Choose heavy fava pods. Remove the beans from the pods, and blanch them in boiling water until the beans soften and the skins loosen, about 3 minutes. Refresh the beans in ice water, then slip off the skins.

peppercress salad with yellow pepper vinaigrette

SERVES 4

The vinaigrette is flavored with a pepper puree. This is a great trick that can be applied to any number of vegetables—for example, Asparagus Vinaigrette (page 35). Purees are also good soup bases; see Sorrel Soup (page 83) and Mushroom Puree (page 48).

FOR THE VINAIGRETTE

½ cup plus 2 tablespoons olive oil
1 small onion, peeled and coarsely chopped
1 large yellow bell pepper, cored, seeded, and coarsely chopped (plus the chopped trimmings from the pepper for the salad, below)
Kosher salt
½ cup Champagne vinegar

FOR THE SALAD

2 Yukon Gold potatoes, peeled and sliced
Kosher salt
¼ pound haricots verts, trimmed
¼ pound peppercress or watercress
1 yellow bell pepper, cored, seeded, and cut into thin lengths (trimmings reserved and chopped)
Freshly ground black pepper
1 tablespoon extra virgin olive oil
Juice of ½ lemon

Peppercress is a spicier, less domesticated relative of watercress. Use watercress when it is unavailable.

Making the vinaigrette.
Heat 2 tablespoons of the oil in a large skillet over medium heat. Add the onion and chopped pepper (including the reserved trimmings from the pepper used in the salad) and cook, stirring, until the pepper softens, about 3 minutes. Season with salt, reduce the heat to medium-low, cover, and cook, stirring occasionally, until the onion and pepper are very tender, about 20 minutes.

Add the vinegar and ¼ cup water and gently simmer, uncovered, until the liquid is reduced by about three-fourths, about 15 minutes.

Puree the pepper mixture in a blender or food processor until smooth, then gradually add the remaining ½ cup olive oil. Season the vinaigrette with salt, press it through a fine sieve, and set aside.

Preparing the vegetables.
Cook the potatoes in boiling salted water until just tender, about 10 minutes. Remove the potatoes from the water and place them in a large bowl.

Add the haricots verts to the boiling water and cook until they are tender, 3 to 5 minutes. Drain, rinse under cold water, and set aside in a second bowl.

Trim and clean the cress. Combine with the haricots, add the pepper lengths, and salt and pepper to taste.

Assembling the salad.
Heat the vinaigrette over very low heat just until it is warm. Lightly coat the potatoes with the vinaigrette (any remaining vinaigrette can be refrigerated; reheat before serving). Season the potatoes with salt and pepper. Dress the cress salad with the olive oil and lemon juice to taste. Mound the salad on top of the potatoes and serve.

layered bread and tomato salad with tapenade vinaigrette

FOR THE VINAIGRETTE

2 large shallots, peeled and sliced
1 clove garlic, peeled and sliced
½ cup sherry vinegar
30 Niçoise olives or other medium
   salty black olives, pitted
3 anchovies, rinsed if salt-packed
1 tablespoon capers
½ cup extra virgin olive oil
Fine sea salt

FOR THE SALAD

4 medium tomatoes, thinly sliced
Kosher or fine sea salt and freshly
   ground black pepper
2 tablespoons extra virgin olive oil
2 large shallots, peeled and thinly
   sliced
8 Croutons (page 127)
2 cups spicy greens, such as
   arugula (see the chart, page 61)

This dish was inspired by panzanella, the Italian bread and tomato salad. It is fantastic made with garden-fresh tomatoes, but still surprisingly flavorful when made with store-bought. The trick is curing the tomatoes. The salt draws moisture from them and intensifies their flavor (see also Slow-Roasted Tomatoes, page 55). The flavor of the extracted juice is subtle and delicious. I soak the croutons in it before adding them to the salad.

Making the vinaigrette.
Combine the shallots, garlic, vinegar, and ¼ cup water in a small saucepan and gently simmer over medium-low heat until the shallots are soft and the liquid is reduced slightly, about 10 minutes. Remove the pan from the heat and allow to cool.

Pulse the olives, anchovies, and capers in a food processor, then add the shallot and vinegar mixture. With the machine running, add the olive oil and puree until smooth. Season to taste with sea salt and set aside.

Preparing the tomatoes.
Arrange the tomatoes in a single overlapping layer in a shallow dish. Season them with about ½ teaspoon salt, a liberal amount of pepper, and the olive oil. Top them with the sliced shallots. Spoon about ¼ cup of the vinaigrette over the tomatoes and set them aside to marinate for about 2 hours at room temperature (or overnight in the refrigerator).

Assembling the salad.
Drain the tomatoes, reserving the juices. Dunk the croutons in the reserved tomato juices (let them soak a bit if you like softer bread).

Place the greens in a small bowl; add about 2 tablespoons of the vinaigrette, salt to taste, and a little pepper; toss to coat. Place a piece of bread on each plate and top with 2 or 3 tomato slices and a small handful of greens. Repeat, adding another layer of bread and tomatoes and ending with greens. Drizzle each plate with a little vinaigrette and serve.

This is a nice first course on which you can build by adding fava beans, white beans, leeks, or an herb salad. At dinner, I serve the salad with pan-roasted tuna. I usually make a double batch of the vinaigrette. It is good tossed with pasta and Slow-Roasted Tomatoes (page 55) or served as a sauce for grilled fish or chicken.

flavor chart for cruciferae

The Cruciferae family, sometimes called the mustard or cabbage family, is most clearly defined by its assertive flavors: hot, spicy, and peppery. Notice that the leaves of arugula, cress, and mustard greens are close flavor relatives to the peppery roots of radish, turnip, and horseradish. These are all in the same family. Although cabbages, broccoli, and cauliflower are not spicy, they are similarly robust.

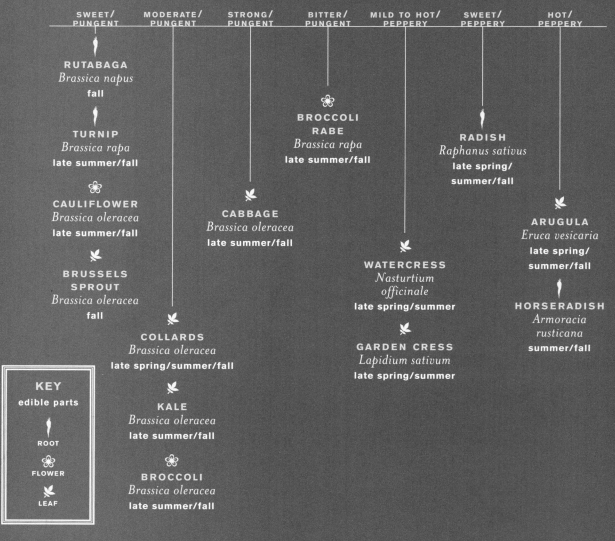

| SWEET/ PUNGENT | MODERATE/ PUNGENT | STRONG/ PUNGENT | BITTER/ PUNGENT | MILD TO HOT/ PEPPERY | SWEET/ PEPPERY | HOT/ PEPPERY |

RUTABAGA
Brassica napus
fall

TURNIP
Brassica rapa
late summer/fall

CAULIFLOWER
Brassica oleracea
late summer/fall

BRUSSELS SPROUT
Brassica oleracea
fall

COLLARDS
Brassica oleracea
late spring/summer/fall

KALE
Brassica oleracea
late summer/fall

BROCCOLI
Brassica oleracea
late summer/fall

CABBAGE
Brassica oleracea
late summer/fall

BROCCOLI RABE
Brassica rapa
late summer/fall

WATERCRESS
Nasturtium officinale
late spring/summer

GARDEN CRESS
Lapidium sativum
late spring/summer

RADISH
Raphanus sativus
late spring/ summer/fall

ARUGULA
Eruca vesicaria
late spring/ summer/fall

HORSERADISH
Armoracia rusticana
summer/fall

KEY
edible parts

ROOT

FLOWER

LEAF

sautéed greens {**COLLARDS, KALE**} 43, parmesan broth with sautéed greens {**COLLARDS, KALE**} 82
KALE pesto 44, sunchoke ravioli with **KALE** pesto 105
HORSERADISH dumplings 43, ruby risotto with winter greens {**KALE, HORSERADISH**} 104
spicy green salad with strawberry vinaigrette {**WATERCRESS**} 62
PEPPERCRESS salad with yellow pepper vinaigrette 64
layered bread and tomato salad with tapenade vinaigrette {**ARUGULA**} 65
roasted winter vegetable stew {**TURNIP, RUTABAGA**} 91
CABBAGE and lentil stew with spaetzle 88, borscht {**RED CABBAGE**} 79
farfalle and **CAULIFLOWER** with bread crumbs 103

flavor chart for compositae

The members of the Compositae family have a variety of edible plant parts. This family includes flowers such as chamomile as well as edible roots, tubers, thistles, and leaves. Flavors swing from bitter to sweet. Bitter flavors are found among the chicories (radicchio, endive). Artichokes bridge the bitter-to-sweet divide, and sweetness characterizes Bibb and romaine lettuces, sunchokes, and salsify. Note that most salad greens are found in this family, except the peppery ones, which are in the Cruciferae family.

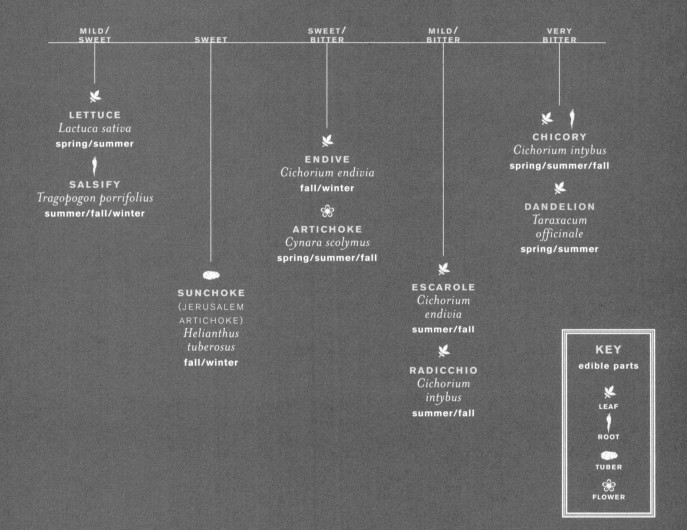

MILD/SWEET

LETTUCE
Lactuca sativa
spring/summer

SALSIFY
Tragopogon porrifolius
summer/fall/winter

SWEET

SUNCHOKE
(JERUSALEM ARTICHOKE)
Helianthus tuberosus
fall/winter

SWEET/BITTER

ENDIVE
Cichorium endivia
fall/winter

ARTICHOKE
Cynara scolymus
spring/summer/fall

MILD/BITTER

ESCAROLE
Cichorium endivia
summer/fall

RADICCHIO
Cichorium intybus
summer/fall

VERY BITTER

CHICORY
Cichorium intybus
spring/summer/fall

DANDELION
Taraxacum officinale
spring/summer

KEY
edible parts

LEAF

ROOT

TUBER

FLOWER

tomato and cucumber salad with avocado cream

SERVES 4

This is the perfect summer appetizer. You can add Shrimp Confit (page 138) or pair it with Scallop Ceviche with Chili Vinaigrette (page 134) for a more complex dish.

Gelatin leaves can be substituted for powdered. Use one leaf per 1½ to 2 cups cold liquid (the exact amount depends on the firmness desired). Allow the gelatin leaf to soften, then proceed.

FOR THE SALAD

1 cucumber
2 tablespoons extra virgin olive oil
Fine sea salt
7 small to medium tomatoes
Freshly ground black pepper
1 teaspoon powdered gelatin
2 tablespoons roughly chopped
   flat-leaf parsley
2 tablespoons roughly chopped
   cilantro

FOR THE AVOCADO CREAM

1 Hass avocado
Juice of 1 lemon
2 tablespoons Crème Fraîche
   (page 204)
Kosher salt
Pinch of cayenne pepper

This is a tall salad that began as a deconstructed guacamole and became a celebration of perfectly ripe juicy tomatoes. It is also a study of textures. Begin with the best-tasting tomatoes you can find. Look for heirloom varieties toward the end of August, and try to balance taste, color, and size. Then add the very slightly jelled cucumber juice, which is remarkably refreshing. Finally, add avocado whipped with crème fraîche. As the salad is eaten, it rearranges and the taste changes.

Marinating the cucumber and making the jam.
Peel the cucumber. Using the vegetable peeler, shave the cucumber into thin lengths, stopping short of the seedy core. Place the core in a food processor and the cucumber lengths in a bowl. Add the olive oil and a pinch of salt to the cucumber lengths. Cover the bowl and refrigerate.

Core and quarter 2 of the tomatoes and add them to the food processor. Puree the mixture until smooth, then strain through a medium strainer into a bowl. Season with salt and pepper.

Sprinkle the gelatin over 2 tablespoons warm water in a small bowl and set aside for a minute or so.

Heat the strained vegetable puree in a small saucepan just until the mixture feels warm (do not allow it to boil). Remove the pan from the heat and stir in the gelatin. Season the mixture with salt and pepper, then transfer it to a bowl and chill until the "jam" sets, about 1 hour. (It will be softly jelled, not firm.)

Making the avocado cream.
Shortly before serving, peel and pit the avocado. Combine the avocado, lemon juice, and crème fraîche in a food processor or blender and puree until smooth. Season the mixture with salt and cayenne, then press it through a medium strainer into a small bowl.

Assembling the salad.

Add the parsley and cilantro to the marinated cucumber lengths, adjust the seasoning with salt and pepper, and mix well. Core the remaining 5 tomatoes and cut them into 4 wedges each. Season with salt and pepper.

Arrange 3 tomato wedges on each plate. Dress the tomatoes first with some of the tomato-cucumber jam and then with avocado cream, then top with half the marinated cucumbers. Place 2 more tomato wedges on each salad; dress with the remaining jam and avocado cream. Finish with the remaining cucumbers and serve.

bibb, endive, and blue cheese salad with apple vinaigrette

SERVES 6

FOR THE VINAIGRETTE

2 tablespoons sugar
1 Granny Smith apple, cored and chopped
1/2 cup flat-leaf parsley leaves
1/4 cup rice wine vinegar
1 cup grapeseed oil
Kosher salt and freshly ground black pepper

FOR THE SALAD

2 heads Bibb lettuce, leaves separated
3 endives, sliced crosswise about 1/2 inch thick, stopping short of the core
1/2 Granny Smith apple, peeled, cored, cut into julienne, and tossed with a little lemon juice to prevent darkening
6 ounces Stilton or other blue cheese, rind removed and crumbled
1/4 cup pomegranate seeds (optional)
Flat-leaf parsley leaves for garnish (optional)

A neutral oil, grapeseed, rather than a more powerful oil such as olive, allows the clean tastes of the green apple and parsley vinaigrette to reign. Adding an ice cube to the vinaigrette keeps it bright green.

Making the vinaigrette.

Heat the sugar with 2 tablespoons water in a very small saucepan just until the sugar dissolves. Allow the sugar syrup to cool.

Combine the apple, parsley leaves, vinegar, and sugar syrup in a blender or food processor. Add an ice cube and process until smooth. With the machine running, slowly add the oil. Season with salt and pepper and refrigerate until ready to use. (The vinaigrette will keep for 2 to 3 days.)

Making the salad.

Combine the lettuce, endive, apple, and cheese in a bowl and mix well. Dress with about the half the vinaigrette, mixing well, then add just enough of the remaining vinaigrette so the salad is coated but not soggy. Serve garnished with pomegranate seeds and parsley leaves, if desired.

Any peppery or bitter green can be substituted for the endive in this salad; see Spicy Green Salad with Strawberry Vinaigrette (page 62) for suggestions.
This salad works before or after a hearty entrée. For lunch, you might serve it accompanied by smoked trout or sturgeon. It could also stand up to Duck Confit (page 163).

carpaccio of quince with endive salad and pecan vinaigrette

Unlike apples and pears, quinces must be cooked beyond initial softness until they really get rosy—they should look like poached peaches when done.

Save the quince seeds and peels. They are high in pectin (a natural thickening agent) and make a lovely glaze when stewed: Combine the seeds and peels of 1 quince with 1¾ cups water (or, better yet, quince poaching liquid) in a small saucepan. Season with 2 tablespoons rice wine vinegar, ¼ cup fresh lemon juice, and ½ cup sugar. Gently simmer until the mixture is rosy and syrupy, at least an hour. Strain, then serve over ice cream or use to glaze game or poultry.

Quinces combine well with strong-tasting ingredients—here, meaty pecans and bitter endive. As quinces are wonderful with game and pork, prosciutto would be a nice addition to this salad.

FOR THE CARPACCIO

1 cup sugar
½ cup rice wine vinegar
Juice of 1 lemon
2 large quinces (see the sidebar)

FOR THE VINAIGRETTE

¾ cup pecans, coarsely chopped
½ cup grapeseed oil
½ cup balsamic vinegar
Kosher salt and freshly ground
   black pepper

FOR THE SALAD

3 endives, outer leaves removed
¼ cup parsley leaves
¼ cup ½-inch chive lengths
Kosher salt and freshly ground
   black pepper

Because of its high sugar content, the balsamic vinegar must be reduced with care. Take the pan off the stove to check the consistency. Add a little water if you fear the vinegar has reduced too much.

Poaching the quinces.
Combine the sugar, rice wine vinegar, and lemon juice in a medium saucepan and add 2 cups water. Peel and seed the quinces. Cut each quince into 8 pieces and immediately drop them into the liquid. Bring to a boil, cover the quinces with a dish towel to keep them submerged, reduce the heat, and simmer until the quinces are completely soft, about 1 hour. Remove from the poaching liquid and cool.

Making the vinaigrette.
Combine the pecans and oil in a small saucepan and heat until the oil is hot but not bubbling. Reduce the heat to low and cook until the oil tastes like pecans, about 15 minutes. Allow the oil to cool.

Meanwhile, pour the balsamic into a small saucepan and reduce at a gentle simmer for about 5 minutes, until it is slightly thicker and reduced by about half. (If the vinegar reduces too much it will solidify when it cools. Check the consistency occasionally.) Remove it from the heat. Allow it to cool for 5 minutes, then add the pecan oil and season with salt and pepper.

Making the salad and finishing the carpaccio.
Slice the endive into rounds, discarding the cores. Combine the endive, parsley, and chives in a bowl and dress with a little of the vinaigrette. Season with salt and pepper and mix well, adding only enough additional vinaigrette to coat the endive.

Place 3 to 4 pieces of quince on a large plate. Cover with plastic wrap and gently press down with the bottom of a glass or measuring cup, forming a single ⅛-inch-thick layer. Season with pepper. Repeat with the remaining quinces on three other plates. Place a small mound of salad on top of each, drizzle with vinaigrette, and serve.

pickled beet salad with oranges and taleggio cheese

Pickled Beets (page 38)
4 small seedless oranges
2 ounces Taleggio cheese, rind
   removed, cut into small pieces
1/4 to 1/2 cup heavy cream
Freshly ground black pepper
2 large or 4 small endives
1/4 cup flat-leaf parsley leaves
1/4 cup 1/2-inch chive lengths
Kosher salt
2 tablespoons extra virgin olive oil

The dressing for this salad is a Taleggio cheese fondue, an easy melted cheese sauce. Taleggio, a soft cow's milk, mold-ripened Italian cheese, has a strong, creamy taste with a slight wine flavor. It melts evenly. Be careful not to get the fondue too hot and to whisk constantly as the cheese melts; the sauce will break (the solids separating from the liquids) if it begins to boil. Any leftover cheese mixture can be refrigerated and then reheated or used at room temperature as a spread.

Drain the beets, reserving the shallots and 1 tablespoon of the pickling liquid. Place the beets and the shallots in a salad bowl. (The remaining pickling liquid can be reused for pickling beets or reserved to make Borscht or a Beet Vinaigrette; see page 79 or 38.)

With a sharp knife, peel the oranges, removing all the bitter white pith. Slice between the membranes to release the orange segments; discard the membranes. Add the orange segments to the pickled beets.

Combine the cheese and 1/4 cup cream in the top of a double boiler set over simmering water. Whisking constantly, gently warm the cheese until it melts. Add more cream if the mixture is too thick. Season the mixture with pepper and remove the pan from the heat. Keep the cheese warm over the hot water.

Slice the endives, discarding the cores. Add the endive, parsley, chives, and salt and pepper to taste to the beet mixture and mix gently. Dress the salad with the reserved pickling liquid and the olive oil, and arrange on plates. Give the cheese mixture a stir, then drizzle a spoonful or so over each salad. Serve.

In past incarnations of this recipe, I used diced roasted and pickled beets (see Ruby Risotto with Winter Greens, page 104) rather than sliced. I have also served the cheese on Croutons (page 127) rather than as a sauce. I always use blood oranges when they are in season.

salads   71

shallot vinaigrette

⅓ cup extra virgin olive oil
2 shallots, peeled and thinly sliced
1 garlic clove, peeled and minced
2 tablespoons Champagne vinegar
1 teaspoon Dijon mustard
1 teaspoon chopped tarragon
1 teaspoon chopped flat-leaf parsley
Kosher salt

Very good with sweet soft lettuces, this vinaigrette also works well as a dressing for potato salad.

Heat the oil in a small skillet over low heat. Add the shallots and cook until they begin to brown, about 10 minutes. Add the garlic and cook until it is soft, about 3 minutes more. Remove the pan from the heat. Add the vinegar and mustard, then add the herbs. Season with salt and serve, or refrigerate for up to 3 days.

lemon–mustard vinaigrette

1½ tablespoons juice of fresh or
   roasted lemon
2 tablespoons red wine vinegar
½ tablespoon Dijon mustard
¼ teaspoon dry mustard
¼ teaspoon coarsely ground
   mustard seeds
Kosher salt and freshly ground
   white pepper
¼ cup canola oil
¼ cup extra virgin olive oil

This is our house vinaigrette. It can be varied by adding herbs or substituting a flavored oil for a portion of the olive oil. I like this dressing best made with roasted lemon juice. Roasting citrus fruits sweetens the juice and results in a more complex flavor (see Butternut Squash Ravioli with Roasted Orange Reduction, page 100).

Combine the lemon juice, vinegar, Dijon mustard, dry mustard, and ground mustard seeds in a medium bowl. Season with salt and white pepper. In a small bowl, combine the oils. Gradually whisk the oil into the lemon mixture. Adjust the seasoning if necessary and serve, or refrigerate for up to 1 week.

Vinaigrettes

I use different vinaigrettes for different purposes. Here I've included a warm shallot vinaigrette, an all-purpose lemon-mustard vinaigrette, and Green Goddess mayonnaise—an herby emulsified vinaigrette.

the anatomy of a dish

green goddess mayonnaise

MAKES ABOUT
2 ¼ CUPS

2 egg yolks, lightly beaten
1 tablespoon capers, rinsed
1 tablespoon Dijon mustard
1 tablespoon chopped tarragon
2 tablespoons chopped chives
2 tablespoons chopped flat-leaf
 parsley
2 tablespoons Champagne vinegar
¼ cup extra virgin olive oil
¾ cup grapeseed oil
2 tablespoons lemon juice
Kosher salt and freshly ground
 black pepper
Pinch cayenne

To make this dressing, my favorite with chilled seafood, simply add capers and fresh herbs to homemade mayonnaise. For a basic mayonnaise recipe, see the variation that follows.

Combine the egg yolks, capers, mustard, tarragon, chives, and parsley in a food processor and pulse until blended. Add the vinegar; then, with the motor running, add the olive and grapeseed oils. Stir in the lemon juice, salt, pepper, and cayenne to taste and refrigerate up to 3 days until ready to use.

VARIATION

mayonnaise

Combine 2 egg yolks and 1 tablespoon of Dijon mustard in a food processor and pulse. Add the vinegar, oils, and seasoning as specified above.

Green goddess mayonnaise is an ingredient in Baked Clams (page 139).

In addition to herbs, mayonnaise can be flavored with Slow-Roasted Tomatoes (page 55), Garlic Confit (page 41), or chopped anchovies.

flavor chart for chenopodiaceae

The Chenopodiaceae family includes a small group of edibles, among them spinach, Swiss chard, and beets, all braising greens with particular personalities though somewhat neutral in flavor and high in oxalic acid. Quinoa, often grouped with grains, is really a seed that belongs to this family.

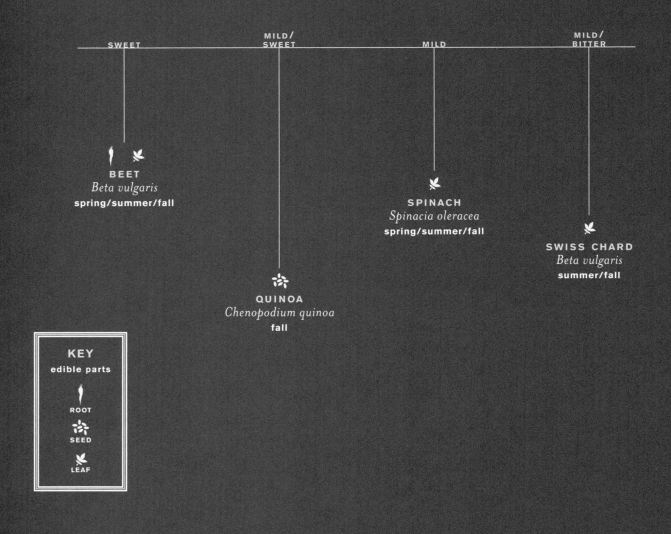

SWEET

MILD/
SWEET

MILD

MILD/
BITTER

BEET
Beta vulgaris
spring/summer/fall

SPINACH
Spinacia oleracea
spring/summer/fall

SWISS CHARD
Beta vulgaris
summer/fall

QUINOA
Chenopodium quinoa
fall

KEY
edible parts

ROOT

SEED

LEAF

pickled **BEETS** 38, roasted **BEETS** 38
pickled **BEET** salad with oranges and taleggio cheese 71, borscht {**BEETS**} 79
ruby risotto with winter greens {**BEETS**} 104
QUINOA 53, **QUINOA**-crusted chicken 176
SPINACH and herb sauce 54, **SPINACH** and ricotta dumplings in broth 95, sorrel soup {**SPINACH**} 83
braised greens tart {**SWISS CHARD, SPINACH**} 112

flavor chart for solanaceae

Solanaceae is familiarly known as the nightshade family. Some plants in this family have toxic leaves and fruits. Tomatoes, potatoes, and eggplants are members of the family, as are all peppers, gooseberries, and tomatillos. This family has an unusually wide range of flavors from sweet to sour to hot. There is also considerable range within some individual species such as peppers. Note the common astringent or acidic quality found in the fruits of this family and the lack thereof in potatoes—a tuber. A tuber, because it is a different plant part, has different texture and flavor characteristics.

SWEET	MILD/ SWEET	PUNGENT/ SWEET	SOUR/ SWEET	BITTER/ SWEET	VARIABLE/ SWEET–HOT

CAPE GOOSEBERRY
Physalis peruviana
spring/summer/fall

TOMATILLO
Physalis ixocarpa
spring/summer

CHILE PEPPER
Capsicum annuum
summer/fall

TOMATO
Lycopersicon esculentum
summer/fall

EGGPLANT
Solanum melongena
summer/fall

POTATO
Solanum tuberosum
summer/fall/winter

KEY
edible parts

FRUIT

TUBER

roasted **EGGPLANT** puree 41, baby lamb chops with roasted **EGGPLANT** salad 171
EGGPLANT and garlic stew with merguez sausage 90
parsnip and **POTATO** galette 51, flame-roasted **PEPPERS** 52, sunchoke and **POTATO** puree 54,
POTATO galette with duck confit 179
peppercress salad with **YELLOW PEPPER** vinaigrette 64
slow-roasted **TOMATOES** 65, layered bread and **TOMATO** salad with tapenade vinaigrette 65
TOMATO and cucumber salad with avocado cream 68, halibut with **TOMATO**-cumin sauce 150
green gazpacho {**TOMATILLO**} 80
mackerel with **PAPRIKA** sauce 153
spiced tuna with romesco sauce {**RED PEPPER, TOMATO**} 155

soups and stews

Soups and stews begin the same way and pose the same culinary challenge. With very few exceptions, all start by cooking a combination of aromatic vegetables. This serves as a flavor foundation and provides the finished soup or stew with sweetness, richness, and authority. The problem facing the cook is how to make the most of this important first step.

In France, the name for this vegetable combination is *mirepoix*. In my kitchen a basic mirepoix, like the French original, consists of chopped onions, leeks, carrots, and celery.

Like many American chefs, I also use the borrowed term to describe a number of other vegetable combinations. I might use an onion, leek, celery, and fennel mirepoix or an onion and garlic mirepoix.

To cook properly, the vegetables for any mirepoix must all be cut to the same size. This allows the vegetables to cook evenly without burning. My mirepoix cooks moderately slowly, in a skim of oil over medium or medium-low heat. Adding a little water when the contents of the pot begin to sputter allows me to cook the vegetables longer without burning and without adding too much oil. Sometimes I brown the vegetables, for a richer, sweeter taste. More often I cook them until they are soft but not caramelized for a cleaner vegetable flavor.

Salting food changes the way it cooks, so I add salt and fresh pepper as I go. Salt promotes the release of liquid, allowing the vegetable juices to mingle in the pot. Adding salt throughout cooking, rather than only at the end, also avoids imparting a sharp salty taste to the finished food. I generally use kosher salt during cooking, then finish with a little sea salt.

Once the flavor foundation is established, constructing the rest of the dish begins. This follows a standard pattern for both soups and stews, with or without meat. I add warm-tasting, quick-cooking flavorings, such as garlic and ginger, if inclined, and then, and only then, add the leading performer—the mushrooms and barley in Mushroom Barley Soup (page 81), for example, or the

Soup vegetables: the Umbelliferae family—fennel, carrot, celery root, celery

roasted vegetables in Roasted Winter Vegetable Stew (page 91).

The amount and type of liquid added depends on what's in the pot and the results you seek. If you are making soup and have a pot full of barley, add a generous quantity of liquid, enough to allow the barley to expand and soften while still leaving some broth. If you're making a stew and your pot contains roasted vegetables, add a good deal less liquid. In either case, simmer, rather than boil, the liquid long enough so that it captures some of the essence of what has preceded it into the pot.

borscht

2 tablespoons extra virgin olive oil
2 medium onions, peeled and
    diced
2 medium carrots, peeled and
    diced
2 stalks celery, diced
¼ head red cabbage, chopped
Kosher salt and freshly ground
    black pepper
1½ pounds roasted beets
    (about 12), peeled and diced
    (see page 38)
¼ to ¾ cup sugar
1 cup dry red wine
1 cup red wine vinegar
Sachet filled with:
    1 bay leaf
    1 sprig thyme
    1 cinnamon stick
    2 cloves
    1 teaspoon black peppercorns
4 cups Chicken Stock (page 170)
1 Idaho or other russet potato,
    peeled and diced

Roasting coaxes a deeper, more subtle sugar flavor from many vegetables, particularly those, such as beets, that grow underground. I balance the sweetness with red wine and vinegar and am always mindful of the fact that the soup will become sweeter if refrigerated overnight.

Heat the oil in a large pot over medium heat. Add the onions, carrots, celery, and cabbage, season with salt and pepper, and cook, stirring frequently, until the vegetables soften, about 15 minutes.

Add the diced beets, ¼ cup sugar, the wine, vinegar, sachet, stock, and 4 cups water. Season generously with salt and pepper and bring to a simmer. Simmer until the broth is flavorful, about 15 minutes.

Add the diced potato and continue cooking until the potato is tender, about 15 minutes longer. Just before serving, adjust the seasoning with salt, pepper, and sugar. Serve warm or chilled.

Serve the borscht warm, topped with Horseradish Crème Fraîche (page 105) as a first course, or topped with shredded Beer-Braised Short Ribs (page 169) as a main course.

soups and stews   79

SERVES
4 TO 6

green gazpacho

For large parties, try serving hors d'oeuvre portions of soup in demitasse cups. Garnish with pepper puree: Puree 1 roasted red bell pepper (see page 52), peeled, seeded, and cored, with ¼ cup olive oil, and drizzle over the soup before serving.

4 cups basil leaves
Kosher salt
¼ cup Champagne vinegar
¼ cup extra virgin olive oil
¾ pound tomatillos, husked and washed
6 scallions, white parts only
8 cups peeled chopped cucumbers (about 2 pounds)
1 teaspoon paprika
¼ teaspoon cayenne pepper, or to taste
3 tablespoons honey, or to taste

My tomatoless gazpacho, made with cucumbers and tomatillos, is light and tart. Tomatillos, like tomatoes, are members of the Solanaceae family. They are not immature green tomatoes but a different fruit, prized by Mexican cooks for their citrus taste. Less seedy and juicy than tomatoes, tomatillos, also known as husk tomatoes, are available at gourmet markets.

Blanch the basil in a pot of boiling salted water. Drain, then refresh the basil in ice water. Squeeze dry.

Combine the vinegar, oil, and 1 cup water in a blender or food processor. Add the basil, then add the tomatillos, scallions, and cucumbers in small batches, pureeing as you go. Add the paprika, cayenne, and honey and blend well. Thin the soup if necessary with water, then adjust the seasoning with salt, cayenne, and honey. Chill and serve.

the anatomy of a dish

mushroom barley soup

SERVES
6 TO 8

About 6 tablespoons extra virgin olive oil
¼ cup hulled barley
¾ pound mixed wild and cultivated mushrooms, such as shiitake, portobello, hen-of-the-woods, and oyster mushrooms, trimmed and sliced
Kosher salt and freshly ground black pepper
1 large onion, peeled and finely diced
2 cloves garlic, peeled and minced
2 tablespoons butter
1¾ cups Mushroom Puree (page 48)
Sachet filled with:
  1 bay leaf
  1 clove garlic
  1 teaspoon black peppercorns
  2 allspice berries
  3 large sprigs thyme
  a handful of parsley stems
1 tablespoon finely chopped flat-leaf parsley
1 tablespoon finely chopped thyme

Barley can be purchased simply hulled or polished. I prefer the former for this rustic soup and the latter for more refined purposes.

Toasting the barley.
Heat 1 tablespoon of the oil in a medium skillet over medium heat. Add the barley and toast, stirring occasionally, until it is fragrant and golden, about 10 minutes. Transfer the barley to a bowl and set aside.

Sautéing the mushrooms.
Add another 2 tablespoons oil to a large pot and increase the heat to medium-high. Add about half the mushrooms (just enough to fill but not crowd the pan) and cook until the edges begin to crisp, about 2 minutes. Flip the mushrooms, season with salt and pepper, and continue cooking just until they are tender, about 1 minute more, then transfer to a plate. Repeat with the remaining mushrooms, adding more oil to the pan if necessary.

Starting the soup.
Add 2 tablespoons of the oil to the pot over medium heat. Add the onion, season with salt and pepper, and cook, stirring and scraping browned bits from the bottom, until the onion softens slightly, 3 to 5 minutes. Add the garlic and butter and cook, stirring every so often, until the onions are very soft and beginning to brown, about 15 minutes more. Add the mushroom puree and cook, stirring frequently, until fragrant, about 5 minutes.

Add 10 cups water, the toasted barley, and the sachet and bring the soup to a simmer, stirring occasionally to prevent the puree from settling. Skim the soup, reduce the heat, and gently simmer, stirring occasionally, until the barley is soft, about 1 hour.

Finishing the soup.
Add the sautéed mushrooms to the soup. Adjust the seasoning with salt and pepper and cook for 5 to 10 minutes longer. Remove the sachet, add the parsley and thyme, and serve.

Toasting grains is a useful technique. It gives them a nutty flavor and seals in the starch. Toasted grains hold their shapes after cooking. This technique also works well with small or delicate pastas; see Toasted Angel Hair Pasta in Shiitake Broth (page 97) and Couscous with Artichokes and Gigante Beans (page 89).

81

parmesan broth with sautéed greens

SERVES 4

Instead of cocktail meatballs, whisk one beaten egg into the simmering broth.

FOR THE BROTH

2 tablespoons extra virgin olive oil
1 large onion, peeled and chopped
1 large leek, white part only, chopped
2 stalks celery, chopped
2 cloves garlic, peeled
2 medium tomatoes, peeled and chopped
6 cups Chicken Stock (page 170)
Sachet filled with:
  about ¼ cup smoked ham or a ham bone
  a piece of Parmigiano-Reggiano rind
  3 sprigs oregano
  3 sprigs thyme
Freshly ground black pepper

Sautéed Greens (page 43)
12 Cocktail Meatballs (page 164) (optional)
Freshly grated Parmigiano-Reggiano for serving (optional)

This simple enhanced chicken broth is flavored with leftover Parmesan cheese rinds. I use this as a starting point for a number of different soups. Beans, pasta, sautéed pancetta, and diced sautéed vegetables are favorite additions.

Making the broth.
Heat the oil in a large pot over medium heat. Add the onion, leek, celery, and garlic and cook, stirring occasionally, until the vegetables soften, about 20 minutes.

Add the tomatoes and cook for about 5 minutes, then add the chicken stock and sachet. Bring to a simmer and cook, skimming as necessary, until the broth is flavorful, about 1 hour. Strain the broth.

Finishing the soup.
Return the broth to the stove, season with pepper, and bring to a simmer. Skim any fat that rises to the surface. Add the greens and the meatballs, if using, and heat through for 5 minutes. Ladle the soup into bowls and serve topped with the cheese, if desired.

the anatomy of a dish

sorrel soup

2 tablespoons extra virgin olive oil
2 onions, peeled and chopped
4 leeks, chopped
Kosher salt and freshly ground
    black pepper
1 pound sorrel, stems trimmed
2 cups Chicken Stock (page 170)
1 lemon
1 pound spinach, stems trimmed

Sorrel is a favorite of mine in both soups and sauces. It is a natural thickener (it seems to melt as it cooks) and has a subtle citrus flavor. This recipe includes spinach (no botanical relation) because, unlike sorrel, it softens but retains its form when cooked, providing a nice textural dimension.

Heat the oil in a large pot over medium heat. Add the onions and leeks and cook, stirring occasionally, until the vegetables soften slightly, 3 to 5 minutes, then add ¼ cup water and salt and pepper. Cook until the vegetables are completely soft and the pan is dry, about 15 minutes more.

Add the sorrel. When the sorrel is wilted, add the stock and 1 cup water and bring to a simmer. Gently simmer the soup until the sorrel begins to dissolve, about 20 minutes.

Finely grate the lemon zest; halve the lemon and set aside. Add the spinach and the zest to the soup and cook until the spinach has softened, about 10 minutes more. Puree the soup in a blender or food processor. Thin the soup with up to 1 cup water, then adjust the seasoning with salt, pepper, and lemon juice to taste. Serve warm or chilled.

You can serve this soup warm with Spinach and Ricotta Dumplings (page 95) or chilled, topped with Crème Fraîche (page 204).

To use sorrel to make a sauce, simply "melt" it in olive oil over medium-low heat, puree it, thin it with chicken stock, and season with lemon juice and sea salt (see Spinach and Herb Sauce, page 54). This is also wonderful with salmon, sturgeon, or skate.

flavor chart for umbelliferae

Umbelliferae is another family that boasts a natural culinary grouping. The sweet and aromatic soup or mirepoix vegetables, as well as most of the herbs included in a French bouquet garni, are found here (see the Herbs and Spices Chart, page 111). Fennel, carrots, parsnips, celery, celery root, parsley, chervil, and coriander are some of the plants in this family.

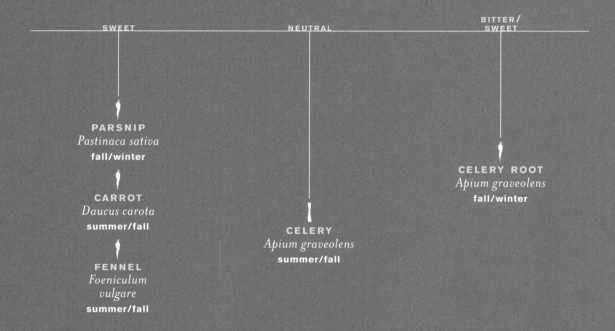

SWEET NEUTRAL BITTER/SWEET

PARSNIP
Pastinaca sativa
fall/winter

CARROT
Daucus carota
summer/fall

FENNEL
Foeniculum vulgare
summer/fall

CELERY
Apium graveolens
summer/fall

CELERY ROOT
Apium graveolens
fall/winter

KEY
edible parts

ROOT

STALK

CELERY ROOT mash 39, seared **CELERY ROOT** and smoked trout salad 142

PARSNIP and potato galette 51, **PARSNIP** puree 51

spinach and herb sauce {**PARSLEY**} 54, cod poached in herbed clam broth {**PARSLEY**} 148

roasted winter vegetable stew {**CELERY ROOT, CARROT, PARSNIP**} 91

poached chicken {**CARROT, CELERY, FENNEL, PARSLEY, CORIANDER**} 174

vegetable stock {**CARROT, FENNEL**} 57

green goddess mayonnaise {**PARSLEY, CHERVIL**} 73

halibut with tomato-**CUMIN** sauce 150

flavor chart for cucurbitaceae

The Cucurbitaceae family is most noted for its climbing, twisting vines and its vegetable fruits.
Cucumber, summer and winter squashes, and melons are all related—and they look that way.
All these fruits share a natural sweetness, though generally a savory one.

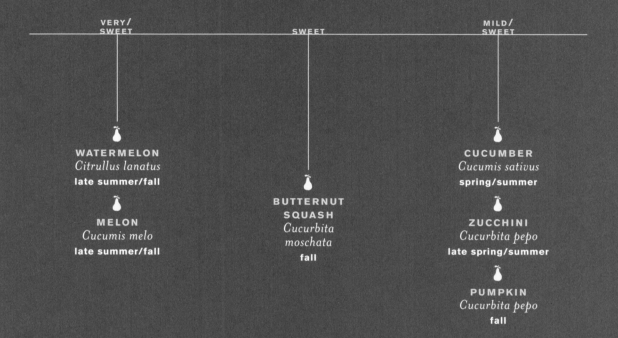

VERY/
SWEET

SWEET

MILD/
SWEET

WATERMELON
Citrullus lanatus
late summer/fall

CUCUMBER
Cucumis sativus
spring/summer

**BUTTERNUT
SQUASH**
*Cucurbita
moschata*
fall

MELON
Cucumis melo
late summer/fall

ZUCCHINI
Cucurbita pepo
late spring/summer

PUMPKIN
Cucurbita pepo
fall

KEY
edible parts

FRUIT

tomato and **CUCUMBER** salad with avocado cream 68, green gazpacho {**CUCUMBER**} 80
ZUCCHINI soup with rosemary 81
roasted winter vegetable stew {**BUTTERNUT SQUASH, ACORN SQUASH**} 91
BUTTERNUT SQUASH ravioli with roasted orange reduction 100

sweet pea soup with mint

The same technique also produces a sauce that is delicious with flounder and halibut— just reduce the water in the recipe by about 3/4 cup.

2½ cups freshly shelled peas
2 tablespoons extra virgin olive oil
1 onion, peeled and diced
2 stalks celery, diced
Kosher salt and freshly ground
    black pepper
2 cups chicken stock (page 170)
¼ cup flat-leaf parsley
10 mint leaves (use black mint
    if available)
Pinch of cayenne pepper
Pinch of freshly grated nutmeg
1 tablespoon sugar (optional)
½ cup heavy cream
1 cup pea shoots (optional)

This soup, which is great both warm and chilled, is best made with very fresh small peas (such as petits pois)— these are the sweetest. Although frozen peas can be substituted, shelling garden fresh is definitely worth the effort. The subtle flavor of black mint makes this a late-spring and early-summer treat.

Blanch ½ cup of peas in a large pot of boiling salted water until tender, 1 to 3 minutes. Drain the peas, refresh them in ice water, drain again, and reserve.

Heat the oil in a large pot over medium heat. Add the onion and celery, season with salt and pepper, and cook, stirring occasionally, until the oil sizzles, about 3 minutes; then add 3 tablespoons of water and gently sweat until the vegetables are tender, about 15 minutes. Add the stock and 2 cups of water and bring to a boil. Reduce the heat to medium-low and simmer for 10 minutes. Add the remaining 2 cups of peas and cook until bright green and tender, about 3 minutes. Add the parsley and mint and simmer until the leaves soften, about 2 minutes.

Puree the soup in a blender or food processor; add cayenne, nutmeg, sugar, if using, and salt and pepper to taste. To serve warm, strain the soup through a medium sieve and whisk in the cream. To serve cold, strain into a bowl set over an ice water bath (chilling the soup helps to fix the bright green color), then whisk in the cream. Warm or chilled, garnish the soup with the reserved peas and pea shoots, if using.

zucchini soup with rosemary

2 tablespoons extra virgin olive oil
1 large onion, peeled and chopped
Kosher salt and freshly ground
  black pepper
3 medium zucchini, peeled and
  chopped
Sachet filled with:
  1 bay leaf
  2 sprigs rosemary
  1 tablespoon black peppercorns
  1 teaspoon coriander seeds
  4 allspice berries
1 cup Chicken Stock (page 170)
Pinch of freshly grated nutmeg

It is a good idea when making pureed vegetable soups like this one to put all the vegetables in the blender, then add the broth in stages. This ensures that you don't add too much. If your soup is too thick after adding all the liquid, add water rather than stock. It is the evaporation of water that has left you with too little broth, so that is all that should be replaced.

Heat the oil in a medium pot over medium heat. Add the onion and cook until it softens slightly, 3 to 5 minutes. Add ¼ cup water and salt and pepper and cook, stirring occasionally, until the onion is soft and the pan dry, about 10 minutes more. Add the zucchini and a little more salt. Reduce the heat to medium-low, cover, and cook until the zucchini softens, about 15 minutes.

Add the sachet, chicken stock, and 1 cup water. Bring to a simmer, uncovered, over medium heat and simmer until the broth is flavorful, about 15 minutes. Discard the sachet and puree the soup in a blender or food processor.

Adjust the seasoning with salt and nutmeg and serve warm.

Early summer, when the zucchini are young and sweet, is the time to try this straightforward soup. It is delicious over couscous as a first course.

cabbage and lentil stew with spaetzle

You might garnish this main-course stew with Sautéed Greens (page 43) or serve it with pan-roasted wild striped bass. The meaty and woodsy flavors go together nicely. You can also substitute flat ribbon noodles or potato gnocchi for the spaetzle. A tablespoon of caraway seeds can be added to the spaetzle rather than the stew for a slightly different effect.

FOR THE SPAETZLE

1 cup all-purpose flour
½ teaspoon kosher salt
Pinch of freshly ground black pepper
2 eggs
¼ cup milk
About 2 tablespoons extra virgin olive oil

FOR THE STEW

About ¼ cup extra virgin olive oil
2 large onions, peeled, quartered, and sliced
½ head Savoy cabbage, cored and shredded
Kosher salt and freshly ground black pepper
2 tablespoons butter
2 tablespoons mustard seeds
1½ teaspoons dry mustard
1 tablespoon caraway seeds
¼ cup balsamic vinegar
2 cups cooked Lentils (page 36)
½ cup flat-leaf parsley (optional)

Spaetzle are Eastern European free-form noodles made by poaching batter in salted water. Once parboiled, the spaetzle can be added to broths or stews, as here, or pan-fried until crisp. A nice alternative to more familiar pastas, they are quite easy to make. You can press the batter through a colander or flat cheese grater if you don't have a spaetzle maker. Just remember that this batter, like most, benefits from a rest so the gluten in the flour can relax.

Making the spaetzle batter.
Combine the flour, salt, and pepper in a large bowl. In a separate bowl, mix together the eggs and milk.

Make a well in the center of the flour, pour the egg mixture into the well, and gradually incorporate it into the dry ingredients. When the batter is smooth, cover the bowl with a dish towel and set it aside at room temperature for about 1 hour.

Starting the stew.
Heat a very large pot over medium-high heat. Heat the oil, then add the onions and cook, stirring, until they soften slightly, 3 to 5 minutes. Add the cabbage, salt, pepper, and butter and cook, stirring frequently, until the cabbage softens and begins to brown, about 20 minutes.

Add a little more salt, the mustard seeds, dry mustard, and caraway seeds and cook, stirring, until fragrant, about 5 minutes longer. Add the balsamic vinegar and 2 cups water and simmer just until the flavors blend, about 15 minutes.

Cooking the spaetzle.
Meanwhile, bring a large pot of salted water to a boil. Working in batches, push the spaetzle batter through a spaetzle maker into the boiling water. Once the

spaetzle float to the surface, allow them to cook about 1 minute longer, then lift them out of the water with a slotted spoon. Dress the cooked spaetzle lightly with oil to prevent sticking. Repeat until all the batter has been cooked.

Finishing the stew.
Add the lentils and spaetzle to the stew and simmer for about 5 minutes. Adjust the seasoning and serve garnished with the parsley leaves, if desired.

couscous with artichokes and gigante beans

SERVES
4 TO 6

1 tablespoon butter
2 cups Israeli couscous
1 fennel bulb, cored and thinly sliced
½ teaspoon turmeric
2 cups cooked gigante beans, with their cooking liquid (see page 35)
4 to 5 cups Chicken Stock (page 170) or Vegetable Stock (page 57)
Kosher salt and freshly ground black pepper
Grated zest of 1 lemon
4 braised or steamed artichokes (see page 30 or 31), sliced
2 cups chopped dandelion greens or Swiss chard

Couscous, a rolled beadlike pasta made from semolina, is eaten throughout the Middle East and North Africa. Israeli couscous is larger than most. Its size gives it a meatier taste. If Israeli couscous is unavailable, substitute small couscous or pastina and adjust the cooking time.

Melt the butter in a large saucepan over medium-low heat. Add the couscous and toast, stirring, until golden, about 3 minutes. Add the fennel and turmeric and cook, stirring frequently, until the fennel softens slightly, about 5 minutes.

Drain the beans, reserving the cooking liquid. Measure the liquid and add it and enough stock to equal 6 cups to the couscous. Season with salt and pepper and bring to a simmer over medium-high heat. Reduce the heat to medium-low, cover, and cook until the couscous is tender, 10 to 15 minutes (there will still be plenty of liquid in the pot). Add the lemon zest, beans, artichokes, and greens and cook just until the greens wilt, about 3 minutes. Adjust the seasoning, if necessary, then serve.

I like to cook pasta in a flavorful broth. The bean cooking liquid, supplemented by a little stock, is ideal. You can substitute the liquid you used to braise the artichokes.

eggplant and garlic stew with merguez sausage

Served with Wheat Berries (page 42) or rice, this is a hearty main course. Naan (page 124) would be a good accompaniment.

3 large or 6 small eggplants, halved lengthwise
6 tablespoons extra virgin olive oil
Kosher salt
½ pound merguez or other spicy sausage, casings removed and crumbled
1 large onion, peeled and diced
¼ cup dry white wine
¼ cup dry vermouth
6 sun-dried tomato halves, chopped
2 cups Chicken Stock (page 170)
Sachet filled with:
  3 sprigs thyme
  1½ teaspoons black peppercorns
  1 tablespoon coriander seeds
10 cloves Garlic Confit (page 41), chopped
Freshly ground black pepper
3 tablespoons chopped flat-leaf parsley

Merguez—spicy lamb sausage fragrant with cloves, cinnamon, coriander, and garlic—and eggplant is a great combination. If merguez is unavailable, substitute spicy pork sausage. Use purple Japanese eggplants when you can find them; they are the most consistently sweet variety. For more about eggplants, see Roasted Eggplant Puree (page 41).

Roasting the eggplant.
Preheat the oven to 425°F.

Place the eggplants cut side up on a baking sheet. Score the flesh, making crosshatch incisions through the eggplant but stopping short of the skin (this helps the eggplant to cook evenly). Drizzle the eggplant with ¼ cup of the olive oil and season with salt. Roast until the eggplant is soft, about 1 hour for large eggplants, about 20 minutes for smaller ones.

Making the stew.
Heat the remaining 2 tablespoons oil in a large pot over medium-high heat. Add the sausage and cook just until it is browned, about 10 minutes. Remove the sausage with a slotted spoon and reserve.

Add the onion to the pot and cook, stirring frequently, until it is soft and beginning to brown, about 15 minutes. Add the wine, vermouth, and sun-dried tomatoes and simmer until the pot is almost dry, 3 to 5 minutes.

Scoop the eggplant out of the skin and add it to the onion mixture. Add the stock, sachet, and garlic confit, season with salt and pepper, and cook, stirring occasionally, until the flavors have blended, about 10 minutes more. Return the sausage to the stew, stir in the parsley, and serve.

roasted winter vegetable stew

1 large carrot, peeled and cut into
  1-inch pieces
1 cup 1-inch dice acorn or
  butternut squash (or a mixture)
¼ rutabaga, peeled and cut into
  1-inch pieces
2 parsnips, peeled and cut into
  1-inch pieces
1 turnip, peeled and cut into
  1-inch pieces
About ½ cup extra virgin olive oil
½ teaspoon ground cinnamon
Kosher salt and freshly ground
  black pepper
1 large onion, peeled, quartered,
  and sliced
½ fennel bulb, cored and sliced
½ cup wakame (see the sidebar)
Sachet filled with:
  ½ cinnamon stick
  1½ teaspoons coriander seeds
  2 allspice berries
  1½ teaspoons black
    peppercorns
  1 sprig rosemary
  a handful of parsley stems
1 cup cooked Chickpeas (page 35)

The key to this dish is careful roasting. The vegetables
should be soft and golden, never mushy or blackened.
Experiment with different vegetable mixtures (starchy
root vegetables work best); you need 7 to 8 cups of
cut-up vegetables in all.

Roasting the vegetables.
Preheat the oven to 400°F.

Combine the carrot, squash, rutabaga, parsnips,
and turnip in a bowl and toss with 4 tablespoons
of the oil. Season with the cinnamon, salt to taste,
and a generous sprinkling of pepper. Spread the
vegetables in a single layer on a baking sheet. Roast
the vegetables, turning them once or twice, until they
are tender and beginning to brown, about 1 hour.

Starting the stew.
Meanwhile, heat ¼ cup of the oil in a very large pot
over medium heat. Add the onion, fennel, and salt
and pepper. Give the vegetables a stir, then cover and
cook, stirring regularly, until the onion and fennel
are very soft, about 45 minutes.

Finishing the stew.
Place the wakame in a bowl and add enough cold
water to cover by about 1 inch. Set aside until the
wakame has absorbed the water, about 15 minutes.

Meanwhile, add the roasted vegetables to the onion
mixture. Add the sachet and 4 cups water and bring
to a rapid simmer, then reduce the heat and cook
gently over medium-low heat until the vegetables soften
almost to the point of falling apart, about 20 minutes.

Add the chickpeas and heat through, 5 to 10 minutes.
Adjust the seasoning if necessary with salt and pepper,
and serve in large bowls, garnished with the wakame.

*Wakame is a type of
seaweed available dried
at most health food
stores. The sea vegetable
is a nice counterpoint
to the sweet winter root
vegetables. If wakame
is unavailable, the
stew is different but
equally good topped
with Sautéed Greens
(page 43). I like
collards, chard, or kale
with this stew.*

*This is a fully satisfying
vegetable meal.
Try it preceded by Bibb,
Endive, and Blue Cheese
Salad with Apple
Vinaigrette (page 69).*

seeds: grains and pasta

To a botanist, grains—wheat, rice, corn, barley, oats, etc.—are all seeds of plants in the Gramineae family. Beans are also seeds, but they come from plants in the Leguminosae family. In this chapter I focus on whole-grain recipes, recipes that use processed grains (bulghur wheat and white rice, for example), and pasta recipes (pasta is, of course, made with flour ground from wheat). Bean recipes are scattered throughout the book, but are written about here because of the culinary similarities of these various seeds.

Whole dried grains such as barley, wheat berries, and posole (corn) should be cooked in much the same way as dried beans: very slowly in a lot of flavorful liquid. Well-cooked beans have a consistent creamy texture throughout; the center is not al dente and the skin is not chewy or hard to digest. To achieve this goal I soak dry beans overnight (unless they are especially small and quick-cooking, like lentils). This makes the outer layer more porous so the beans absorb water evenly. Then I drain the beans and place them in a large pot. I add water or stock to cover by about 2 inches, add aromatic vegetables—generally, onion, carrot, and celery—and a handful of herbs. I also add some fat, most often olive oil but sometimes duck fat. Fat softens the texture and flavor of the finished beans.

I season with pepper and set the pot over medium heat to slowly come up to a gentle burble. Once the beans begin to simmer, I lower the heat and let them cook with an occasional bubble, replenishing the water as necessary to maintain at least an inch over the expanding beans. When they are almost soft, I add salt, then continue to cook the beans until they are fully tender. I cool and store them in their liquid.

For whole grains, I follow the same procedure—with two major differences. I don't soak grains before cooking, and I don't cool or store them in the cooking liquid. Unlike beans, most grains do not have a protective skin that must be softened and made elastic. Also unlike beans, most grains will continue to absorb even cold liquid until they disintegrate. Otherwise, the

Although sometimes grains, beans, and pasta are thought of as food groups distinct from vegetables and one another, they are, I have come to realize, all of a piece. Grains are the dried fruit of the members of the Gramineae family and beans the pods and/or seeds of the Leguminosae. Pasta is, of course, primarily ground grain.

Grains and beans: the Gramineae and Leguminosae families—corn and cranberry bean

method (and goal) is much the same. I start with a big pot and cover the grains by an inch or so with water or stock, then add oil, butter, or some other fat and bring the liquid to a slow simmer. As with beans, I don't watch the clock but instead check the pot every now and then, adding more water or stock as necessary, though less than I would with beans: When I cook whole grains, I try to add just the quantity of liquid the grain should absorb. Often I cook grains covered so that they steam as well as simmer. Ideally, by the time the grain is tender, the pot is dry. When I misjudge, I simply drain the cooked grain (although it loses a little flavor this way).

Processed grains, such as rice or cracked wheat, must be considered separately, with the cooking method dependent on the nature of what is being cooked (short-grain Arborio rice cooks quite differently from long-grain Carolina). The one common thread is the goal of adding flavor to what you are cooking through simmering in aromatic, well-seasoned liquid.

Pasta (processed then ground grain, generally durum wheat), combined with other ingredients to form a new quick-cooking whole, cooks entirely differently. A quick bath in rapidly boiling salted water is all that is required. In most pasta dishes, rich flavor comes from fillings and sauces. Though many pasta dishes at Verbena follow this scheme, I find myself unable to resist applying the logic of beans and whole grains, so I cook my pasta in a flavored liquid whenever possible (see Toasted Angel Hair Pasta in Shiitake Broth, page 97).

spinach and ricotta dumplings in broth

2 tablespoons extra virgin olive oil
1 small onion, peeled and diced
Kosher salt and freshly ground
   black pepper
1 tablespoon butter
1 pound spinach, trimmed and
   chopped
1 tablespoon chopped tarragon
1 tablespoon chopped flat-leaf
   parsley
1 tablespoon chopped chives
2 eggs, lightly beaten
¼ cup freshly grated Parmigiano-
   Reggiano, plus additional
   for serving
⅓ cup ricotta cheese
¼ cup all-purpose flour
Pinch of freshly grated nutmeg
⅓ cup matzoh meal
6 cups Chicken Stock (page 170)
   or broth from Poached Chicken
   (page 174)

These dumplings are made with matzoh meal, the perfect light binder.

Heat the oil in a large skillet over medium heat. Add the onion and cook until it sizzles, then add 2 tablespoons water and salt and pepper. Cook until the onion is soft and the pan dry, about 10 minutes.

Add the butter and spinach and cook until the spinach is soft, about 5 minutes. Add the tarragon, parsley, and chives and remove the pan from the heat.

Combine the eggs, Parmigiano-Reggiano, and ricotta in a medium bowl and mix well. Drain the spinach mixture, squeeze it dry, and add it to the ricotta. Mix in the flour and nutmeg and season with salt and pepper. Fold in the matzoh meal, about half at a time. Set the batter aside to rest for 15 minutes.

To serve, bring the chicken stock to a simmer and season with salt and pepper; keep warm over low heat.

Bring a large pot of salted water to a simmer. Using a tablespoon and working in batches, drop spoonfuls of the dumpling mixture into the water. Cook the dumplings until they are hot at the center, 3 to 5 minutes after they float to the surface. Divide the dumplings among four warm bowls, ladle the broth over the dumplings, and serve.

An excellent garnish for Sorrel Soup (page 83), these dumplings are also good simply topped with melted butter and freshly grated Parmigiano-Reggiano.

lemon porridge with asparagus and basil

This dish can be varied in several ways. Add a little more liquid and you have soup, a little less and you have a dry rice dish. It is also perfect for a still-chilly spring night. Peas, leeks, fava beans, and morel mushrooms would all work instead of, or in addition to, the asparagus.

½ **pound asparagus, tough ends trimmed, halved lengthwise if large, and cut into 2-inch lengths**
Kosher salt
2 **tablespoons extra virgin olive oil**
½ **onion, peeled and chopped**
Freshly ground black pepper
1 **cup Arborio or other short-grain rice**
Finely grated zest and juice of 2 lemons
2 **cups Chicken Stock (page 170)**
2 **eggs**
¼ **cup chopped flat-leaf parsley**
¼ **cup chopped basil**
1 **cup diced, cooked lump crabmeat or lobster (optional)**
2 **tablespoons butter (optional)**

This recipe grew out of an impulse to create a cheese-less risotto for my spring menu. For inspiration I looked to the lemon-perfumed Greek soup *avgolemono*. The only cautionary word concerning the preparation of this soothing dish is to be sure to let the rice cool slightly and only then stir in the egg mixture. Add the eggs too quickly to rice that is too hot, and you will wind up with egg ribbons rather than an emulsified broth.

Preparing the asparagus.
Blanch the asparagus in a large pot of boiling salted water until tender, about 5 minutes. Refresh the asparagus in ice water, drain, and set aside.

Making the porridge.
Heat the oil in a medium saucepan over medium heat. Add the onion, season with salt and pepper, and cook until the onion softens slightly, 3 to 5 minutes. Add ¼ cup water and cook until most of the water has evaporated and the onion is soft, about 15 minutes more.

Add the rice and lemon zest. Stir to coat the rice with oil. Add the stock and bring to a simmer. Cook uncovered, stirring occasionally with a wooden spoon, until most of the stock has evaporated, about 20 minutes.

Add 1½ cups water. Simmer until the rice is almost but not quite tender, about 5 to 10 minutes more. At this point, the rice should be brothy. If it is dry, add another ½ cup warm water. Remove the pan from the heat. Let the rice cool for about 1 minute.

Beat the eggs with half the lemon juice in a small bowl. Gradually stir the egg mixture into the rice. Return the rice to the stove and heat over medium, stirring constantly, until the broth thickens slightly and turns opaque, about 5 minutes.

Add the asparagus, parsley, basil, and seafood, if using. Finish with the butter, if desired. Season with salt, pepper, and a little more lemon juice and serve.

toasted angel hair pasta in shiitake broth

SERVES 4

¼ **pound angel hair pasta or capellini**
3 **tablespoons extra virgin olive oil**
½ **pound shiitake mushrooms, stems removed and reserved, caps sliced**
1 **bunch flat-leaf parsley, leaves picked, stems reserved**
½ **head garlic**
3 **sprigs thyme**
1 **teaspoon black peppercorns**
4 **large shallots, peeled and sliced**
Kosher salt
2 **cups Chicken Stock (page 170)**
¼ **cup ½-inch chive lengths**

I borrowed the idea of toasting pasta from the Spanish dish *fideo*, in which thin noodles are cooked paella-style. Precooking in oil works with pasta the same way it does with rice, forming a protective seal sufficient to prevent too much liquid from being absorbed. The result of the experimentation is this flavorful mushroom dish.

Toasting the pasta.
Preheat the oven to 350°F.

Put the pasta on a baking sheet, coat it with 1 tablespoon of the oil, and then spread it out in a single layer. Bake until the pasta is golden, about 10 minutes. Let cool.

Making the broth.
Wrap the mushroom stems, parsley stems, garlic, thyme, and peppercorns in a square of cheesecloth and set the sachets aside.

Heat the remaining 2 tablespoons oil in a large skillet over medium-high heat. Add the shallots and cook, stirring occasionally, until soft and golden, about 10 minutes. Add the sliced shiitakes and cook until they begin to brown, about 10 minutes. Season the mushrooms with salt, then transfer them to a large saucepan.

Add the sachet, the stock, and 2 cups water to the mushrooms. Bring to a simmer and cook until the broth has a nice mushroom taste, about 15 minutes. Discard the sachet.

Cooking the pasta.
Break the pasta in half and add it to the simmering broth. Cook just until the pasta is done, about 5 minutes. Adjust the seasoning with salt and pepper if necessary, then ladle the broth and pasta into bowls. Serve garnished with the parsley leaves and chives.

Because they are always available, shiitake mushrooms are called for in this recipe. In fact, virtually any mushroom will work—cultivated mushrooms such as cremini or portobellos are always good. In the fall and spring, when wild mushrooms are available, you should use them. Morels, porcini, and mousserons are delicious, but should be used singly, not together. Hen-of-the-woods, oyster, and chanterelle mushrooms are nice, especially as a garnish.

A large bowl of this pasta is the perfect cold-weather dinner. For more formal occasions, whisk in a spoonful of truffle butter and serve the pasta as an appetizer topped with shaved white truffles.

flavor chart for leguminosae

The Leguminosae family includes beans and peas. Botanically, legumes are really seeds enclosed in pods. Seasonally, most pods ripen in late summer and early fall—this is when plants develop their fruits in order to disperse their seeds before the frost. Beans are often grouped as fresh or dry. The fresh beans are generally sweeter because sugar converts to starch as the bean dries.

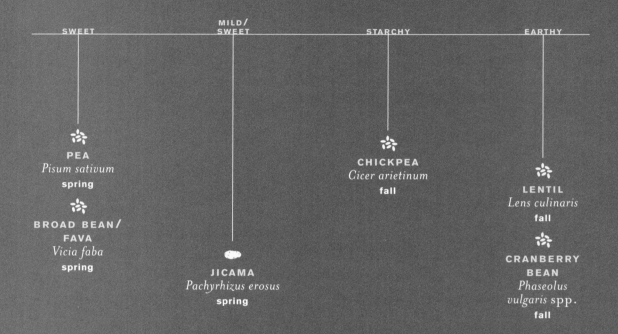

SWEET   MILD/SWEET   STARCHY   EARTHY

PEA
Pisum sativum
spring

BROAD BEAN/FAVA
Vicia faba
spring

JICAMA
Pachyrhizus erosus
spring

CHICKPEA
Cicer arietinum
fall

LENTIL
Lens culinaris
fall

CRANBERRY BEAN
Phaseolus vulgaris spp.
fall

KEY
edible parts

SEED

TUBER

flavor chart for gramineae

The word *cereal* comes from the name of the Roman goddess of agriculture, Ceres.
It refers to any plant from the Gramineae or grass family that yields an edible seed.
As with legumes, grain is really a dry fruit with the seed lying within. Because grains
are harvested and dried, the seasons have less of an effect on availability.

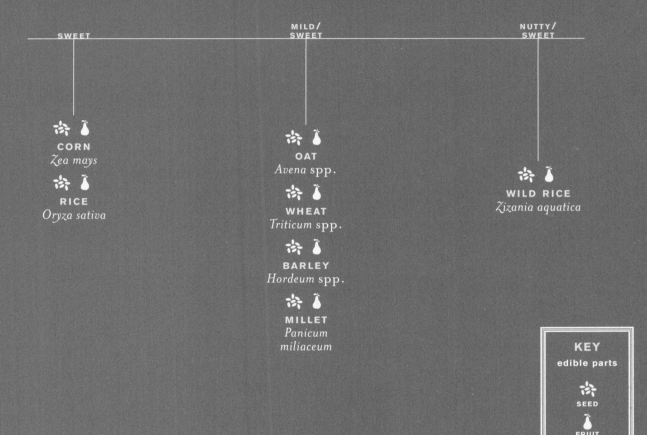

SWEET

CORN
Zea mays

RICE
Oryza sativa

MILD/ SWEET

OAT
Avena spp.

WHEAT
Triticum spp.

BARLEY
Hordeum spp.

MILLET
Panicum miliaceum

NUTTY/ SWEET

WILD RICE
Zizania aquatica

KEY
edible parts

SEED

FRUIT

posole {**CORN**} 39
corn bread {**CORNMEAL**} 122
sautéed salmon with **CORN** sauce 149
mixed grain pilaf {**BROWN RICE, MILLET**} 42
ruby risotto with winter greens {**ARBORIO RICE**} 104
WILD RICE "soufflé" 109
mussels in curried broth with coconut **JASMINE RICE** 135
WHEAT BERRIES 42
BULGUR WHEAT salad with fava beans 63
mushroom **BARLEY** soup 81

butternut squash ravioli with roasted orange reduction

SERVES
4 TO 6

The sauce is more difficult than the ravioli because its success depends on balancing contrasting flavors. It is, however, a great example of the wonderful possibilities of reductions. I don't recommend substituting frozen orange juice for fresh—there is no substitute for the intriguing flavor of the roasted oranges—but if you must, reduce the amount of juice by half and add additional stock. The combined stock and juice reduction can be made up to a day in advance; just warm it and whisk in the butter and cheese when you are about to sit down to eat.

FOR THE RAVIOLI

1½ butternut squash, peeled, seeded, and cubed (about 6 cups)
1½ tablespoons dark brown sugar
¼ teaspoon ground cinnamon
⅛ teaspoon ground allspice
Pinch of ground cloves
Kosher salt and freshly ground black pepper
⅓ cup Homemade Bread Crumbs (page 127)
⅓ cup ricotta cheese
⅓ cup freshly grated Parmigiano-Reggiano
Semolina Pasta Dough (page 102)
1 egg, beaten with 2 teaspoons water, for egg wash
Cornmeal for dusting the baking sheet

FOR THE SAUCE

4 navel oranges
3 cloves garlic, peeled
Kosher salt and freshly ground black pepper
About 2 tablespoons extra virgin olive oil
½ fennel bulb, cored and diced
2 stalks celery, diced
1 cup Chicken Stock (page 170)
1 tablespoon balsamic vinegar
1 cup fresh orange juice
½ cup freshly grated Parmigiano-Reggiano, plus additional for serving
2 tablespoons butter
1 teaspoon slivered sage

These ravioli are easy but time-consuming to make. However, you can prepare a large batch and freeze some. (Freeze in a single layer on a baking sheet, then transfer to storage bags.) A sauce of melted brown butter, chopped sage, and grated Parmigiano-Reggiano is an easy and delicious alternative to the orange reduction.

Starting the filling.
Preheat the oven to 375°F.

Toss the squash with the brown sugar, cinnamon, allspice, and cloves and arrange in a single layer on a baking sheet. Season with salt and pepper and roast until the squash is tender, about 1 hour.

Starting the sauce.
Meanwhile, place the 4 oranges, whole, on another baking sheet. Season the garlic with salt and pepper and a little olive oil, wrap it in aluminum foil, and place it on the baking sheet with the oranges. Roast the oranges, turning once or twice, until they are slightly inflated and browned, about 1 hour. Roast the garlic until it is very soft and golden, also about 1 hour.

Halve and juice the roasted oranges and set aside. Chop the roasted garlic and set aside.

Finishing the filling.
Combine the roasted squash, bread crumbs, ricotta, and Parmigiano-Reggiano in a food processor and pulse until smooth. Season with salt and pepper.

Making the ravioli.
Divide the dough in half. Roll out the first half through a pasta machine, stopping at the next-to-the-last setting (or you can roll it out very thin by hand). Cut the dough into 24 squares (cut the pasta sheet lengthwise in half, then cut each half into 12 squares).

the anatomy of a dish

Place a heaping teaspoonful of filling in the center of half of the pasta squares. Brush the dough around the mounds of filling with egg wash, then lay 1 pasta square on top of each. Run a finger around the filling, pressing out any air bubbles and sealing the edges. Place the ravioli on a baking sheet dusted with cornmeal. Roll out the remaining dough and fill with the remaining squash mixture.

Finishing the sauce.
Heat 2 tablespoons of the olive oil in a medium saucepan over medium heat. Add the fennel and celery, season with salt and pepper, and cook, stirring frequently, until the vegetables are soft, about 20 minutes.

Add the stock, vinegar, and roasted garlic and bring to a simmer. Simmer until the mixture is reduced by about three-fourths, dark, and very slightly syrupy, about 12 minutes. Strain the reduction through a fine sieve. (You should have just over ¼ cup reduction. If you have too much, reduce it further; too little, add water.)

Rinse the pan. Return the reduction to the pan. Add the juice from the roasted oranges and the fresh orange juice. Bring the mixture to a simmer and reduce by half, about 15 minutes (measure if you are unsure—you should have about ¾ cup liquid). Taste the sauce and add salt and pepper. Reduce the heat to low and whisk in the grated cheese and butter. Add the sage and keep warm over very low heat.

Cook the ravioli in a large pot of boiling salted water until they float to the surface and the pasta is tender, 3 to 5 minutes. Drain the ravioli and divide them among warm bowls. Spoon the sauce over the ravioli, and serve topped with additional cheese, if desired.

semolina pasta dough

MAKES
1 ½ POUNDS

Flavoring the pasta dough can be a nice way to vary a recipe. The trick is to adjust the amount of liquid correctly. Black olive pasta, for example, can be made by adding ¼ cup black olive paste and omitting half of the olive oil in the basic recipe. Freshly chopped fines herbes added toward the end of the kneading process are another flavoring option.

1½ cups semolina flour
1½ cups all-purpose flour
1 teaspoon kosher salt
2 eggs
2 tablespoons extra virgin olive oil

Wheat varieties run the gamut from "hard," meaning full of a protein called glutenin, to "soft," low in protein but high in starch. The latter is best for making delicate, crumbly, and flaky baked goods like cakes and biscuits. The former is good for making chewy breads. Pasta requires even more elasticity than bread. It is ideally made with the hardest wheat variety—durum. Semolina is finely ground durum wheat flour. It provides the resilience, flavor, and color necessary for pasta dough (for more information, see About Flour, page 121).

Combine the semolina and all-purpose flours in a food processor, add the salt, and pulse to mix.

Lightly beat the eggs in a bowl. Add the oil, mix well, and add to the flours. Add ⅓ cup water and pulse until the dough begins to come together (if the dough seems too dry, add another tablespoon or so of water). Remove the dough from the food processor and knead until it is smooth, about 3 minutes.

Wrap the dough in plastic and set it aside to rest for at least an hour (you can make the dough up to a day in advance and refrigerate—bring it to room temperature before rolling). Roll out according to the individual recipe.

farfalle and cauliflower with bread crumbs

¼ cup Homemade Bread Crumbs (page 127)
1 head cauliflower, cored and broken into florets
5 tablespoons extra virgin olive oil
1 onion, peeled and diced
Kosher salt and freshly ground black pepper
1 pound farfalle
2 tablespoons chopped chives
2 tablespoons chopped flat-leaf parsley
½ cup freshly grated Pecorino (optional)

This dish was born of my fondness for cauliflower gratin, but I wanted greater integration of the vegetable and the crumbs. The solution: Pulverize the cauliflower and mix it with the crumbs so the cauliflower becomes part of the topping, and vice versa.

Toast the bread crumbs in a dry skillet until golden. Set aside.

Chop or process the cauliflower until it is the consistency of coarse crumbs. Set aside.

Heat 2 tablespoons of the oil in a large skillet over medium-high heat. Add the onion and cook, stirring frequently, until it is golden, about 15 minutes. Add the cauliflower, season with salt and pepper, and cook, stirring frequently, until the cauliflower begins to brown lightly, about 15 minutes.

Meanwhile, bring a large pot of salted water to a boil over high heat. Add the farfalle and cook, stirring once or twice, until it is done, about 7 minutes; then drain.

Stir the bread crumbs, chives, parsley, and Pecorino cheese, if using, into the cauliflower mixture. Toss with the farfalle and serve.

Here the cauliflower mixture is tossed with pasta. You can also bake it in a gratin dish topped with additional cheese, or even add a little matzoh meal and turn the mixture into dumplings (see Horseradish Dumplings, page 43).

ruby risotto with winter greens

SERVES 6

Periodic stirring of risotto is sufficient to agitate the starchy coating of the rice and cause it to thicken, creating a nice saucy risotto.

This risotto is delicious topped with Sautéed Greens (page 43) and Horseradish Crème Fraîche (page 105). Usually this is a first course, but it would be a lovely main course topped with shredded Beer–Braised Short Ribs (page 169). In that case, replace half the chicken stock used to make the risotto with 1 cup of the short rib braising liquid.

FOR THE PICKLED BEETS

8 Roasted Beets (page 38), peeled and diced
1 cup dry red wine
1 cup red wine vinegar
¾ cup sugar
2 shallots, peeled and sliced
Sachet filled with:
  1 bay leaf
  1 sprig thyme
  1 tablespoon black peppercorns
  2 cloves
  1 cinnamon stick

FOR THE RISOTTO

2 tablespoons extra virgin olive oil
1 medium onion, peeled and diced
1 fennel bulb, diced
Kosher salt and freshly ground black pepper
Juice of 2 lemons, plus grated zest of 1 lemon
1 cup dry white wine
¼ teaspoon anise seeds
2 cups Arborio or other short-grain rice
2 cups Chicken Stock (page 170)
10 juniper berries, chopped
Kosher salt and freshly ground black pepper
1 to 2 tablespoons butter
½ recipe Sautéed Greens (page 43; use kale) (optional)
About ¾ cup Horseradish Crème Fraîche (page 105) (optional)

In this recipe I pickle roasted beets. The finished pickle has a very concentrated flavor and texture. Use the pickling liquid to finish the risotto, which turns it pink— I first served this dish on Valentine's Day.

Pickling the beets.
Place the beets in a saucepan, add the wine, vinegar, sugar, shallots, sachet, and ½ cup water, and bring to a simmer over medium heat. Reduce the heat to low and cook until the beets are very tender, about 20 minutes. Strain the beets and shallots, reserving the pickling liquid; discard the sachet.

Starting the risotto.
Heat the olive oil in a large deep skillet over medium-low heat (you can also use a saucepan—the risotto will just take a bit more time and attention). Add the onion and fennel, season with salt and pepper, and cook, stirring occasionally, until the vegetables begin to soften, 10 to 15 minutes. Add the lemon juice and white wine and cook, stirring occasionally, until the pan is almost dry and the vegetables are tender, about 15 minutes more.

Add the lemon zest, anise seeds, and rice and season with salt and pepper. Stir to coat the rice with oil. Add 1 cup of the chicken stock and simmer, stirring frequently with a wooden spoon, until most of the liquid has been absorbed, about 5 minutes. Add 1 cup water and continue cooking, stirring frequently, until the rice no longer looks soupy and is even threatening to stick to the pan. Add the juniper berries and the remaining 1 cup chicken stock. Allow the rice to absorb the stock, then add another cup of water. When the rice is again threatening to stick to the pan, add 1 cup of the reserved pickling liquid and a little more salt and pepper. Cook, stirring frequently, until the pickling liquid looks saucy and very slightly syrupy and the rice is almost tender, about 2 minutes more. Stir in the butter and remove the pan from the heat.

Gently stir in the pickled beets and shallots. Serve topped with the sautéed greens and the horseradish crème fraîche, if desired.

horseradish crème fraîche

¾ cup crème fraîche (page 204)
1½ to 2 tablespoons freshly
   grated horseradish
Kosher salt and freshly ground
   black pepper
Freshly squeezed lemon juice
   (optional)

Stirring freshly grated horseradish into homemade (or store-bought) crème fraîche creates a tangy garnish for Ruby Risotto with Winter Greens (page 104).

In a small bowl, mix together the crème fraîche and horseradish until blended. Add salt and pepper to taste, then add lemon juice if desired. Mix well. Serve or refrigerate until ready to use.

sunchoke ravioli with kale pesto

48 wonton skins
2 cups Sunchoke and Potato Puree
   (page 54)
Kosher salt
Kale Pesto (page 44)
Freshly grated Parmigiano-
   Reggiano for serving (optional)

Vegetable purees make wonderful pasta fillings. Wonton skins have a silky texture and are easy to work with.

Making the ravioli.
Lay 16 of the wonton skins out on a work surface. Place a heaping spoonful of the puree in the center of 8 of the wonton skins. Brush the remaining 8 wonton skins with water and place them on top of the filled skins. Run your finger around the edges of each to force out air and seal the ravioli. Place the ravioli on a dry baking sheet. Repeat with the remaining wonton skins and filling.

Cooking the ravioli.
Bring a large pot of salted water to a boil over high heat. Cook the ravioli until they float to the surface and are tender, about 5 minutes. Drain, reserving about ¼ cup of the cooking water.

Place the ravioli in a serving bowl. Add the pesto and enough of the reserved cooking water to moisten it, and mix gently. Serve topped with cheese, if desired.

Serve these ravioli as a first course, entrée, or side dish. For a different effect, try parboiling them, then browning them in butter and serving them topped with grated Parmigiano-Reggiano.

savory pastries

When I was fourteen, my mother took me to France, where I bought a copy of Gaston Lenôtre's *Desserts and Pastries*. This book became my bible. When we got home, I steadfastly cooked each recipe. Meals at my parents' house, always delicious, took on an added formality when they began to routinely conclude with fruit tartlets, homemade ice creams, and chocolate petits fours.

Ten years later, when I was living and cooking in New York, I got a job at the newly opened Gotham Bar and Grill as pastry chef.

Most of the recipes that follow contain eggs. I include them in this section of the book because I nevertheless think of them as primarily vegetable dishes.

I thrived, no little thanks due to those early studies of Lenôtre's pâte brisée, pâte sucrée, and génoise.

I returned to the savory side of kitchen life when I left Gotham, progressing through various "stations" and kitchens until I opened Verbena in the fall of 1994. Since then, I have had little opportunity to focus my undivided attention on the magic of sweets, cakes, and confections. But early lessons are rarely forgotten. My appetizer and entrée menus almost always hint at my earlier vocation. I serve individual Wild Rice Soufflés (page 109) as an appetizer and accompany sautéed foie gras with a delicate Mushroom Torte (page 113). My mixed culinary heritage greatly widened my kitchen vocabulary.

I advise cooks to familiarize themselves with both pastry and savory cooking techniques. Learn a little about what happens to egg yolks and whites as they are beaten, and become aware of the different characteristics of various common and not so common flours (see page 121). Once you understand the nature of your ingredients, you can handle them to best effect. Cooking is not a matter of common sense. It is a matter of understanding chemistry (though usually not identified by that name) and knowing how to plan and control outcomes. Observing and beginning to comprehend the various implications of the combination of protein, fat, and starch in eggs and flour, whether in savory or sweet dishes, is a great place to start.

Eggs—many shapes and sizes

rolled soufflé

SERVES 4

Spinach and Herb Sauce (page 54) can be substituted for the Mushroom Puree (page 48). Sautéed vegetables also make a nice filling; see Sautéed Mushrooms (page 48) and Sautéed Greens (page 43).

The soufflé can easily be transformed into a sweet. Omit the cheese and add ½ cup sugar to the warm milk mixture. Fill the soufflé with a fruit puree, warm fruit compote, or melted chocolate.

5 eggs, separated
6 tablespoons butter (plus additional for greasing the pan)
¼ cup all-purpose flour
2 tablespoons semolina flour
1¼ cups milk
½ cup heavy cream
½ cup freshly grated Parmigiano-Reggiano
About ½ teaspoon kosher salt
Mushroom Puree (page 48)

When I was growing up, my mother used to serve a rolled soufflé for Sunday brunch. Years later, I created my own version, adding semolina to all-purpose flour to give the batter—the same for my traditional soufflés—a more interesting flavor and a little more vigor.

Preheat the oven to 350°F.

Lightly butter a 12-inch ovenproof skillet, then line it with parchment paper. Butter the parchment paper (the butter will hold the paper in place).

Beat the egg whites in a large bowl until they hold soft peaks.

Melt the butter in a medium saucepan over medium-low heat. Whisk in the all-purpose and semolina flours and cook, whisking, until the mixture is bubbly and fragrant but still pale, 2 to 3 minutes. Remove the pan from the heat and whisk in the milk, then the cream.

Return the pan to the stove and, whisking constantly, bring the mixture to a simmer. Cook, stirring, until it thickens, 2 to 3 minutes.

Transfer the milk mixture to a bowl and add the cheese and salt. Mix well. Stir in the egg yolks one at a time. Fold about one third of the egg whites into the yolks, then incorporate the mixture into the remaining whites.

Pour the batter into the prepared pan and bake just until the soufflé is set, about 15 minutes.

Meanwhile, warm the mushroom puree in a small skillet over medium-low heat.

Remove the soufflé from the oven and invert it onto a clean kitchen towel. Carefully peel away the parchment paper. Spread the puree evenly over the soufflé, then gently roll, pushing and molding the soufflé with the towel until it resembles a jelly roll. (Don't worry if the soufflé cracks a little as you roll it; just wrap it tightly in the towel and allow it to sit for a few minutes before serving—it will re-form.) Remove the towel and slice the soufflé. Serve warm or at room temperature.

the anatomy of a dish

wild rice "soufflé"

¾ cup plus 2 tablespoons
   extra fancy wild rice
Kosher salt
2 tablespoons quick-cooking grits
¼ teaspoon ground allspice
⅛ teaspoon ground cardamom
Pinch of freshly grated nutmeg
Freshly ground black pepper
3 eggs, separated

Though all are members of the Gramineae family, wild rice and the various familiar and exotic short-, medium-, and long-grain white and brown rices are not otherwise related. Wild rice is the seed of an aquatic plant and is higher in protein than the land-born grain it is often incorrectly grouped with.

Making the "porridge."
Combine ½ cup of the rice with 3 cups water in a medium pot and bring to a boil. Reduce the heat to medium, add ½ teaspoon salt, and simmer until the rice is tender, about 45 minutes. Drain off any remaining water, cover, and set aside.

Meanwhile, finely grind the remaining 6 tablespoons rice in a spice grinder. Combine the ground rice, grits, allspice, cardamom, nutmeg, ½ teaspoon salt, and a generous pinch of pepper and mix well.

Bring 2½ cups water to a boil in a medium pot. Whisking constantly, gradually add the ground rice mixture. Reduce the heat to low and cook, stirring frequently with a wooden spoon, until the porridge is smooth, about 30 minutes.

Remove from the heat, stir in the cooked rice, and allow to cool slightly, about 10 minutes.

Making the soufflés.
Preheat the oven to 375°F. Thoroughly butter and flour six 4-ounce ramekins.

Beat the egg yolks in a small bowl until they are thick and pale. Beat the whites in a medium bowl until they hold soft peaks.

Stirring constantly, gradually add the yolks to the porridge. Add a pinch each of salt and pepper, then fold in the beaten whites.

Divide the soufflé batter among the ramekins and bake until the soufflés are slightly puffed, browned on top, and cooked through, 35 to 40 minutes (test for doneness by inserting a metal skewer—if it comes out clean, the soufflés are ready). Allow the soufflés to rest for 5 to 10 minutes, then unmold by running a knife around the edges. Invert onto plates and serve warm.

Wild rice is graded according to size, ranging from select, the smallest, to extra fancy, mid-sized, to giant, largest. This recipe calls for extra fancy.

In this recipe you grind uncooked wild rice and combine it with cooked wild rice and grits. The powdered rice acts as an earthy-flavored substitute for the flour in a traditional soufflé. The soufflé base can be made a day in advance and refrigerated; just fold in the eggs immediately before baking.

asparagus crepes

The potato starch in this recipe makes the batter silky. Mixing just so the ingredients are combined, then allowing the batter to rest, makes it more delicate and the result-ing crepes tender.

For lunch or brunch, serve these crepes with Asparagus Vinaigrette (page 35) or a drizzle of Taleggio fondue (see Pickled Beet Salad with Oranges and Taleggio Cheese, page 71).

FOR THE CREPES

½ cup all-purpose flour
½ cup potato starch
Pinch of kosher salt
2 eggs
1¼ cups milk
5⅓ tablespoons butter, melted and cooled

FOR THE FILLING

1 pound asparagus, tough ends trimmed and cut into 3- to 4-inch pieces
Kosher salt
1 to 2 tablespoons butter
1 cup freshly grated Parmigiano-Reggiano

This recipe calls for adding asparagus to crepe batter and cooking the two together. It must be made at the last minute. If you want to work ahead, make the batter but don't add the asparagus. Cook the crepes on both sides without filling them. Roll blanched asparagus in the crepes, arrange them seam side down in a baking dish, and top with grated cheese. Bake the crepes in a preheated 350°F oven until heated through and browned.

Making the batter.

Combine the flour, potato starch, and salt in a large bowl. Mix well, then make a well in the center. In a separate bowl, beat the eggs with the milk. Pour the egg mixture into the well, then, using a whisk, incorporate it into the flour mixture. Gradually add the butter, whisking just until the ingredients are combined and the batter is smooth (it is better to pass a lumpy batter through a sieve than to overbeat). Set the batter aside for at least 1 hour. (The batter can be made up to 2 days in advance and refriger-ated. Bring it to room temperature before cooking.)

Making the filling and crepes.

Blanch the asparagus in boiling salted water until just tender, about 2 or 3 minutes. Refresh the asparagus in ice water, drain, and then dry. If you are using jumbo asparagus, split them lengthwise. Divide the asparagus into eight groups of 3 or 4 pieces each.

Heat the oven to 200°F.

Heat a crepe pan or medium nonstick skillet over medium-high heat. Add a little bit of butter (you just want a thin film) and allow it to melt. When the butter stops bubbling, pour in just enough batter to coat the bottom of the pan, about ¼ cup. Allow the bottom to set slightly, about 2 minutes, then place 3 or 4 pieces of asparagus and 2 tablespoons of the cheese in the still somewhat runny center of the crepe. Cook the crepe until the center is set, about 2 minutes, and then fold the sides over the filling. Flip the crepe over and continue cooking until the bottom is golden. Keep the finished crepes warm on a baking sheet in the oven. Repeat, forming 8 crepes in all. Serve warm.

herbs and spices chart

Several families contain herbs and spices, each with a distinct personality. The members of the Labiatae family, commonly called the mint family, share a fresh taste. The Umbelliferae family contains the aromatic herbs used in sachets for soup and stocks, and Zingiberaceae contains hot spices. Note that herbs and spices come from various plant parts: seeds, leaves, stems, pods, flowers, and bark. The chart is organized by flavor and by botanical family.

INGREDIENT	FAMILY	GENUS/SPECIES	FLAVOR
BASIL	Labiatae	*Ocimum basilicum*	sweet
MINT	Labiatae	*Mentha* spp.	sweet
ROSEMARY	Labiatae	*Rosmarinus officinalis*	sweet
SAGE	Labiatae	*Salvia officinalis*	sweet
SUMMER SAVORY	Labiatae	*Satureia hortensis*	pungent/sweet
THYME	Labiatae	*Thymus* spp.	pungent/sweet
CHAMOMILE	Compositae	*Matricaria recutita*	sweet
TARRAGON	Compositae	*Artemisia dranunculus*	sweet
CARAWAY	Umbelliferae	*Carum carvi*	bitter/sweet
CHERVIL	Umbelliferae	*Anthriscus cerefolium*	sweet
CORIANDER	Umbelliferae	*Coriandrum sativum*	bitter/sweet
CUMIN	Umbelliferae	*Cuminum cyminum*	bitter
PARSLEY	Umbelliferae	*Petroselinum* spp.	sweet
CARDAMOM	Zingiberaceae	*Elettaria cardamomum*	sweet/peppery
GINGER	Zingiberaceae	*Zingiber officinale*	sweet/peppery
TURMERIC	Zingiberaceae	*Curcuma longa*	pungent/sweet
HORSERADISH	Cruciferae	*Armoracia rusticana*	hot/peppery
MUSTARD	Cruciferae	*Brassica* spp.	hot/peppery
JUNIPER BERRY	Cupressaceae	*Juniperus communis*	sweet
SAFFRON	Iridaceae	*Crocus sativus*	pungent/sweet
NUTMEG	Myristicaceae	*Myristica fragrans*	spicy/sweet
ALLSPICE	Myrtaceae	*Pimenta dioica*	spicy/sweet
CLOVE	Myrtaceae	*Syzygium aromaticum*	spicy/sweet
BAY	Lauraceae	*Laurus nobilis*	sweet
CINNAMON	Lauraceae	*Cinnamomum zeylanicum*	bitter/sweet
PAPRIKA	Solanaceae	*Capsicum annuum*	sweet to hot
CHILI PEPPER	Solanaceae	*Capsicum annuum* spp.	sweet to hot
PEPPERCORN	Piperaceae	*Piper nigrum*	hot
LEMON GRASS	Gramineae	*Cymbopogon citratus*	sour/sweet
TAMARIND	Leguminosae	*Tamarindus indica*	sour
VANILLA	Orchidaceae	*Vanilla* spp.	sweet
CACAO	Sterculiaceae	*Theobroma cacao*	bitter

braised greens tart

*The ultra-flaky dough
for this tart is made by
precooking a portion of
the dough, chilling it,
and then mixing it with
the remainder of the
dough. This dough is so
flaky that it only works
as a bottom crust.*

*A good buffet or picnic
dish, this tart also
makes a tasty lunch,
accompanied by a salad.*

FOR THE CRUST

1 cup all-purpose flour
¼ teaspoon baking powder
Pinch of kosher salt
4 tablespoons chilled butter,
  cut into small pieces
⅓ cup solid vegetable shortening

FOR THE FILLING

¼ cup extra virgin olive oil
2 onions, peeled, halved, and
  sliced
1 fennel bulb, cored and sliced
1 pound Swiss chard (about
  1 bunch), leaves removed and
  chopped, stems sliced
1 clove garlic, peeled and thinly
  sliced
Sachet filled with:
  1 teaspoon fennel seeds
  1 teaspoon black peppercorns
  1 tablespoon coriander seeds
  1 bay leaf
  2 allspice berries
  3 sprigs thyme
Kosher salt
2 cups chopped spinach

This tart has a wonderfully crumbly crust. It is filled with braised greens. Use whatever greens you can find, the wilder and more bitter the better.

Making the crust.

Combine the flour, baking powder, and salt in a bowl. Cut in the butter and rub the shortening into the mixture until it resembles coarse crumbs.

Place half the flour mixture in a skillet and toast it over medium heat, stirring occasionally, until it is golden and smells nutty, about 15 minutes. Let cool, then chill both the toasted and raw flour mixtures thoroughly.

Combine the two flour mixtures. Add a tablespoon of ice water and lightly and quickly work the water into the dough with your hands. Repeat, adding up to 3 tablespoons ice water, stopping as soon as the dough can be formed into a ball.

On a floured surface, roll out the dough to an 11- to 12-inch round. Fit it into a 9-inch pie plate and trim the excess dough (for a more rustic crust, just press the crust into place without first rolling). Chill the crust.

Making the filling.

Heat the oil in a large pot over medium heat. Add the onions, fennel, and chard stems and cook, stirring frequently, until the vegetables are coated with oil, 3 to 5 minutes. Add the garlic, sachet, salt, and ½ cup water, bring to a simmer, and cook until all the vegetables are slightly softened, about 10 minutes. Add the chard leaves, cover, and gently simmer until all the vegetables are tender, about 15 minutes more.

Add the spinach, season with salt, and cook uncovered, stirring occasionally, until the spinach is wilted and the pan dry, about 10 minutes. Remove from the heat; discard the sachet.

Finishing the tart.

Preheat the oven to 375°F.

Bake the crust (it is not necessary to weight it) until it is lightly browned, about 20 minutes.

Spoon the filling into the crust and bake until heated through, about 10 minutes. Serve warm.

the anatomy of a dish

mushroom torte

1 cup hazelnuts, toasted
1 cup all-purpose flour
8 tablespoons (1 stick) butter,
    melted and cooled
Mushroom Puree (page 48)
4 egg whites
Sautéed Mushrooms (page 48)

For this luxuriously earthy cake, I have made my own hazelnut flour by grinding the nuts to a powder. Pulsing the nuts with flour or with sugar allows for the finest possible grind while preventing the nut oils from forming a paste. Commercially ground hazelnut flour will result in a slightly smoother texture. Wedges of the torte pair well with Roasted Chicken (page 175) or Roasted Leg of Venison (page 172).

Preheat the oven to 375°F. Butter and flour a 9-inch round cake pan.

Process the hazelnuts in a food processor until coarsely ground. Add the flour and grind the mixture as fine as possible. Transfer to a bowl, add the butter and mushroom puree, and mix well.

Beat the egg whites to soft peaks in a medium bowl. Fold the whites into the batter. Spoon the batter into the prepared pan, spreading it evenly with the back of a spoon (the pan will only be about half full). Bake the cake until a toothpick inserted in the center is clean when removed, the sides begin to pull away from the pan, and the top is firm and lightly golden, about 35 minutes.

Cool the cake for about 5 minutes, then carefully remove it from the pan and let cool completely. Turn the cake upside down and slice it into two thin layers. Spread the sautéed mushrooms over the bottom layer and reassemble the cake. Serve at room temperature, cut into wedges, or reheat in a preheated 300°F oven until warm in the center.

Bake the batter in tiny cupcake tins to create individual tortes. Serve them topped with seared foie gras or foie gras terrine—a great hors d'oeuvre.

breads

Space is tight in New York City, and few restaurants have enough room to bake their own bread. Nevertheless, since I spent a considerable portion of my apprenticeship in France concentrating on the art of the *boulangerie* and have always felt that the simplest and most reliable measure of a restaurant is its bread, I hoped to make house-baked loaves a part of mine.

Bread in its most basic form contains four ingredients—flour, water, leavening, and salt. These ingredients are completely transformed

Bread is made with flour ground from grain, which, as I have mentioned (see Seeds: Grains and Pasta, page 93), is the dried fruit of the Gramineae family.

through four steps—mixing, kneading, rising, and baking. This simplicity disguises the alchemy involved. Magic—the scientific variety—is the source of my fascination with this simple but exacting culinary discipline.

Successful baking is a consequence of knowing as much as you can about what you are using and how. I like to begin here, as I do elsewhere, by considering my ingredients. First comes flour: Start by looking at labels, but don't stop there. The designation "all-purpose white flour," for example, guarantees only that the bag contains white wheat flour that the manufacturer feels can be used for a wide range of purposes. It does not guarantee that the bag contains only one type of wheat, and it certainly does not guarantee that one brand is anything like another. Some all-purpose

flour is very soft (meaning it is low in gluten) and some very hard (meaning it is high in gluten). Gluten is what gives flour flexibility and what makes a bread chewy rather than flaky. A chewy baguette is wonderful, a chewy biscuit is not, so choosing the correct flour is essential. (For more about flour, see page 121.)

Leavening is the next thing to consider. Bread is divided into two broad categories: quick breads and slow-rising breads. Quick breads are chemically leavened with baking powder or soda. Slow-rising breads are organically leavened with some form of yeast. Yeast is a microorganism that eats glucose and expels gas. The gas causes bread to rise, while the gluten in the flour gives it the flexibility to expand. The length of time yeast feeds (and expels) affects

Grains:
Most grains are
really seeds.

the texture and flavor of bread.

Yeast is produced in different ways. Commercial yeast is a bacterial by-product of brewing beer. It is dried and packaged in one of several easy-to-store, easy-to-use forms. It is reliable (meaning that the baker can be sure her bread will rise) and fast-acting (bread will rise in 1 to 2 hours). Starters (noncommercial yeasts) are home-grown microorganisms kept alive by daily feeding and careful climate control. (What are called dormant starters can be fed less frequently but must be revived by regular feeding before they can be used.) Starters may be passed down from cook to cook; I have one that originated in France. Starters work much more sluggishly than commercial yeast (a rise can take 12 to 24 hours), but the slower leavening can result in the development of a more interesting flavor and texture. Starters require regular maintenance and are less dependable than commercial yeast. I use both yeast and starters in the little windowed nook that has become my restaurant's bakery.

blini

2 eggs
¼ cup potato starch
½ cup all-purpose flour
1½ teaspoons baking powder
2 teaspoons kosher salt
¾ cup milk, warmed
4 tablespoons butter, melted and
  cooled
About 2 tablespoons vegetable oil

Blini are light pancakes used to form luxurious hors d'oeuvres. Although some blini are very thin, I prefer mine thicker—a taste I developed while working as the sous-chef of New York's Petrossian restaurant. Serve the blini topped with Crème Fraîche (page 204) and caviar or Cured Salmon (page 143).

Making the batter.
Place the eggs in a bowl of warm water and set aside for about 5 minutes. Combine the potato starch, flour, baking powder, and salt in another bowl.

Beat the eggs with the milk in the bowl of an electric mixer until almost doubled in volume. Add the butter, then, with the mixer running, add the dry ingredients. Allow the batter to rest at room temperature for about 20 minutes.

Making the blini.
Heat a small skillet over medium heat. Add just enough oil to coat the surface. Add 2 tablespoons of the batter, swirling it to spread it, and cook until the top is bubbly and the bottom lightly browned, about 2 minutes. Flip the blini over and cook until the second side is golden, about 1 minute longer. Transfer the blini to a plate and cover it with a clean towel to keep warm. Continue cooking blini until all of the batter has been used. Serve warm.

Warming the eggs allows them to accommodate more air when beaten. This makes for a lighter batter.

chive popovers

I bake popovers in cast-iron muffin tins. Popovers made in pans designed for the purpose are too large. Cast iron holds heat better than aluminum, and a hot pan ensures nicely puffed popovers. Cast iron also promotes even browning.

Serve for brunch with scrambled eggs and Cured Salmon (page 143). Popovers also work well as a side dish for roasted meats.

1 cup all-purpose flour
½ teaspoon salt
1 cup milk
2 eggs, lightly beaten
2 tablespoons butter, melted and cooled
2 tablespoons chopped chives
6 tablespoons olive oil

Successful popovers (and Yorkshire pudding) require forethought, heat, and fat. The *rested* batter must be poured into *hot* molds filled with *hot* fat. I use olive oil (blended rather than extra virgin olive oil because it is milder), but you can substitute any fat with a high burning point (poultry drippings work nicely). If you want to use butter, which has a low burning point, it must be clarified first. (Melt 1 pound butter over low heat, skimming the foam as it rises to the top. Continue skimming until the remaining butter is clear dark yellow. Clarified butter can be used immediately or refrigerated for later use.)

Making the batter.
Combine the flour and salt in a small bowl.

In a medium bowl, whisk the milk with the eggs, butter, and chives. Gradually add the flour mixture, whisking just until the batter is smooth (overmixing will make the popovers tough). Allow the batter to rest at room temperature for about an hour.

Preheat the oven to 425°F. Place a muffin tin (cast iron if you have one) in the oven to preheat for at least 30 minutes.

Pour about 2 teaspoons oil into each mold, then return the pan to the oven for 5 minutes.

Place the pan on a baking sheet (in case of drips) and pour the batter into the molds, filling each one about two-thirds full. Bake the popovers until they are puffed and brown, about 30 minutes. Serve warm.

biscuits

5 cups all-purpose flour
1 tablespoon baking powder
1 teaspoon kosher salt
½ pound (2 sticks) butter, diced and frozen
2¼ cups buttermilk

There are three tricks to light biscuits. First, freeze the butter for about an hour. Second, don't overmix the dough. The dough should hold together but small butter lumps should still be visible. Third, use a soft (high-starch, low-gluten) flour (see page 121).

Combine the flour, baking powder, and salt in a bowl and mix well. Using a pastry cutter or your fingertips, work in the butter until the mixture resembles coarse crumbs. Add 2 cups of the buttermilk, a little at a time, mixing first with a wooden spoon and then with your hands, just until the dough comes together.

Turn the dough out onto a lightly floured board and roll it out about ½ inch thick. Cut the dough into rounds with a 2- to 3-inch biscuit cutter and place them on a parchment-lined baking sheet. Allow the biscuits to rise for about 15 minutes (the biscuits can be cut out a day in advance and refrigerated until ready to bake; they can also be frozen for up to 1 month; thaw before baking).

Preheat the oven to 400°F.

Brush the biscuit tops with the remaining ¼ cup buttermilk. Bake until the biscuits are golden, 30 to 45 minutes. Serve warm, plain or with butter or preserves.

VARIATION

cobblers

Biscuit dough becomes tough if rerolled, so use any scraps to top cobblers. Simply toss peaches, plums, or berries with sugar and a little spice, top with the scraps of dough, and bake at 375°F for about 20 minutes.

You can vary the recipe by adding cheese (sharp cheddar or Roquefort) or replacing half the butter with flavorful sausage drippings.

Serve these biscuits for dinner with Roasted Chicken (page 175) or for brunch with scrambled eggs and bacon.

scones

The same rules that apply to making biscuits apply to scones (see the headnote on page 119).

I also use this dough for my version of strawberry shortcake. Omit the raisins. Split the scones and top them with strawberries cooked in balsamic vinegar and seasoned with black pepper (see Spicy Green Salad with Strawberry Vinaigrette, page 62; omit the oil and add 2 tablespoons sugar). Top with Crème Fraîche (page 204) or whipped cream.

1 cup raisins
4 cups all-purpose flour
2 teaspoons baking powder
2 teaspoons baking soda
1 teaspoon kosher salt
½ cup sugar
5 ounces butter, diced and frozen
½ cup grapeseed oil
¾ cup buttermilk
2 tablespoons heavy cream

This recipe contains both baking soda and baking powder. Baking soda is a leavening made from finely ground alkaline salts, used since the nineteenth century to make quick breads and biscuits. It must be combined with an acid to avoid a chemical reaction that, practically speaking, produces a bitter aftertaste. In this recipe, buttermilk solves the problem. Baking powder, developed shortly after baking soda, is a combination of finely ground alkaline and acidic salts. It is a faster-acting, more reliable leavening than baking soda, free of the risk of aftertaste. The two are used here together to take advantage of the reliability of baking powder and the distinctive tang of baking soda. Chill the dough before adding the buttermilk.

Put the raisins in a small saucepan, cover with water, and bring to a boil. Remove the pan from the heat and set the raisins aside to plump.

Combine the flour, baking powder, baking soda, salt, and sugar in a large bowl and mix well. Using a pastry cutter or your fingertips, work the butter into the flour mixture until it resembles coarse crumbs. Stir in the oil. Refrigerate the dough for at least 30 minutes.

Preheat the oven to 350°F.

Drain the raisins and add them to the dough. Add the buttermilk a little at a time, mixing first with a wooden spoon and then your hands, just until the dough comes together.

Turn the dough out onto a lightly floured board (it will be quite sticky). Roll it out about ½ inch thick. Cut the dough into rounds with a 3-inch floured biscuit cutter and place them on a parchment-lined baking sheet. (The scraps can be gathered and used to top a cobbler; see page 119.)

Brush the tops of the scones with the cream and bake until they are golden, about 25 minutes. Serve warm.

About Flour

Wheat is an annual plant grown worldwide. Winter wheat is planted in the fall and grown in temperate climates. Spring wheat is planted in the spring and fares better in warmer places. Both winter and spring wheats include hard and soft varieties.

When used to describe flour, the labels "hard" and "soft" refer to the amount of protein a particular variety contains. These terms are used primarily to differentiate between types of *white* flour. Hard flours contain just under 12 to over 13 percent protein; soft, under 10 percent.

The word *gluten* is used to describe the elasticity produced by the interaction of two proteins (gliadin and glutenin) when mixed with water. Hard flour is more elastic (higher in gluten) than soft. Hard flour is used to make chewier baked goods, like bread. Soft flour is best for baking tender and flaky things such as cakes. All-purpose flour is a mixture of hard and soft, designed to be used for many different types of baking.

Wheat Flours

WHOLE WHEAT FLOUR Ground hulled wheat berries (includes the bran, germ, and endosperm)

GRAHAM FLOUR Ground hulled, sometimes degerminated, wheat berries with added ground bran.

WHITE FLOUR Ground wheat endosperm (the hull, the bran, and germ are removed before milling). Buy unbleached white flour; chemical whitening, or bleaching, is unnecessary and, I believe, unhealthy.

ALL-PURPOSE FLOUR A blend of hard and soft white flours; different brands contain different proportions. The best way to predict results is to check the percentage of protein. This is indicated in the nutritional information on the label.

SELF-RISING FLOUR All-purpose flour mixed with a chemical leavening, usually baking powder.

CAKE FLOUR Very finely ground soft white flour.

PASTRY FLOUR Finely ground (but not quite as fine as cake flour), fairly soft white flour.

BREAD FLOUR Moderately finely ground hard white flour (usually a blend of varieties).

SEMOLINA FLOUR Moderately coarsely ground endosperm of durum wheat. Harder than bread flour, semolina is used for making pasta and couscous.

corn bread

This batter, sharp with pepper and cheese, is great for muffins or corn pone; simply adjust the baking time.

4 cups all-purpose flour
2 teaspoons baking powder
1½ cups yellow cornmeal
1 tablespoon kosher salt
2¼ cups milk
4 eggs
12 tablespoons (1½ sticks) butter, softened
2 cups sugar
¼ cup maple syrup
¼ cup honey
1 cup freshly grated Parmigiano-Reggiano
2 teaspoons freshly ground black pepper

Cornmeal is dried corn ground to various degrees of coarseness—medium cornmeal is best for this recipe. Corn flour is much more finely ground and is not a substitute.

Preheat the oven to 350°F. Line two 9- by 13-inch baking pans with parchment paper.

Combine the flour, baking powder, cornmeal, and salt in a bowl. Beat the milk with the eggs in a second bowl.

Cream the butter with the sugar in the bowl of an electric mixer (the batter can also be made by hand). With the mixer on low speed, add a little of the flour mixture, then a little of the milk mixture, alternating three or four times until all of each mixture has been added. Mix in the syrup, honey, cheese, and pepper.

Spoon the batter evenly into the prepared pans. Bake until the corn bread is golden, the edges begin to pull away from the sides, and a toothpick inserted in the center comes out clean, about 45 minutes. Cut into squares and serve warm or at room temperature.

corn bread stuffing

Corn Bread (page 122), cut into
  1½-inch cubes
2 tablespoons extra virgin olive oil
6 tablespoons butter
2 onions, peeled and diced
Kosher salt and freshly ground
  black pepper
4 stalks celery, diced
⅓ cup chopped sage
½ cup chopped flat-leaf parsley
4 cups cubed country or other
  white bread
4 cups Chicken Stock (page 170),
  heated
½ teaspoon cayenne pepper, or
  to taste

*Serve with Roasted
Chicken (page 175) or
Rolled Roasted Turkey
with Mushroom Gravy
(page 180).*

Here is a hint: Roast turkey (or chicken) on a rack set over the stuffing and you will get great flavor without having to fill the bird.

Preheat the oven to 350°F.

Spread the corn bread on two baking sheets and dry in the oven for about 20 minutes. Transfer the dried bread to a very large bowl (you may need to use two bowls). Leave the oven on.

Heat the oil and 3 tablespoons of the butter in a large skillet over medium heat. Add the onions, season with salt and pepper, and cook, stirring occasionally, until the onions soften, about 15 minutes. Add the celery, sage, and parsley and continue cooking until the onions are completely soft and the celery tender, about 10 minutes more. Add to the corn bread.

Melt the remaining 3 tablespoons butter in the same skillet over medium heat. Add the country bread cubes and toast on all sides. Add them to the corn bread mixture. Add the stock and season with salt, the cayenne, and black pepper.

Butter a large roasting pan. Put the stuffing in the pan and bake until heated through, about 1½ hours.

naan

Serve naan with
spicy dishes such as
Eggplant and Garlic Stew
with Merguez Sausage
(page 90). It is also
good for sandwiches.

½ teaspoon active dry yeast
1 tablespoon sugar
3½ to 4½ cups bread or other
    high-gluten flour (for more about
    flour, see page 121)
1¾ tablespoons kosher salt
1 cup plain yogurt
About 3 tablespoons vegetable oil

Naan is an East Asian flat bread. It is traditionally baked in a super-hot chimney-shaped oven. I use a griddle or grill.

Combine the yeast, sugar, and 1 cup tepid water in a small bowl, stirring to mix. Set aside for 10 minutes.

Combine 3½ cups of the flour and the salt in a large bowl. Make a well in the center and stir the yeast mixture into the flour a little at a time, then gradually mix in the yogurt. When the dough begins to form a ball, turn it out onto a floured board. Knead the dough for 10 minutes, adding the remaining cup of flour as necessary, until the dough is smooth and elastic. Place the dough in an oiled bowl, cover it with plastic wrap, and set aside in a warm place to rise until doubled, about 2 hours.

Punch the dough down. Divide it into 8 pieces (4 ounces each). Shape each one into a ball. Flatten and stretch each ball out until you have a round about ¼ inch thick. Oil the dough on both sides.

Heat a large skillet over medium heat and add one or two of the dough rounds. Cook until crisp and lightly browned on one side, 2 to 3 minutes, then flip over and cook the remaining side. Serve immediately, brushed with butter or olive oil. Repeat to cook the remaining naan.

parkerhouse rolls

1 ⅛ teaspoons active dry yeast
3 tablespoons sugar
1 cup plus 2 tablespoons milk
4 tablespoons butter
3 ½ to 4 cups all-purpose flour
1 teaspoon kosher salt
Sea salt (optional)

The Parker House Hotel in Boston became so famous for its soft, folded yeast dinner rolls in the late nineteenth century that imitators began offering the rolls by name. This dough is like the original, light but chewy and a little sweet. At the restaurant, the dough is formed into rolls. In this recipe, the cut dough is fitted into two pans following the fashion of the original recipe.

Combine the yeast, sugar, and ¼ cup warm water in a small bowl.

Combine the milk and 2 tablespoons of the butter in a small saucepan and heat, stirring occasionally, just until the butter melts. Remove the milk from the heat and allow it to cool enough so that it feels warm but not hot (the temperature should be between 100° and 110°F).

Combine 3½ cups of the flour and the kosher salt in a large bowl. Add the yeast mixture to the milk and butter, then add to the flour and mix until the dough comes together into a ball. Turn the dough out onto a floured work surface. Knead it until smooth, about 10 minutes, adding additional flour only if necessary. Place the dough in a large, lightly floured bowl, cover with plastic wrap, and set aside to rise until doubled, about 2 hours.

Punch down the dough. Using a pastry cutter or sharp knife, cut the dough into 18 pieces. Butter an 8- by 10-inch baking dish and arrange the dough in the dish in a single layer, with the pieces touching one another. Cover with a clean towel and set aside to rise for about 30 minutes.

Preheat the oven to 400°F.

Melt the remaining 2 tablespoons butter. Brush the rolls with the butter; sprinkle with sea salt, if desired. Bake until golden, about 30 minutes. Serve warm.

These dinner rolls are also great sandwich rolls—a favorite for soft-shell crab sandwiches.

grissini

One ½-ounce packet active dry
  yeast
2 tablespoons molasses
½ cup extra virgin olive oil
1 egg
5¾ cups bread or other high-
  gluten flour (for more about
  flour, see page 121)
2 teaspoons kosher salt
2 tablespoons chopped marjoram
2 tablespoons chopped thyme
2 tablespoons chopped rosemary

Grissini are thin Italian breadsticks. I roll the dough with a pasta machine and use the fettuccine attachment to cut it into lengths. The dough can instead be cut into squares and baked to be served as crackers.

Combine the yeast and 1 cup warm water in a small bowl. Stir in the molasses and set aside for about 10 minutes. In another small bowl, mix the oil with the egg.

Combine the flour, salt, and herbs in the bowl of an electric mixer. Using the dough hook, mix in the egg and yeast mixtures, then transfer to a lightly floured work surface. Knead the dough until it is smooth, about 10 minutes. Form the dough into a ball, place it in a lightly oiled bowl, cover with plastic wrap, and set it aside to rise until doubled, about 1 hour.

Preheat the oven to 375°F. Dust two baking sheets with flour or semolina.

Punch down the dough and divide it into 8 pieces. One at a time, roll out each piece as thin as possible into a square about 6 by 6 inches. Using a pizza cutter or sharp knife, cut the square into thin lengths, each about ½ inch wide. Repeat with the remaining dough. Arrange the breadsticks about ½ inch apart on the baking sheets and let rise in a warm place for about 10 minutes (the breadsticks will be slightly rounded when ready).

Bake the grissini in batches until they are golden, 10 to 15 minutes. Let cool, then serve.

croutons

Eight ½-inch-thick slices white
country bread, crusts removed
if desired
2 tablespoons extra virgin olive oil
Kosher or sea salt and freshly
ground black pepper

Do not neglect to season your croutons. Salt, pepper, and olive oil can make the difference between bland and flavorful. Vary the seasoning according to the dish; freshly ground cumin, caraway, and celery seeds can add a nice aroma and flavor. (I always grind spices as I need them in a coffee grinder, cleaning the grinder by wiping it out, then grinding a piece of soft bread to gather any remaining spice dust.)

Preheat the oven to 375°F.

Place the bread in a single layer on a baking sheet. Brush with the oil, season with salt and pepper, and toast in the oven, turning each piece once, until golden and crunchy, about 25 minutes in all.

homemade bread crumbs

1 day-old baguette

Preheat the oven to 250°F.

Break the baguette into pieces. Place the pieces on a baking sheet and dry the bread thoroughly in the oven, about 35 minutes.

Transfer the bread to a food processor and finely grind. Store in a cool, dry place.

developing a menu

adding shellfish and fish

I am always surprised when I hear people say they are reluctant to prepare fish because they find it harder to cook than meat. My experience indicates otherwise. The first job a cook can expect on the hot line in a restaurant is the job of *poissonier,* or fish cook. Why? Because fish and shellfish, unlike meat and poultry, cook obviously and quickly.

Fish, whether salt- or freshwater, are differently constituted than mammals and birds. Fish muscle is more fragile (a consequence of its groupings of shorter protein fibers)

and is bound by less tough, fibrous connective tissue (connective tissue makes up about 3 percent of an average fish's weight, as opposed to 15 percent of a typical land animal's). This difference explains why the application of heat transforms fish protein more quickly and visibly than hardy meat protein. It generally takes just a few minutes, confirmed by a glance and a quick touch, to gauge a fish fillet's readiness for the table. A roast takes longer to cook and is more difficult to read.

Cooking fish isn't the trick; choosing and storing it is. The delicacy of fish protein makes it subject to quick spoiling. It is therefore necessary to keep a few simple rules in mind. Buy the freshest fish you can find. I know my fish purveyor but trust myself. Fresh fish looks fresh. This is

easiest to see with whole fish. Look for clear eyes, red gills, and shiny scales. If you're buying fillets or steaks, look for firm, shimmering flesh. In any case, choose fish that smells like the sea—not like a pier. Store all fish with care. Wrap the fish in clean plastic. Refrigerate it, set over ice—this keeps the fish extra cold—for no more than two days.

Shellfish is even more subject to spoilage than fish. Clams, mussels, lobsters, and crabs should be alive when cooked. Buy clams and mussels with tightly closed shells, and active lobsters and crabs, the day you plan to cook them. Store live shellfish in unsealed bags (to allow air circulation) in the refrigerator. Shrimp, shelled scallops, squid, and octopus should be stored like fish, again for as short time as possible.

At this point the focus shifts from building a dish to developing a menu, and from recipes that are at heart vegetable combinations to those that integrate shellfish, fish, meat, and poultry. Generally, the recipes in this chapter and the next are, whether for appetizers or entrées, fully realized dishes. The appetizer recipes that begin these chapters are each accompanied by an entrée and wine suggestion. And I've accompanied the entrée recipes with links to complementary appetizers and side dishes as well as a wine recommendation.

Liliaceae family members— onion, scallion, garlic, leek

As I said, seafood cooks quickly. In most instances, a very short time over high heat (in a skillet or on a grill) or a somewhat longer time over low heat (maybe in a broth) will produce the best results. Shellfish—shrimp, scallops, mussels, clams, oysters, lobsters, and crabs—all move from raw to overcooked in the blink of an eye, so you need to pay close attention. Fish and shellfish look different when cooked. Fish becomes opaque and firmer, shrimp turn pink, clams and mussels open. (Lobster and crab shells change color, but because their meat is hidden, rely on past experience to determine doneness.)

Looking back, I realize that I began my hot line training aided by these visual cues. As I continued to work, I developed a sense of how exposure to different types of heat changes proteins. This awareness readied me for cooking meats and birds that boast less obvious signs of culinary transformation.

flavor chart for liliaceae

Liliaceae is commonly known as the onion family. Onions, shallots, garlic, and leeks are all in this family of edible bulbs. Asparagus, although in a different genus, is also in this family.

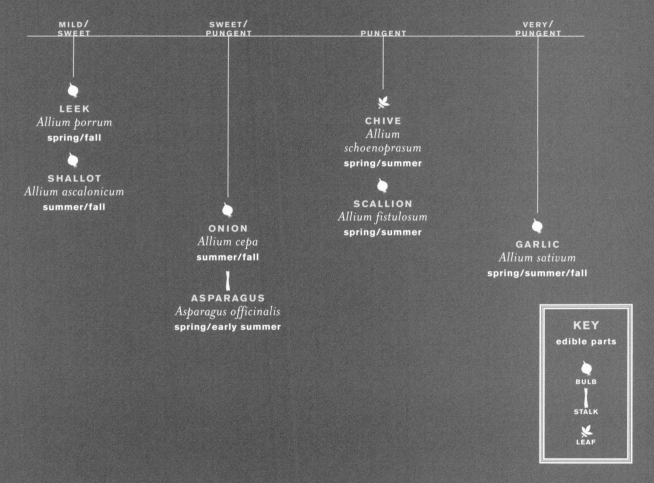

MILD/
SWEET

SWEET/
PUNGENT

PUNGENT

VERY/
PUNGENT

LEEK
Allium porrum
spring/fall

SHALLOT
Allium ascalonicum
summer/fall

CHIVE
*Allium
schoenoprasum*
spring/summer

SCALLION
Allium fistulosum
spring/summer

ONION
Allium cepa
summer/fall

GARLIC
Allium sativum
spring/summer/fall

ASPARAGUS
Asparagus officinalis
spring/early summer

KEY
edible parts

BULB

STALK

LEAF

poached eggs in **ASPARAGUS** nests 34, lemon porridge with **ASPARAGUS** and basil 96

ASPARAGUS crepes 110, **ASPARAGUS** vinaigrette 35

GARLIC confit 41

eggplant and **GARLIC** stew with merguez sausage 90

braised **LEEKS** 45, sorrel soup **{LEEK}** 83

smoked **ONION** puree 50, farfalle and cauliflower with bread crumbs **{ONIONS}** 103

sautéed scallops with **ONION** pan gravy 140

CHIVE popovers 118

SHALLOT vinaigrette 72

vegetable stock **{ONION, LEEK}** 57, chicken stock **{ONION, LEEK}** 170

scallop ceviche with chili vinaigrette

Appetizer
Scallop Ceviche
with
Chili Vinaigrette

Wine
Chardonnay—
California

Main Course
Tamarind-Marinated
Flank Steak
(page 167)

*Small bay scallops
are preferable for this
recipe; larger sea
scallops also work, but
dice or slice them
before adding them to
the vinaigrette. Either
way, look for "dry"
scallops, which have
not been whitened in a
chemical bath (see the
headnote on page 140).
Diced lean white fish
fillets, such as flounder
or fluke, or shrimp can
be substituted.*

FOR THE VINAIGRETTE

2 tablespoons chili powder
1 tablespoon coriander seeds
1 tablespoon cumin seeds
1 tablespoon paprika
1 teaspoon dried mustard
1 chipotle chile (canned in adobo)
1 red bell pepper, cored, seeded,
  and diced
1 cup extra virgin olive oil
2 tablespoons Champagne vinegar
Grated zest and juice of 2 limes
Grated zest and juice of 2 lemons
½ cup cilantro leaves, chopped

FOR THE CEVICHE

Kosher salt
1 pound bay scallops

1 bunch watercress, tough stems
  removed
Avocado Cream (page 68)
  (optional)

Typically, ceviche recipes call for curing seafood in spiced citrus juice. I find that scallops prepared this way can be somewhat tough. Instead, I cook scallops gently in salted water and only then dress them with a citrus-chili vinaigrette. The finished dish of silky scallops flavored with a spicy and tangy sauce is a favorite warm-weather starter.

The chili oil is a worthy recipe on its own. It makes a nice dressing for seafood or shrimp salad and is delicious with grilled fish. Just take care to follow the instructions for decanting the oil, or it will be gritty.

Making the chili oil.
Place the chili powder, coriander seeds, cumin seeds, paprika, and mustard in a medium saucepan and toast lightly over medium-low heat until fragrant, about 1 minute. Add the chipotle, half the bell pepper, and the oil and bring to a simmer. Remove the pan from the heat and allow the oil to steep for about 1 hour.

Pour the oil through a fine sieve into a bowl, leaving behind any spice sediment in the bottom of the pan. Allow the strained oil to settle again for at least 15 minutes.

Making the vinaigrette.
Combine the vinegar, lime and lemon juices, and the remaining bell pepper in a bowl. Whisking constantly, pour in the chili oil, leaving behind any sediment. Add the cilantro leaves and citrus zests.

Making the ceviche.
Bring a pot of well-salted water to a boil over high heat. Remove the pot from the stove and add the scallops. Leave the scallops in the hot water just until they are opaque and a little warm at the center (taste one to check), about 3 minutes.

Add the scallops to the vinaigrette, cover, and refrigerate for an hour or so to let the flavors blend.

Serve on a bed of watercress leaves, topped with a spoonful of avocado cream, if desired.

mussels in curried broth with coconut jasmine rice

FOR THE RICE

1 cup jasmine or other long-grain
  rice, rinsed
1 tablespoon butter
Pinch of kosher salt
¼ cup unsweetened coconut milk

**FOR THE MUSSELS
AND BROTH**

¼ cup extra virgin olive oil
1 onion, peeled, halved, and sliced
½ fennel bulb, cored and sliced
1 carrot, peeled, cut lengthwise
  into thirds and then slivered
Kosher salt and freshly ground
  black pepper
4 cloves garlic, peeled and
  chopped
1 tablespoon curry powder
1 teaspoon coriander seeds
2 tablespoons Pernod
4 sprigs thyme
2 cups Chicken Stock (page 170)
2 bay leaves
Juice of 1 lemon
4 dozen mussels, scrubbed and
  debearded if necessary
6 sprigs cilantro

Prince Edward Island mussels are my choice for this recipe. Purge the mussels early in the day (see the sidebar), then scrub and debeard them just before cooking. (As most mussels available today are cultivated, scrubbing and debearding won't be necessary. However, if you gather your own, be sure not to skip this step.) Throw away any that don't open during cooking.

Making the rice.
Combine the rice, butter, and salt in a small saucepan. Add 1 cup water and bring to a boil. Cover the pan and reduce the heat to low. Cook until the rice is almost dry, about 10 minutes. Add the coconut milk and another ¼ cup water and continue cooking until the rice is just tender, about 5 minutes more. Remove the rice from the heat. Cover with a clean towel and a lid to keep warm.

Making the broth.
Meanwhile, heat 2 tablespoons of the oil in a large pot over medium heat. Add the onion, fennel, and carrot, season with salt and pepper, and cook, stirring frequently, until the vegetables soften slightly, about 5 minutes. Add the garlic and 1 cup water and continue cooking until the vegetables are tender and the pan dry, about 15 minutes more.

Add the curry powder and coriander seeds; cook until the spices are fragrant. Add the Pernod and thyme. When the pan is again almost dry, in 1 to 2 minutes, add the chicken stock and bay leaves. Bring the broth to a simmer and cook until flavorful, about 10 minutes.

Cooking the mussels.
Add the lemon juice, the remaining 2 tablespoons olive oil, and the mussels to the broth. Cover the pot and cook just until the mussels open, 2 to 5 minutes.

Spoon the rice into warm bowls. Ladle the broth and mussels into the bowls and serve, garnished with the cilantro.

Appetizer
Mussels in Curried
Broth with Coconut
Jasmine Rice

Wine
Lillet Blanc
(an aperitif wine)

Main Course
Panfried Soft-Shell
Crabs with Jicama
Slaw (page 141)

Sandy mussels and clams must be purged in salted water to force them to expel sand and grit. Always discard any that are not fully closed. Soak the mollusks in a mixture of 1 cup salt and 3 quarts water for several hours. Drain and rinse well before cooking.

braised octopus

Appetizer
Braised Octopus

Wine
Barbera—
Barbera d'Asti

Main Course
Baby Lamb Chops
and Roasted
Eggplant Salad
(page 171)

*You can slice the
octopus on the bias and
drizzle it with both the
reduced braising liquid
and Puttanesca
Vinaigrette (page 56).*

*Another way to braise
seafood is confit-style,
in olive oil with
garlic and bay leaf;
see Shrimp Confit
(page 138). Squid and
octopus are both very
good cooked this way.
Just be sure to salt-
cure before cooking.*

FOR THE CURE

1 onion, peeled and sliced
½ fennel bulb, sliced
1 bunch flat-leaf parsley, roughly
 chopped
1 bay leaf, crumbled
1 pound octopus legs or baby
 octopus
3 tablespoons kosher salt
3 tablespoons sugar

FOR THE BRAISE

About 1⅓ cups extra virgin olive oil
2 onions, peeled and chopped
1 fennel bulb, cored and chopped
1 carrot, peeled and chopped
1 head garlic, halved
Kosher salt and freshly ground
 black pepper
3 cups dry red wine
2 cups red wine vinegar
Juice of 1 lemon
Sachet filled with:
 1 tablespoon black peppercorns
 1 bay leaf
 1 bunch thyme
 1 bunch flat-leaf parsley

2 cups arugula
Croutons (page 127)
Extra virgin olive oil

This recipe makes use of two techniques I often use together: salting and braising. I salt-cure the octopus overnight in order to flavor and tenderize it. Then I cook it very slowly in an aromatic red wine sauce. Prepared this way, the octopus is salted but not salty and perfectly tender throughout. Squid can be substituted for the octopus in this recipe.

Curing the octopus.
Combine the onion, fennel, parsley, and bay leaf. Lay about half of this mixture in a container large enough to hold the octopus in a single layer. Arrange the octopus on the herbs. Mix the salt with the sugar and sprinkle it over the octopus, then spread on the remaining onion and fennel mixture. Cover the container with plastic wrap and refrigerate overnight.

Braising the octopus.
Heat 3 tablespoons of the olive oil in a large deep skillet over medium heat. Add the onions, fennel, carrot, garlic, salt, and pepper and cook, stirring occasionally, until the vegetables are soft and golden, about 15 minutes.

Add the wine, vinegar, and lemon juice. Bring to a boil and reduce by about one-third, 10 minutes. Reduce the heat to low and add the sachet and 1 cup of the olive oil.

Brush the salt and herb mixture from the octopus. Add the octopus to the pot, then add water to cover (about 1 cup). Cover the pot and simmer very gently until the octopus is tender, about 1 hour. Remove the pot from the heat and allow the octopus to cool in the liquid.

Finishing and serving.
Once it is cool, remove the octopus from the braising liquid. Strain the liquid, return it to the pot, and bring to a boil. Allow it to reduce by three-quarters, or until the sauce can coat the back of a spoon, about 30 minutes. Meanwhile, if using the legs, slice them about ½ inch thick.

Return the octopus to the sauce and allow to cool to room temperature.

Spoon the octopus onto plates and drizzle with olive oil. Serve with the arugula and croutons, dressed with a little olive oil.

oyster stew

2 tablespoons extra virgin olive oil
2 onions, peeled and diced
1 fennel bulb, cored and diced
2 stalks celery, diced
2 leeks, diced
Kosher salt
2 cups dry white wine
Sachet filled with:
  1 bunch thyme
  2 bay leaves
  1 tablespoon black peppercorns
  5 cloves
  1 tablespoon coriander seeds
4 cups Clam Broth (page 139), or
  substitute 2 cups commercial
  clam broth plus 2 cups Chicken
  Stock (page 170)
1 cup milk
½ cup heavy cream
12 large oysters, scrubbed and
  shucked

Use Blue Point or Wellfleet oysters for this version of a traditional New England stew. Using clam broth rather than oyster liquor as a base allows more control and adds a nice light brininess. I puree sweated onion, celery, fennel, and leeks with the broth. Then I enrich this liquid with milk and cream before adding the oysters. The success of the recipe turns on controlling the temperature of the milk. Bring it to a "steam," not a simmer—this ensures plump tender oysters and prevents the milk from curdling.

Starting the broth.
Heat the oil in a large pot over medium-low heat. Add the onions, fennel, celery, and leeks, season with salt, and cook, stirring occasionally, until the oil gently sizzles and the vegetables soften slightly, about 5 minutes. Add ½ cup water and continue cooking until the vegetables are soft, about 20 minutes.

Increase the heat to medium-high and add the wine. Simmer until the pan is almost dry, then add the sachet and clam broth. Bring the broth to a simmer and cook until flavorful, about 15 minutes.

Finishing the stew.
Warm the milk and cream together in a small pan. Remove the sachet from the broth and transfer the broth to a food processor or blender. Add the warm milk mixture and pulse to combine.

Return the stew to the stove and heat just until steaming; do not boil. Add the oysters and poach until just barely firm, 2 to 3 minutes. Spoon into bowls and serve.

Appetizer
Oyster Stew

Wine
Sherry—
Manzanilla or fino

Main Course
Ruby Risotto with
Winter Greens and
Horseradish Cream
(page 104),
topped with Beer-
Braised Short Ribs
(page 169)

*This stew is hearty
enough for a one-
dish supper, though
the recipe would
have to be doubled if
you wanted to serve
four people amply.*

shrimp confit

Appetizer
Shrimp Confit

Wine
Chenin Blanc—
Loire

Accompaniment
Artichoke Griddle
Cakes (page 33)

Main Course
Rolled Soufflé
(page 108)

The oil seasons the shrimp and the shrimp flavor the oil. Any leftover oil can be reused, within 5 days, if refrigerated. I like to heat it a little, then blend it with vinegar for a warm vinaigrette to serve over sautéed fish or pasta.

12 large shrimp, peeled and
   deveined
About 3 cups olive oil
1 clove garlic, peeled and smashed
1 bay leaf
Kosher salt

Shrimp become tough when overcooked. This slow, low-temperature method, which can also be used to cook scallops, squid, and octopus, ensures a moist and creamy texture throughout. When they are available, use head-on shrimp to make this dish.

Place the shrimp in a single layer in a saucepan and add enough oil to cover by about ½ inch. Add the garlic and bay leaf and season with salt. Warm the oil over medium heat until you see one or two bubbles (the oil will register 170°F on an instant-read thermometer). Reduce the heat to low and let steep until the shrimp are pink and firm, about 2 minutes. Remove the shrimp from the oil and serve.

Shrimp Notes

Shrimp are crustaceans that fall into nine different families containing about 150 species. They live in both salt and fresh water and range dramatically in size. They are, like other crustaceans (lobsters, crab, and crawfish), extremely perishable. For this reason, shrimp are generally frozen as soon as they are caught, then sold either frozen or defrosted. Fresh shrimp—though hard to find—are a real treat.

Shrimp are sold by size, which is determined by the number of shrimp in a pound.

MINIATURE	100 or more
SMALL	36 to 45
MEDIUM	31 to 35
LARGE	21 to 30
EXTRA LARGE	16 to 20
JUMBO	11 to 15
COLOSSAL	10 or fewer

Whether they are fresh or frozen, I like to buy head-on shrimp. Cooking shrimp intact produces a more flavorful result.

Even when I plan to shell the shrimp before cooking, I prefer to buy them whole. I freeze the heads and shells; then, when time permits, I can simmer them for about forty minutes to make a fast, potent seafood stock that I use in soups, risotto, and sauces.

Clam Notes

Most edible clams belong to the Veneridae family. Roughly speaking, the bivalve mollusks are divided into hard-shells (all technically quahogs) and soft-shells. Small hard-shells are generally preferred raw; large ones are used for chowder. Soft-shell clams are more likely to be eaten steamed or fried—but these rules are not without exception. Common hard-shell varieties include, from small to large: littlenecks, cherrystones, and chowder clams. Soft-shell clams are not categorized by size. Steamer clams are readily available soft-shell clams.

clam broth and chopped clams

18 chowder clams (quahogs), scrubbed
1 bay leaf
1½ fennel bulbs, cored and quartered
½ onion, peeled and quartered
4 sprigs thyme

This recipe calls for chowder clams (sometimes called quahogs) because they are large—at least 3 inches across—and yield a lot of juice when cooked. Sandy clams must be purged (see the sidebar on page 135).

Place the clams in a large pot. Add the bay leaf, fennel, onion, thyme, and water to cover (about 12 cups). Cover and bring to a boil over high heat. Reduce the heat to medium and simmer until the clams open, about 5 minutes. Remove the clams from the broth and set them aside to cool. Strain the broth, let cool, and refrigerate or freeze until ready to use.

Remove the clams from their shells. Clean them by removing and discarding the necks and bellies, then chop. Store the chopped clams, covered with a little of the clam broth, in the refrigerator for up to 5 days or in the freezer for up to 6 months.

Clam broth is pleasantly salty and eminently useful to poach fish (see Cod Poached in Herbed Clam Broth, page 148), as a soup base, and in seafood sauces. This recipe yields not only broth but also clams. I season and bake them (see below) or quick-braise them with sautéed garlic, a little white wine, some clam broth, parsley, and black pepper and serve them over pasta.

baked clams

1 cup chopped cooked clams (double recipe above), 12 large half clamshells, scrubbed and reserved
2 cloves garlic, peeled and minced
2 slices bacon, cooked until crisp and crumbled
Pinch of cayenne pepper
¾ cup Homemade Bread Crumbs (page 127)
3 to 4 tablespoons Green Goddess Mayonnaise (page 73)
3 tablespoons extra virgin olive oil

Chopped chowder clams are best for this recipe. If you don't want to steam your own clams, buy them already chopped (fresh or frozen). I use herbed Green Goddess Mayonnaise (page 73) rather than olive oil to bind the clams and bread crumbs.

Preheat the oven to 400°F.

Combine the clams, garlic, bacon, cayenne, ½ cup of the bread crumbs, and the mayonnaise in a bowl and mix well. Spoon the clam mixture into the clam shells and set them on a baking sheet.

Mix the ¼ cup remaining bread crumbs with the oil. Cover each clam with a little of the bread crumb mixture, then bake until the tops are golden, about 20 minutes. Serve warm.

Appetizer
Baked Clams

Main Course
Sautéed Salmon with Corn Sauce (page 149)

Wine
Viognier—Rhône

sautéed scallops with onion pan gravy

Appetizer
Sautéed Scallops
with
Onion Pan Gravy

Wine
Chardonnay—
California

Main Course
Pan-Roasted Duck
Breast with
Pineapple Chutney
(page 178)

*I often pair this dish
with the Peppercress
Salad with Yellow Pepper
Vinaigrette (page 64).
Set the scallops around
the greens and drizzle
with both the vinaigrette
and the gravy.*

FOR THE GRAVY

2 tablespoons olive oil
1 large onion, peeled and coarsely
   chopped
Kosher salt and freshly ground
   black pepper
1 teaspoon sugar
1 cup Chicken Stock (page 170)

FOR THE SCALLOPS

¾ pound large "dry" sea scallops
Kosher salt and freshly ground
   black pepper
2 tablespoons olive oil
2 tablespoons butter
½ lemon

Beware of fat, pure white scallops. More likely than not they have been soaked in a chemical solution that plumps, whitens, and extends the delicate creatures' shelf life. Good news for the merchant, but bad news for the cook, who will find herself with scallops that stick to the pan, steam when they should brown, and are flaccid and tasteless when they should be firm, meaty, and delicious.

Starting the onion gravy.
Heat the oil in a large skillet over medium heat. Add the onion, season with salt and pepper, and cook, stirring occasionally, until soft and beginning to brown, about 20 minutes. Reduce the heat to medium-low, add the sugar, and cook, stirring frequently, until the onions are well browned, about 10 minutes more.

Add the stock and cook until the onions are very soft and the skillet is almost but not quite dry, about 15 minutes more. Transfer the onions to a blender and puree until smooth (add up to ¼ cup water if the mixture is too dry—you want the puree to be the texture of gravy).

Cooking the scallops.
Wipe out the skillet and heat it over medium-high heat. Season the scallops with salt and pepper. Add the oil and then the scallops to the pan. Jiggle the pan for a few seconds to keep the scallops from sticking, then cook the scallops without moving them until the first sides are golden, about 2 minutes. Turn the scallops, add the butter, and cook, basting the scallops with the melting butter, until they are well browned on the second side and beginning to firm, about 1 minute more (always cook an extra scallop—the best way to check doneness is to taste). Squeeze the juice of the lemon into the pan and baste the scallops with the lemon-butter sauce for about 30 seconds, then transfer them to plates.

Finishing the gravy.
Add the onion puree to the lemon butter left in the skillet and simmer for a minute or so. Drizzle the scallops with the sauce and serve.

panfried soft-shell crabs with jicama slaw

FOR THE VINAIGRETTE

1 jalapeño pepper, seeded and
  minced
3 scallions, chopped
2 tablespoons fresh lime juice
2 tablespoons fresh lemon juice
1 tablespoon rice wine vinegar
Kosher salt
1/2 cup grapeseed oil

FOR THE SLAW

1 large jicama, peeled and cut
  into julienne
1 scallion, thinly sliced on the bias
Kosher salt
2 cups spicy cress or arugula

FOR THE CRABS

1/4 cup heavy cream
Pinch of kosher salt
Pinch of cayenne pepper
1 cup all-purpose flour
1 cup semolina or finely ground
  cornmeal
8 small soft-shell crabs
  (see the headnote)
Extra virgin olive oil

Soft-shell crabs are blue crabs that have outgrown and shed one shell but have not yet grown a replacement. They are extremely perishable. Buy them live and clean them yourself. Using kitchen shears, snip off the eyes. Pull off the flap that wraps around the belly (known as the apron), then turn the crab over, lift up each side of the shell, and remove the gills. None of these parts is tasty (although it is reassuring to note that none is poisonous either). A good fishmonger can usually be imposed upon to clean soft-shells for you, but make sure that you see the crabs alive and then cook them the same day.

Making the vinaigrette.
Combine the jalepeño, scallions, lime juice, lemon juice, and rice wine vinegar in a blender and add salt. With the motor running, gradually add the oil.

Making the slaw.
Combine the jicama and scallion in a bowl. Season generously with salt, add about 1/2 cup of the vinaigrette, and set aside for 20 minutes to marinate.

Breading and frying the crabs.
Combine the cream, salt, and cayenne in a bowl. Place the flour and semolina on separate plates. Dip each cleaned crab first in the flour, then the cream, then the semolina.

Heat about 1/4 inch of oil in a large skillet over medium heat. Working in batches if necessary, fry the crabs until crisp on both sides, about 6 minutes in all, then drain on paper towels.

Add the cress or arugula to the slaw. Arrange the slaw on plates with the crabs and drizzle with a bit more vinaigrette.

Appetizer
Panfried
Soft-Shell Crabs
with Jicama Slaw

Wine
Vino Verde—
Spain

Main Course
Seared Sirloin
with Mushroom
Worcestershire
(page 168)

The crabs and slaw are also good in a sandwich.

seared celery root and smoked trout salad

Appetizer
Seared Celery Root
and Smoked Trout
Salad

Wine
Riesling—
German Kabinett

Main Course
Roasted Leg of
Venison (page 172)

*This could also be served,
in larger portions,
as an entrée at lunch.*

FOR THE VINAIGRETTE

¾ teaspoon sugar
2 tablespoons Champagne vinegar
¼ teaspoon turmeric
Kosher salt and freshly ground
   black pepper
6 tablespoons grapeseed oil

FOR THE SALAD

1 Yukon Gold potato, peeled and
   diced
Kosher salt
4 leeks, white parts only, halved
   lengthwise and sliced
3 tablespoons extra virgin olive oil
1 medium celery root, peeled and
   sliced ⅛ inch thick
Freshly ground black pepper
4 cups frisée
¼ cup parsley leaves
¼ cup ½-inch chive lengths
2 skinless smoked trout fillets
   (any bones removed), broken
   into pieces

Celery root, slightly bitter eaten raw, becomes wonderfully sweet when gently sautéed in olive oil. The smoky trout and the pungent turmeric vinaigrette harmonize with the celery root in an unfamiliar but addictive way. (See page 50 for directions for home-smoking.)

Making the vinaigrette.
Combine the sugar and vinegar in a small saucepan and heat, stirring occasionally, just until the sugar dissolves.

Place the turmeric in a small bowl and whisk in the hot vinegar mixture. Season with salt and pepper, then whisk in the grapeseed oil.

Making the salad.
Place the potatoes in a medium pot, cover with water, and add salt. Bring to a boil, reduce the heat, and simmer until the potatoes are tender, about 15 minutes; drain and set aside.

Meanwhile, cook the leeks in boiling salted water until tender, about 4 minutes. Drain and refresh in ice water. Drain again and set aside.

Heat the oil in a large skillet over medium-high heat. Working in batches, cook the celery root slices, browning them on each side, 2 to 3 minutes, and adding salt and pepper to taste. Transfer the celery root to paper towels to drain.

Combine the frisée, parsley, chives, potatoes, and leeks in a large bowl and dress with some of the vinaigrette. Add the celery root and trout and a little more vinaigrette. Mix gently and serve.

cured salmon

MAKES
I POUND

¼ cup coriander seeds
One 1-pound salmon fillet (skin on)
Juice of ½ lemon
2 tablespoons coarsely ground
   black pepper
½ bunch parsley (including
   stems), roughly chopped
1 onion, peeled and sliced
½ small fennel bulb, cored and
   sliced
2 cups kosher salt
6 tablespoons sugar

Cured salmon is easy to make at home. The tricky part is slicing it. Make sure the fish is weighted sufficiently while it cures; this helps to ensure that it becomes compact and firm. Use a very sharp long knife. Cut from the tail end, drawing the knife across the fillet toward you. You can lay your hand over the piece you are slicing to help guide you, which allows you to slice the salmon very thin.

Toast the coriander seeds in a small skillet over medium heat until fragrant, about 5 minutes. Transfer to a spice grinder and finely grind.

Place the salmon skin side down in a baking dish lined with parchment paper. Squeeze the lemon over the fish. Combine the pepper and ground coriander and sprinkle over the fish. Combine the parsley, onion, and fennel and spread over the fish, then combine the salt and sugar and sprinkle over the fish. Wrap the salmon in plastic, then weight it with a plate topped with heavy cans.

Refrigerate for 2 days, from time to time pouring off any liquid that accumulates.

When ready to serve, wipe off the salmon (discard the cure). Cut into thin slices and serve.

VARIATION

seared cured salmon

Cured salmon is good seared. Slice the fish about ½ inch thick. Sauté it in olive oil over medium heat on one side only; serve it with a shaved fennel salad. Once cured, the salmon can also be hot-smoked. Follow the instructions for smoking on page 50.

Appetizer
Cured Salmon

Accompaniments
Mustard oil, chopped
radishes, Blini
(page 117),
and Crème Fraîche
(page 204)

Wine
Champagne—
Blanc de Blancs

adding shellfish and fish   143

About Fish

Firm, moderately lean white-fleshed round fish

saltwater

BLACK SEA BASS

The name *bass* is used to refer to a variety of unrelated spiny-finned fish. Black sea bass *(Centropristis striatus)* is a member of the Serranidae family. Like its three close relations, the Southern sea bass, bank sea bass, and rock sea bass, the black bass inhabits the shoreline waters of the Atlantic from Florida to New York.

Sold whole or in fillets. Roasted, braised, fried, sautéed, or grilled. Substitute snapper or striped bass.

STRIPED BASS

The American striped bass *(Morone saxatilis)* is not related to the black sea bass discussed above. It is a member of the Moronidae family and is, like salmon, an *anadromous* fish, meaning it lives in saltwater but reproduces in fresh. Striped bass, left unmolested, can grow very large—over seventy pounds, every sports fisherman's dream. Cooks prefer a more modest (6- to 8-pound) catch. Naturally found in Atlantic waters from the Gulf of St. Lawrence to the Gulf of Mexico, striped bass were successfully introduced into the Pacific in 1879.

Sold whole or in fillets. Roasted, poached, braised, fried, sautéed, or grilled. Substitute snapper or black sea bass.

SNAPPER

There are about two hundred fifty members of the Lutjanidae family. Fifteen varieties of snapper are found in the warm waters of the southern Atlantic from North Carolina to the Gulf of Mexico. The red snapper *(Lutjanus campechanus)* is the most familiar.

Sold whole or in fillets. Roasted, poached, braised, fried, sautéed, or grilled. Substitute black sea bass or striped bass.

GROUPER

Groupers, like black bass, are among the four hundred species that make up the Serranidae family. Though they are found off both U.S. coasts, the commercial catch comes primarily from the warm waters off Florida and the Caribbean islands. Groupers generally boast tough, strong-tasting skin.

Sold in skinned fillets. Fried, braised, sautéed, roasted, and used in soups and stews. Substitute snapper or cod.

Meaty, lean white-fleshed cartilaginous fish

saltwater

MONKFISH

Monkfish *(Lophius americanus)* is a deep-water fish with an extremely large head and meaty tail. It is a chondrichthyan, meaning its skeleton is made of cartilage rather than bone. The tail, the part of this fish of the greatest culinary interest, is divided by a ridge of cartilage and covered by layers of tough skin. The meat is additionally encased in a thin membrane. All the skin and membrane must be removed before eating. The cartilage need not be, but usually is. Properly cooked, monkfish has the firm texture of lobster meat.

Sold in skinned medallions or pieces. Roasted, sautéed, braised, and used in stews. Substitute cod.

MAKO

Mako *(Isurus* spp.) is a type of shark, and another chondrichthyan. Though some consider it a culinary substitute for swordfish, I do not. I find the taste and texture of the two quite different. Mako is much milder tasting and less finely textured than swordfish. Swordfish has been seriously overfished, so I no longer serve it. Mako is therefore worth a second look.

Sold in steaks. Grilled, sautéed, or quick-braised. Substitute mahi-mahi.

Delicate, lean white-fleshed cartilaginous fish

saltwater

SKATE

The common skate *(Raja batis)* is also a chondrichthyan. It is, like the culinarily similar rays, a flatfish, with a broad head and two large "wings" (actually pectoral fins). The entire fish is covered with a tough skin that must be removed. The wings house the sweet meat between small cartilage dividers. Filleting skate, though not difficult, takes some practice.

Sold in skinned fillets. Sautéed, fried, or poached. Substitute sole or flounder.

Delicate, lean white-fleshed flatfish

saltwater

SOLE AND FLOUNDER

Sole is a shortening of the family name Soleidae. This family contains a number of flatfish, the most famous being the Eastern Atlantic native Dover sole. In common usage, the designation *sole* extends to members of two other fish families: Bothidae and Pleuronectidae. A number of culinarily significant mid-sized flatfish found off the Atlantic and Pacific U.S. coasts come from these families. American lemon sole, gray sole, and Lex sole can all be substituted for Dover sole.

Sold whole or in skinned fillets. Whole fish: grilled or sautéed. Fillets: poached, sautéed, or fried.

Meaty, lean white-fleshed flatfish

saltwater

HALIBUT

A large cold-water fish, the Atlantic halibut *(Hippoglossus hippoglossus)* is the largest flatfish. It is, like many flounders (see above), a member of the Pleuronectidae family. Halibut are commercially fished in both the Atlantic and Pacific Oceans. They can grow to more than four hundred pounds. For this reason, halibut is usually seen already cut into skinless fillets or steaks. Smaller halibut, more frequently available from fish farmers than found in the wild, can be cooked whole. Halibut is meaty and lean, with a tendency toward dryness.

Sold in skinned fillets or steaks. Pan-roasted, poached, or braised. Substitute haddock, merluza, or cod.

Firm but flaky, lean white-fleshed round fish

saltwater

COD

It is the Atlantic cod *(Gadus morhua)*, not gold, that probably brought the first Europeans to North America. Spanish, Portuguese, and Italian fishermen worked up the coast of Europe, then moved on to Iceland and Greenland and finally to Newfoundland and south. As recently as fifty years ago, enormous cod were a common sight off Canadian shores—no more. Moderately sized Atlantic cod are still available from other waters, as are Pacific cod (a close relative and fellow member of the Gadidae family).

Sold in skinned fillets or steaks. Poached, pan-roasted, fried, or used in soups and stews. Substitute grouper or haddock. Also sold dried and salted; once rehydrated, good poached, braised, or sautéed.

HADDOCK

Haddock *(Melanogrammus aeglefinus)*, like cod, is a member of the Gadidae family. Haddock are smaller than cod, on average about 4 ½ pounds. They swim in the North Atlantic. In France, haddock is almost exclusively served smoked, but, when fresh, this mild-tasting fish is an excellent substitute for cod.

Sold in fillets. Poached, sautéed, or fried. Substitute halibut or cod.

Meaty, oily red-fleshed round fish

saltwater

TUNA

The Scombridae family contains mackerel and bonito as well as tuna. Tuna are large (hundreds of pounds), tough-skinned fish. They prefer relatively warm waters and are found in the Atlantic and Pacific Oceans. Tuna is graded according to the brightness of its color, the absence of bruises, the percentage of fat, and freshness. "Sashimi quality" or *number 1* grade tuna gets highest marks on all tests. This grade, however, is rarely available to consumers. *Number 2* grade is easier to find and perfectly acceptable for most purposes. Bluefin *(Thunnus thynnus)* is the most highly regarded variety. Yellowfin *(Thunnus albacares)* and bigeye *(Thunnus obesus)* are becoming more important commercially, as bluefins grow scarcer.

Sold in thick fillets or steaks. Raw, grilled, seared, sautéed, or braised. Substitute mahi-mahi.

Firm, flaky, oily dark-fleshed round fish

saltwater

BLUEFISH

Common off the Atlantic coast from Florida to Nova Scotia but also found in the Mediterranean, bluefish *(Pomatomus saltatrix)* is strong tasting and highly perishable. This member of the Pomatomidae family is best eaten the day it is caught.

Sold whole or in fillets. Whole fish: roasted or grilled. Fillets: grilled, braised, baked, or sautéed. Also good cured and then hot-smoked. Substitute mackerel.

MACKEREL

Mackerel is, like tuna, a member of the Scombridae family. From the cook's vantage, however, the various mackerels have more in common with bluefish or sardines than tuna. Mackerel is strong tasting and highly perishable. Varieties are found on both sides of the Atlantic and Pacific Oceans.

Sold whole or in fillets. Roasted, poached, braised, fried, sautéed, or grilled. Substitute snapper or black sea bass.

MAHI-MAHI

Also known as dorado and dolphin fish, mahi-mahi *(Coryphaena hippurus)* are no relation to mammalian dolphins. This warm-water-dwelling fish has long been eaten in the Hawaiian Islands. It is becoming increasingly available in mainland United States.

Sold in fillets or steaks. Grilled, sautéed, or roasted.

Firm, flaky, oily red-fleshed round fish

saltwater

SALMON

Both Atlantic and Pacific salmon are anadromous fish (they live in saltwater but breed in fresh water). Pollution and development are taking a large toll on varieties in both oceans. The stock of wild Atlantic salmon, *Salmo salar,* has been particularly compromised. The five Pacific species (all from the *Oncorhynchus* genus)—chinook (king), coho (silver), sockeye (red), dog (chum), and pink—are faring only a little better. Some consider fish farming the answer. Unfortunately, farmed salmon has neither the strength nor the delicacy of flavor of wild fish. Wild Atlantic salmon is no longer commercially available. Wild chinook, coho, and sockeye are available and worth the extra expense.

Sold whole or in fillets or steaks. Whole fish: poached, roasted, or grilled. Fillets and steaks: poached, braised, grilled, or sautéed, cured, pickled, smoked, or raw. Substitute Arctic char.

Firm, lean beige- to red-fleshed round fish

freshwater (lakes, rivers, and streams)

TROUT

Trout are members of the Salmonidae family and the most extensively farmed fish. Some varieties live exclusively in freshwater, and some migrate to the sea. Rainbow trout *(Onchorhynchus mykiss)* and brook trout *(Salvelinus fontinalis)* are considered the tastiest. Both species originated in North America but have been introduced worldwide. Trout is most often cooked whole (it is easy to bone once cooked), but larger fish can be filleted.

Sold whole or in fillets. Grilled, sautéed, poached, or smoked.

cod poached in herbed clam broth

Appetizer
Artichoke Gratin
(page 32)

Main Course
Cod Poached in
Herbed Calm Broth

Accompaniment
Green salad with
Lemon-Mustard
Vinaigrette
(page 72)

Wine
White Burgundy—
Chablis

4 cups Clam Broth (page 139)
2 teaspoons chopped tarragon
2 teaspoons chopped flat-leaf
  parsley
2 teaspoons chopped chives
Four 6-ounce cod fillets
Kosher salt and freshly ground
  black pepper
Croutons (page 127)

Cod is a good poaching fish because it is firm. It is mild-tasting, so it is best to use a flavorful broth; clam broth, with its briny sweetness, is perfect. Haddock or hake would make a good substitute for the cod.

Heat the clam broth in a large deep skillet over medium heat. When it reaches a simmer, add the tarragon, parsley, and chives. Season the fish with salt and pepper and add it to the simmering broth. Cover the pot, reduce the heat to medium-low, and poach the fish until it is done (test by lifting a fillet out of the broth and sticking a knife in the center—if it flakes rather than resists, the fish is done).

Place a crouton in each bowl and top with a piece of cod. Ladle the broth around the fish and serve.

Although inspired by seafood stews like bouillabaisse, this dish is much simpler, yet satisfying enough to be served as a main course. If you want a more rustic effect, add potatoes. Roasted garlic mayonnaise (see the sidebar on page 41) is a nice accompaniment.

sautéed salmon with corn sauce

FOR THE SAUCE

½ cup milk
½ cup heavy cream
3 ears corn, husked and kernels
   removed, corncobs reserved
Sachet filled with:
   ½ teaspoon coriander seeds
   ½ teaspoon white peppercorns
   1 bay leaf
   1 sprig thyme
Kosher salt
Pinch of cayenne pepper

FOR THE SALMON

2 tablespoons extra virgin olive oil
Kosher salt and freshly ground
   black pepper
Four 6-ounce skinless center-cut
   salmon fillets

Always buy wild salmon when it is available. I like full-flavored Chinook (sometimes called king) or, for a milder taste and more dramatic presentation, deeply colored sockeye. I have recently become very fond of a variety sold as white albino king salmon—it reminds me of sturgeon.

Making the sauce.
Combine the milk and cream in a large pot. Break the corncobs in halves or thirds and add them, the corn, and the sachet to the milk mixture. Bring to a simmer, then reduce the heat to low and steep until the sauce is flavorful, about 30 minutes. Remove the sachet and cobs, and puree the sauce in a blender (a hand blender will also work). Strain the sauce through a sieve into a saucepan, season with salt and cayenne, and keep warm over low heat.

Sautéing the salmon.
Heat the oil in a large skillet over medium-high heat. Salt and pepper the salmon on both sides, then add the fillets cut side down to the skillet. Cook the salmon until the first sides begin to brown slightly, about 4 minutes, then turn and cook about 1 minute more for medium-rare. Serve with the sauce.

Appetizer
Tomato and
Cucumber Salad
with Avocado Cream
(page 68)

Main Course
Sautéed Salmon
with Corn Sauce

Accompaniments
Braised Leeks
(page 45) and
Sautéed Greens
(page 43)

Wine
Sauvignon Blanc—
Bordeaux

halibut with tomato-cumin sauce

Appetizer
Bulgur Wheat Salad
with Fava Beans
(page 63)

Main Course
Halibut with
Tomato-Cumin Sauce

Accompaniment
Steamed white rice

Wine
Viognier—Rhône

Cod or haddock would be good alternate fish choices. A whole 2½- to 3-pound fish, sea bass or snapper, can also be substituted for the fillets: simply adjust the cooking time.

2 tablespoons extra virgin olive oil
1 medium onion, peeled, halved, and sliced
2 stalks celery, trimmed and cut into thin lengths
¾ pound Swiss chard, stems cut into thin 2-inch lengths, leaves chopped
Kosher salt and freshly ground black pepper
1 tablespoon ground cumin
1 tablespoon cracked coriander seeds
4 cups canned tomatoes, with their juice, chopped
2 tablespoons sugar, or to taste
Pinch of cayenne pepper
Four 6-ounce halibut fillets

My grandmother Violet used to make this, a dish that has been in my mother's family for generations. My mother likes to serve small portions of the silky fish chilled as an appetizer on special occasions. I serve my version warm, moistened with fruity olive oil, seasoned with sea salt, and accompanied by rice.

Making the broth.
Heat the oil in a large deep skillet over medium heat. Add the onion, celery, and chard stems, and season with salt and pepper. Cook, stirring frequently, until the vegetables soften slightly, about 5 minutes. Add the cumin and coriander seeds and cook until fragrant. Add the tomatoes and their juice, the sugar, and 3 cups water. Bring to a simmer. Add the chard leaves and cayenne and simmer until the sauce is flavorful and the oil begins to float to the surface, about 40 minutes. (The broth is best made a day in advance, cooled, covered, and refrigerated. Bring to a simmer before proceeding.)

Poaching the fish.
Season the halibut fillets with salt and pepper and add them to the simmering broth. Spoon a little of the broth over the fillets and cook covered until the fish is just done, about 5 minutes (test by lifting a fillet out of the broth and sticking a knife in the center—if it flakes rather than resists, the fish is done).

Spoon the fish and broth into bowls and serve.

sautéed flounder with braised rhubarb

SERVES 4
AS AN ENTREE

FOR THE RHUBARB

2 cups port wine
¼ cup sherry vinegar
½ cup sugar
2 teaspoons black peppercorns
4 stalks rhubarb, peeled and cut
  into 3-inch sticks
2 tablespoons butter (optional)

FOR THE FLOUNDER

1 tablespoon extra virgin olive oil
Four 6-ounce flounder fillets
Kosher salt and freshly ground
  black pepper
3 tablespoons butter

The combination of a tart fruit compote with lean white fish is a favorite of mine. Here I have used flounder, but sole or even halibut would be equally nice.

Braising the rhubarb.
Combine the port, vinegar, sugar, and pepper in a high-sided medium skillet and bring to a simmer over medium-high heat. Reduce the liquid by one-third, about 10 minutes; strain through a fine sieve to remove the pepper. Return the liquid to the skillet and add the rhubarb. Gently simmer over medium-low heat until the rhubarb is tender but still holding its shape, about 5 minutes. Remove the pan from the heat and cover to keep warm.

Sautéeing the flounder.
Heat the oil in a large skillet over medium-high heat. Dry the fillets well with paper towels and season on both sides with salt and pepper. Add the fillets to the pan along with the 3 tablespoons butter. (If your pan is too small to accommodate all the fish, work in batches, wiping out the pan in between and adding fresh oil and butter.) Brown the fish on both sides, about 3 minutes in all. Transfer to four dinner plates.

Finishing the sauce.
Stir the 2 tablespoons butter, if using, into the rhubarb, then spoon the rhubarb and sauce around each serving of fish.

Appetizer
Asparagus Crepes
(page 110)

Main Course
Sautéed Flounder
with Braised Rhubarb

Accompaniments
Jasmine rice and
Sautéed Greens
(page 43)

Wine
Rosato–Sicily

For a more elaborate presentation, serve sorrel sauce (see the sidebar on page 83), in addition to the braised rhubarb and fish.

adding shellfish and fish   151

sea bass in lemon nage

The word nage *comes from the French* nager: *to swim. In culinary terms,* à la nage *refers to cooking in an aromatic liquid.*

½ cup extra virgin olive oil
½ medium onion, peeled and
  sliced
½ fennel bulb, cored and sliced
Kosher salt
1 bay leaf
1 tablespoon coriander seeds
1½ teaspoons white peppercorns
1½ cups dry white wine
6 tablespoons Champagne vinegar
1 bunch tarragon
Four ½-pound sea bass fillets
Freshly ground white pepper
8 slices Quick Preserved Lemon
  (page 47)
2 tablespoons chopped tarragon for
  garnish (optional)

The nage, or broth, in this recipe is flavored with lemon and herbs. This is a quick recipe but for the preserved lemon, which must be left to cure overnight. The extra flavor dimension is worth the effort.

Heat 2 tablespoons of the oil in a large deep skillet over medium heat. Add the onion, fennel, and salt. Cook, stirring occasionally, until the oil gently sizzles and the vegetables begin to soften but not brown, about 5 minutes. Add the bay leaf, coriander seeds, peppercorns, and ½ cup water and cook until the vegetables are tender, about 15 minutes more.

Add the wine and simmer until the pan is almost dry, about 10 minutes. Add the vinegar, the remaining 6 tablespoons oil, and 3 cups water, bring to a simmer, and cook very gently until the broth is flavorful, about 20 minutes. Add the tarragon, then remove the pan from the heat, and allow the broth to steep for 15 minutes; strain.

To serve, bring the broth to a simmer over medium heat in a pot or deep skillet large enough to hold the fish. Season the fish with salt and white pepper. Lower the fillets into the broth. Add the preserved lemon slices, cover, reduce the heat, and gently simmer until the fish is opaque at the center, about 5 minutes.

Spoon the fish and broth into bowls and serve garnished with the preserved lemon slices and freshly chopped tarragon.

mackerel with paprika sauce

FOR THE SAUCE

3 tablespoons extra virgin olive oil
1 large onion, peeled and diced
2 tablespoons paprika
1 tablespoon coriander seeds
1 teaspoon caraway seeds
1 bay leaf
¼ cup sherry vinegar
1 cup canned tomatoes, with their juices
Pinch of cayenne pepper
Kosher salt and freshly ground black pepper

FOR THE FISH

Four 6-ounce mackerel fillets
Kosher salt and freshly ground black pepper
2 to 3 tablespoons extra virgin olive oil

This recipe is for my father. I match mackerel, an oily and wonderfully assertive fish, with a tomato-paprika sauce to create a dish with the warmth and character of my father's native Hungarian cuisine.

Making the sauce.
Heat the oil in a medium saucepan over medium heat. Add the onion and cook, stirring frequently, until it begins to brown, about 15 minutes.

Add the paprika, coriander seeds, caraway seeds, and bay leaf and cook until the spices are fragrant, about 2 minutes. Add the vinegar and tomatoes. Season the sauce with cayenne, salt, and pepper and bring to a simmer over medium heat. Simmer until the oil rises to the surface, about 30 minutes. Strain the sauce through a fine sieve into a saucepan. Keep warm, or reheat before serving (the sauce can be made up to 3 days in advance).

Pan-roasting the fish.
Heat one large or two medium skillets over medium-high heat. Season the fish on both sides with salt and pepper. Add enough oil to film the pan(s), then add the fish skin side down. Cook until the first sides are golden, about 5 minutes, then turn the fish and continue cooking until the fish is opaque at the center, about 5 minutes more. Transfer the fish to plates, dress with the sauce, and serve.

Appetizer
Zucchini Soup
with Rosemary
(page 87)

Main Course
Mackerel with
Paprika Sauce

Accompaniment
Braised Salsify
(page 53) warmed
in Crème Fraîche
(page 204)

Wine
Pinot Gris—
Alsace or Oregon

This is not a dish for the faint of heart, though it could be rendered a little more mannered by a different fish. Rouget, mahi-mahi, and escolar would all be different but good.

roasted monkfish with curried kumquats

SERVES 4
AS AN ENTRÉE

Appetizer
Sorrel Soup
(page 83)

Main Course
Roasted Monkfish
with Curried
Kumquats

Accompaniment
White Lentils
(page 36)

Wine
Pinot Gris—
Alsace

The whole monkfish tails must be specially ordered from a fish-monger. Monkfish medallions, while not quite as flavorful (or dramatic), can be substituted—cook them from start to finish on top of the stove over medium heat.

FOR THE KUMQUATS

2 tablespoons extra virgin olive oil
1 red onion, peeled, halved, and sliced
1/2 cup diced sun-dried tomatoes
1/4 cup sherry vinegar
1/4 cup packed dark brown sugar
2 tablespoons granulated sugar
Sachet filled with:
  1/2 head garlic
  3 sprigs thyme
  1 teaspoon black peppercorns
  1 star anise
1 tablespoon curry powder
20 kumquats, stems removed, quartered, and seeded
4 cups Chicken Stock (page 170)

FOR THE MONKFISH

Two 1 3/4-pound monkfish tails (see the sidebar)
Kosher salt and freshly ground black pepper
2 tablespoons extra virgin olive oil
3 tablespoons butter
1/2 lemon

Monkfish tail is usually sold filleted and cut into medallions. If you can, buy it cut into cross sections on the bone (actually cartilage). When you roast it, the fish seems to baste itself. It remains moist and holds its shape rather than curling up.

Making the curried kumquats.
Heat the oil in a large saucepan over medium heat. Add the onion and cook, stirring frequently, until browned, about 20 minutes.

Add the tomatoes, vinegar, and 3 tablespoons water and cook until the pan is almost dry, about 5 minutes. Add the brown and granulated sugars, the sachet, curry powder, kumquats, and stock and bring to a boil. Adjust the heat and simmer rapidly until the sauce is reduced by two-thirds, about 1 hour.

Remove the sauce from the heat and discard the sachet. Reheat the sauce just before serving.

Roasting the monkfish.
Preheat the oven to 400°F.

Heat a very large ovenproof nonstick skillet over medium-high heat. Season the fish on both sides with salt and pepper. Add the oil to the skillet, then add the fish, bone side up. Cook until the first side is golden, about 2 minutes, then turn the fish and add the butter. Continue cooking the fish, basting it with the browning butter, until the second side is golden, about 2 minutes more.

Transfer the pan to the oven and roast until the fish is opaque at the center, about 7 minutes. Squeeze the juice of the lemon into the pan and baste the fish with it to glaze. Allow the fish to rest for 1 minute, then cut each tail in half and place on warm plates with the curried kumquats.

spiced tuna with romesco sauce

FOR THE SAUCE

3 cloves garlic, peeled
6 tablespoons extra virgin olive oil
3 tablespoons slivered almonds
1 red bell pepper
1 Slow-Roasted Tomato (page 55)
Pinch of cayenne pepper
3 tablespoons red wine vinegar
¼ cup plain yogurt (optional)
Kosher salt

FOR THE TUNA

2 tablespoons coriander seeds
1 tablespoon cumin seeds
1 teaspoon white peppercorns
1 teaspoon sugar
½ teaspoon kosher salt
Four 6-ounce tuna steaks, about
  2 inches thick
3 tablespoons extra virgin olive oil

Romesco sauce is a Catalan classic typically made by combining bread, garlic, tomatoes, nuts, wine, vinegar, chili powder, and paprika in a mortar and grinding them together. Like much Mediterranean cooking, it is subject to considerable variation. My version is made with flame-roasted pepper, roasted tomato, toasted almonds—and, in a clear break with tradition, thinned with yogurt.

Making the sauce.
Preheat the oven to 375°F.

Place the garlic on a square of aluminum foil and add about 1 tablespoon of oil. Wrap the garlic in the foil and roast until the garlic is soft, about 15 minutes. Meanwhile, place the almonds on a small baking sheet and roast them until they are golden, about 7 minutes.

Flame-roast the bell pepper over a burner (alternatively under the broiler). Turn the pepper occasionally, until charred all over, about 10 minutes. Put it in a bowl, cover with plastic wrap, and set aside for 10 minutes. Peel, core, seed, and roughly chop the pepper. Place it, the almonds, and garlic in a food processor. Add the tomato, cayenne, and vinegar and pulse; gradually add the remaining oil until the sauce is about the consistency of a chunky mayonnaise. Transfer to a bowl and refrigerate until ready to use.

Making the tuna spice.
Finely grind the coriander seeds, cumin seeds, and peppercorns in a spice or coffee grinder. Transfer to a bowl and mix in the sugar and salt (the tuna spice will keep in a sealed container for weeks).

Cooking the tuna.
Roll each piece of tuna in the spice mix, thoroughly coating the pieces on all sides. Heat one or two large skillets over medium heat. Add the oil, then the tuna. Cook, turning to brown on all sides, for about 10 minutes for rare. Transfer the tuna to serving plates. Thin the Romesco sauce with the yogurt, if desired, season with salt, and serve.

Appetizer
Braised Greens Tart
(page 112)

Main Course
Spiced Tuna with
Romesco Sauce

Accompaniment
Bulgur Wheat Salad
with Fava Beans
(page 63)

Wine
Cabernet Franc—
Loire

Be careful not to cook the tuna over high heat or the spices will burn. If you prefer your fish done medium or well, finish the cooking in a 375°F oven.

adding meat and poultry

The appetizers that begin this chapter are particular favorites of mine. Most come from the long French tradition of preserving meat that I first learned to love while working at the River Café. The making of charcuterie, which includes confits, rillettes, sausages, pâtés, and terrines, like making pastry, requires a comforting precision from the cook.

It is important to understand that this branch of cooking grew out of the need to store meat before refrigeration was available. Success depended on balancing the need to purify and preserve by eliminating moisture (first with salt, then with heat) with a desire for moist and luscious results. Key to success is beginning with the right cut. Traditional charcuterie is made with what I like to think of as the working parts of the animal: the legs, neck, shoulders, and even tail. This is true whether you are dealing with poultry, beef, pork, or lamb. These cuts contain a lot of strong connective tissue that, when exposed to heat for prolonged periods, is transformed from inedibly tough to tender and delicious as the collagen in the tissue is converted to gelatin. This transformation lubricates from within as the meat's juices evaporate. Tender cuts have no such lubrication and taste unpleasantly dry when fully cooked.

The judicious use of fat was also essential. Traditionally, fat was used to replace the moisture lost by curing and cooking. It also added flavor and worked to seal the meat from bacterial attack. A precise measure (generally 30 percent) of chilled fat is an essential ingredient in such classics as pâté de campagne.

Refrigeration has eliminated the need for charcuterie but not the desire. Like many modern cooks, I use a combination of old techniques and new technology to reinvent this old craft. A quick look at my Short Rib Terrine (page 160) will demonstrate what I mean. My goal as I developed this recipe was a dish without the weightiness of many more traditional preparations. I wanted to reduce the fat without compromising the structure or the texture of the terrine. Because I wanted old-fashioned

The progression of recipes moves from appetizers to entrées and from meat to poultry.

Mushrooms: Their own kingdom (fungi)— oyster, Portobello, hen-of-the-woods, shiitake, cremini (young portobello)

richness, I started by using a traditional—that is, tough—cut of meat (originally oxtails, but here, because they are a bit easier to find, beef short ribs). I brined the ribs to concentrate their flavor by extracting some of the juices. Then I slowly braised the meat in a broth of caramelized aromatic vegetables, stock, and red wine. Once it was cooked, I removed the meat from the bones and strained and defatted the braising liquid. Instead of using fat to hold the terrine together, I added gelatin to the braising liquid, and chilled it to set. Then, just before serving it, I coated the terrine in mustard and bread crumbs and crisped one side, heating it only enough to warm the crust, not to melt the gelatin.

Big flavor comes from the choice of meat, the brining, and the slow, rich, red wine braise. Streamlining comes with the use of gelatin as a binder. And a modern crunch comes from the warm mustard crust. The recipe combines traditional and modern cooking methods, and that's what I like about it. Like much charcuterie, preparing this terrine demands exactitude, but the technical problems presented need not bind the cook to traditional solutions. The ability to adapt to new technology and innovation are shared strengths of the charcutier and the pâtissier.

meat and poultry cooking temperatures

The definitions for rare, medium-rare, medium, and well-done
are not universal. Look at the descriptions as well as the familiar
designations before deciding what temperature you prefer.

MEAT	DEGREE OF DONENESS	TEMPERATURE AND DESCRIPTION
BEEF	rare	120°F; red interior, just-warm center
	medium-rare	125°F to 130°F; red interior, warm center
	medium	135°F to 150°F; pinkish interior, warm center
	well-done	above 150°F; brown interior, hot center
LAMB	rare	120°F; bloody-red interior, just-warm center
	medium-rare	125°F to 130°F; red interior, warm center
	medium	135°F to 150°F; pinkish interior, warm center
	well-done	above 150°F; brown interior, hot center
CHICKEN (breast and leg)		145°F; thoroughly cooked but juicy
TURKEY (breast and leg)		145°F; thoroughly cooked but juicy
DUCK AND DARK MEAT BIRDS	rare	120°F; bloody-red interior, just-warm center
	medium-rare	125°F to 130°F; red interior, warm center
	medium	135°F to 150°F; brown interior, hot center
	well-done	above 150°F; brown interior, hot center, slightly dry

short rib terrine

*The terrine can be
served as an entrée.
The wine-braised
short ribs themselves
are delicious served
as you would Beer-
Braised Short Ribs.
(page 169).*

FOR THE SHORT RIBS

Kosher salt
6 pounds beef short ribs
2 tablespoons extra virgin olive oil
Freshly ground black pepper
2 onions, peeled and chopped
2 carrots, peeled and chopped
2 stalks celery, peeled and
    chopped
1 small rutabaga, peeled and
    chopped (or 1 cup chopped
    parsnip)
1 head garlic, halved
2 tablespoons tomato paste
4 sprigs thyme
1 tablespoon black peppercorns
2 bay leaves
1 cup dry red wine
1 cup red wine vinegar
4 anchovies, rinsed
4½ cups Chicken Stock
    (page 170)

1¼ teaspoons powdered gelatin

FOR THE OPTIONAL
BREADING

2 eggs
1 tablespoon Dijon mustard
½ cup all-purpose flour
½ cup finely ground Homemade
    Bread Crumbs (page 127)
2 tablespoons extra virgin olive oil

I usually make this terrine with oxtails, which can be hard to find, but short ribs make a fine substitute. If you want to try it with oxtails, use about 5 pounds. The tails should be braised the same way as the ribs. The only difference, aside from the amount of meat, is the quantity of gelatin you will need to set the terrine. As they cook, the oxtails will release more gelatin into their braising liquid than short ribs give off. How much to use? Experiment. Measure out ½ cup of the strained braising liquid, chill, and see how solid it gets. If it jells completely, don't add any gelatin. If it is still liquid, add the full amount called for in the recipe. In between?—add a little of the liquid at a time.

Brining the short ribs.
Dissolve 3 tablespoons salt in 6 cups warm water in a large bowl. Let cool, then add the short ribs. Cover and refrigerate overnight.

Braising the short ribs.
Drain the ribs and blot them dry. Heat the oil in a large, deep, flameproof roasting pan over medium-high heat. Season the ribs with pepper. Working in batches, brown the ribs on all sides, 30 to 40 minutes per batch. Transfer the ribs to a large plate and pour off all but about 2 tablespoons of the fat from the pan.

Add the onions, carrots, celery, rutabaga, and garlic to the pan and cook, stirring occasionally, over medium heat until the vegetables soften, about 15 minutes.

Preheat the oven to 325°F.

Add the tomato paste, thyme, peppercorns, and bay leaves to the roasting pan and cook, stirring frequently, for about 5 minutes. Return the ribs to the pan and add the wine, vinegar, and anchovies. Bring to a simmer and reduce the liquid by half, about 15 minutes.

Add the stock and enough water to just cover the meat, season with salt, and bring to a simmer. Cover the pan with aluminum foil and transfer to the oven. Gently simmer until the meat is tender enough to be cut with a fork, 3 to 4 hours. Remove the braise from the oven and allow it to cool. Bone and shred the meat and discard the bones. Strain and defat the braising liquid; reserve 2 cups. (The meat can be braised 1 day ahead.)

Assembling the terrine.
Warm half the reserved braising liquid. Sprinkle the gelatin over the remaining room-temperature broth in a small bowl. Stir, then mix in the warm liquid.

Line a 12- by 3½- by 3½-inch terrine mold with plastic wrap. Place a quarter of the meat in the terrine and sprinkle evenly with about ½ cup of the gelatin mixture. Season with salt and pepper. Press another quarter of the meat into the terrine in an even layer, then sprinkle with ¼ to ½ cup of the liquid and adjust seasoning. Repeat twice, using enough of the liquid so all the meat is just moistened.

Cut a piece of cardboard to just fit inside the top of the terrine. Wrap the cardboard in plastic, then use it to press down the meat. Evenly weight the terrine (cans or bottles will work), and refrigerate it overnight.

Unmold the terrine. Serve at room temperature, cut into 1-inch-thick slices with a very sharp knife, or bread the slices and warm as follows.

Breading the terrine.
Preheat the oven to 375°F.

Mix the eggs and mustard together in a medium bowl. Place the flour and bread crumbs on separate plates. Cut the terrine into slices about 1 inch thick (if not serving the whole terrine, just slice as many as you need, then wrap the remaining terrine in fresh plastic and refrigerate for up to 1 week). Dip one side of each slice first in the flour, then in the eggs, then in the bread crumbs.

Heat the oil in a very large ovenproof skillet over medium heat. Working in batches if necessary, add slices of the terrine, coated side down, and cook until the crust begins to crisp, about 3 minutes. Transfer the slices crisped side down to a baking sheet and place in the oven just until the terrine is heated through, about 5 minutes. Serve with Honey Mustard Sauce (page 162) and Pickles (page 40), if desired.

honey mustard sauce

MAKES ABOUT
1 ¼ CUPS

*Serve honey mustard
with the terrine (page
160) or Cured Salmon
(page 143). Warmed
and then thinned slightly
with cream or butter-
milk, it is also excellent
with fish or poultry.*

1 tablespoon dry mustard
2 tablespoons red wine vinegar
1½ teaspoons mustard seeds
½ cup Dijon mustard
½ cup honey

Three types of mustard are used here: the dry mustard
adds sharpness; the prepared mustard, roundness; and
the mustard seeds, texture.

Combine the dry mustard and vinegar in a small
bowl and mix until the mustard dissolves. Add the
mustard seeds and Dijon mustard, then whisk in
the honey. Serve, or refrigerate for up to 1 week.

duck rillettes

MAKES ABOUT
1 CUP

Appetizer
Duck Rillettes

Wine
Pinto Noir–Rhône

Main Course
Roasted Monkfish
with Curried
Kumquats
(page 154)

2 whole legs Duck Confit
  (page 163)
¼ cup duck fat from the confit,
  chilled
2 tablespoons whole-grain mustard
1 tablespoon finely chopped thyme
1 tablespoon chopped chives
1 clove garlic, roasted (see the
  headnote) and minced
2 ounces fresh goat cheese
  (optional)
Kosher salt and freshly ground
  black pepper

Before refrigeration, pork and game, including duck,
were cooked in fat, then mixed with additional fat and
finally sealed with still more fat to preserve the meat
through the winter. The resulting potted meat was
creamy and delicious—a treat rather than a necessity.
These rillettes are a little less rich than traditional
recipes are. They also call for roasted rather than raw
garlic (wrap peeled garlic cloves in aluminum foil and
roast at 375°F until soft, about 20 minutes), and herbs.
For extra creamy spread, add some goat cheese. Serve
on Croutons (page 127) or crackers.

Warm the confit in a small skillet over low heat.
Remove the duck, strain any rendered fat, and reserve.

Remove the meat from the bones. Combine the
duck, the fat, mustard, thyme, chives, and garlic in
a food processor. Add the cheese, if using, and salt
and pepper. Pulse until the mixture holds together.

duck confit

⅓ cup kosher salt
¼ cup coriander seeds
2 star anise, ground
2 tablespoons freshly ground
  black pepper
1 bunch chopped flat-leaf parsley
  leaves and stems
1 onion, peeled and sliced
8 whole duck legs (legs and thighs)
2 pounds duck fat
Olive oil to cover
1 head garlic, halved
1 bunch thyme

Commercially prepared duck confit is available at gourmet stores, but it is easy to make at home. Either way, duck confit is delicious. Serve warm, seared in a hot skillet until the skin is crisp, or serve the meat shredded at room temperature in salads.

Curing the duck.
Combine the salt, coriander seeds, star anise, and black pepper in a small bowl. Combine the parsley and onion, and spread half the mixture over the bottom of a container large enough to hold the duck in a single layer. Season the duck legs on both sides with the salt mixture, then place them on the parsley mixture. Cover with the remaining parsley and onion, cover, and refrigerate for 24 hours.

Cooking the duck.
Brush the salt and herb mixture from the duck. Melt the duck fat in a large deep skillet. Add the duck and enough olive oil to cover. Add the garlic and thyme and gently simmer over low heat until the meat pulls easily from the bone, at least 2 hours.

Allow the duck to cool in the fat. Store in the refrigerator covered with fat until ready to serve. The confit will last at least 1 month.

Duck confit is the starting point for Duck Rillettes (page 162) and Potato Galette with Duck Confit (page 179).

adding meat and poultry   163

cocktail meatballs

When serving cocktail meatballs for hors d'oeuvres at large parties, I usually accompany them with a sauce, maybe warm Romesco Sauce (page 155). The meatballs also work well in Parmesan Broth with Sautéed Greens (page 82).

3 tablespoons extra virgin olive oil
2 shallots, peeled and minced
3 cloves garlic, peeled and minced
Kosher salt and freshly ground black pepper
1 tablespoon finely chopped oregano
½ cup Homemade Bread Crumbs (page 127), lightly toasted
2 tablespoons heavy cream
1 tablespoon Dijon mustard
1 egg, lightly beaten
2 teaspoons paprika
1 tablespoon dry mustard
½ pound ground chicken
Pinch of cayenne pepper

Ground chicken is a nice alternative to ground beef, veal, or pork for meatballs. Its lighter, less assertive taste allows the cook more flavoring options. Chicken is also leaner than the meat of four-legged animals, which means extra care must be taken to avoid dryness. This recipe solves the problem by adding cream and bread crumbs to the meat mixture—a French technique.

Heat 1 tablespoon of the oil in a small skillet over medium heat. Add the shallots, garlic, and salt and pepper and cook just until the oil begins to sizzle, about 2 minutes. Add 2 tablespoons water and cook until the shallots are soft and the pan dry, about 5 minutes. Set aside to cool.

In a large bowl, combine the shallot mixture, oregano, bread crumbs, cream, Dijon mustard, egg, paprika, and dry mustard and mix well. Add the chicken, season with salt and cayenne, and mix again. Form the chicken mixture into small meatballs.

Heat the remaining 2 tablespoons oil in a large skillet. Working in batches, cook the meatballs over medium-low heat until browned on all sides and cooked through, about 10 minutes per batch. Serve warm.

croque monsieur

2 cups milk
6 eggs
Freshly ground black pepper
About 20 slices white sandwich
   bread, crusts removed
6 tablespoons mascarpone cheese
½ pound baked or boiled ham,
   thinly sliced
½ pound Fontina cheese, thinly
   sliced
¼ cup chopped chives
4 tablespoons extra virgin olive oil

I love croque monsieur, a French ham and cheese sandwich. I build my version in a terrine, evenly distributing the ham, cheese, and bread in each cross section. Custard keeps the terrine moist (and makes it like a bread pudding). A quick sauté immediately before serving crisps the bread.

Combine the milk and eggs in a medium bowl, season with pepper, and whisk until well mixed.

Line a 12- by 3½- by 3½-inch loaf pan or terrine mold with parchment paper, cutting separate pieces for the sides (you want sharp corners) and leaving about 3 inches of overhang; cut a piece to cover the top.

Cut the bread into pieces that fit into the bottom of the pan. Place a layer of bread in the bottom of the pan. Spread the bread with a third of the mascarpone, top with a third of the ham, cover with a third of the Fontina, and sprinkle with a third of the chives. Repeat the layers twice, then make a final layer of bread. Pour the egg mixture evenly over the top. Lay the cover piece of parchment on top and fold the overhanging parchment over. Cover the entire pan with aluminum foil, and chill thoroughly (at least 2 hours, or, better yet, overnight).

Preheat the oven to 350°F.

Place the loaf pan in a larger baking pan and fill the larger pan with enough boiling water to come halfway up the sides of the loaf pan. Bake until the cheese is melted and the custard set, about 1 hour. Let cool, then chill thoroughly (at least 2 hours).

To serve, unmold the croque monsieur and peel off the parchment. Cut into slices about 1 inch thick.

Heat the oil in a large skillet over medium heat. Brown the slices of croque monsieur in batches for about 5 minutes per side, and serve.

Appetizer
Croque Monsieur

Accompaniments
Slow-Roasted
Tomatoes (page 55)
and a green salad

Wine
Sparkling, fermented
apple cider

Slices of croque monsieur are delicious for brunch. For hors d'oeuvres, cut the croque monsieur into small cubes, skewer them, brown in a skillet, and serve with a glass of wine.

About Steak

A truism: Great steaks and chops begin with great meat. The cook's challenge is learning what to look for. Begin here as elsewhere by getting to know your ingredients. Meat, whether beef, pork, lamb, or poultry, is muscle tissue harnessed by connective tissue and surrounded and permeated by fat. The more active the muscle, the thicker and tougher it becomes. It also becomes more flavorful. Muscle is tender; connective tissue, tough; fat, soft and moist. Heating dries and toughens muscle tissue, softens connective tissue, and melts fat. A balance must be struck, and knowing the extent and location of fat is the secret to success.

The most tender parts of an animal are the parts it uses least. In four-legged animals, the back is least heavily worked and therefore has less-developed muscles and less connective tissue. The short loin, sirloin, and ribs thus provide the most appealing steaks and chops. Younger animals have finer (that is, more tender) muscle, a higher proportion of connective tissue to muscle, and less fat. Their meat is also less tasty. Great steak comes from the back of a youthful but not young animal and is marbled with fat that moistens the meat as it cooks, preventing the tender lean tissue from drying and toughening.

The United States Department of Agriculture grades meat. The grades run from prime to choice to select. When you plan to slowly braise lamb shanks or short ribs to luscious brown doneness, don't hesitate to buy select. But when you are planning to grill a steak, buy prime if you can find it and choice if you can't. Establish a relationship with a good butcher and don't be afraid to learn what you can from him or her. Get to know as much as you can about where your meat is raised. Ask for beef that is tenderized by the process known as dry-aging. And don't shy away from meat with some fat nicely marbled through it.

When you are ready to cook your purchase, do so with focus and care. Overcooked steak is just not very good. Don't hesitate to use an instant-read thermometer to determine when your steak is a perfect medium-rare (see the chart, page 159). Always allow meat to rest and reabsorb juices forced out by the cooking process. Keep in mind that the meat will continue to cook as it rests—expect the temperature at the center to rise from 2 to 5 degrees.

tamarind-marinated flank steak

¼ cup extra virgin olive oil
1 large onion, peeled, halved, and sliced
Kosher salt and freshly ground black pepper
1 head garlic, halved
2 tablespoons brown sugar
½ cup Champagne vinegar
1 lemon, sliced
2 tablespoons tomato paste
¼ cup molasses
1½ tablespoons strained tamarind paste (see the sidebar)
6 green cardamom pods, crushed
12 black peppercorns
1 teaspoon coriander seeds
1 bunch flat-leaf parsley
1 bay leaf
1 teaspoon dry mustard
2 pounds flank steak, cut into 4 pieces

The tamarind tree produces large pods; each one contains several seeds and a fibrous but magically bittersweet acidic pulp. A tamarind marinade is ideal for a chewy full-flavored cut such as flank steak.

Making the marinade.
Heat 2 tablespoons of the oil in a medium saucepan over medium-high heat. Add the onion, season with salt and pepper, and cook, stirring occasionally, until the onion softens and browns, about 10 minutes. Add the garlic and cook until fragrant, 3 to 5 minutes more. Stir in the brown sugar and vinegar and bring to a boil. Add the lemon, tomato paste, molasses, tamarind, cardamom, peppercorns, coriander seeds, parsley, bay leaf, mustard, and 2 cups water. Bring to a boil, then reduce the heat to low and simmer until the mixture is reduced by about one-third, about 15 minutes. Allow the marinade to cool.

Brush the steaks on both sides with the marinade, wrap them in plastic, and refrigerate overnight.

Cooking the steak.
Unwrap the steaks and wipe off any spices that adhere. Heat two large heavy skillets over medium-high heat. Add 1 tablespoon of the oil to each and brown the steaks on both sides, about 7 minutes in all. Transfer the steaks to a platter and allow to rest in a warm place for 5 to 10 minutes.

Slice the steaks and serve.

Appetizer
Scallop Ceviche with Chili Vinaigrette (page 134)

Main Course
Tamarind-Marinated Flank Steak

Accompaniment
Sunchoke and Potato Puree (page 54)

Wine
Bandol—France

This recipe uses the strained tamarind paste sold in Asian markets and sometimes at health food and gourmet stores.

seared sirloin with mushroom worcestershire

*If you prefer a thicker
steak, just cook it
for a longer time over
lower heat.*

4 tablespoons extra virgin olive oil
Six 10-ounce sirloin steaks, each
  about 1 inch thick
Kosher salt and freshly ground
  black pepper
¾ cup Mushroom Worcestershire
  Sauce (page 49)
4 tablespoons butter
Sautéed Mushrooms (page 48)

Some steaks are noted for their tenderness (filets) and some for their meaty flavor (flank steak). A good sirloin steak is both tender and flavorful. I like mine cut fairly thin and served with a sharp and sour sauce.

Cooking the steaks.
Heat two large heavy skillets over high heat. Divide the oil between the skillets. Season the steaks on both sides with salt and pepper. Working in batches if necessary, cook the steaks for 2 to 3 minutes per side for medium-rare. Set them aside on a platter to rest for about 5 minutes.

Making the pan sauce.
Pour the fat from one skillet into the other. Add the Worcestershire and butter, then add any meat juices that have accumulated as the steaks rested. Whisking constantly, gently warm the sauce over medium-low heat. Add the sautéed mushrooms and heat through.

Serve the steaks with the sauce.

the anatomy of a dish

beer-braised short ribs

SERVES 6 TO 8
AS AN ENTRÉE

Kosher salt
6 pounds beef short ribs
2 tablespoons extra virgin olive oil
Freshly ground black pepper
2 onions, peeled and cut into
   large dice
2 carrots, peeled and cut into
   large dice
2 stalks celery, peeled and cut
   into large dice
3 turnips, peeled and cut into
   large dice
2 shallots, peeled and chopped
1 head garlic, halved
4 sprigs thyme
1 tablespoon black peppercorns
2 bay leaves
1 cup dry red wine
1 cup dark beer
4½ cups Chicken Stock
   (page 170)

This recipe uses a combination of beer, wine, and stock. The stock reinforces the meaty flavor and the beer draws out another dimension. Additional wine can replace the beer, as can vermouth, vinegar, or cider. The stock—veal, beef, lamb, chicken, or even water—controls the weight of the sauce.

Brining the short ribs.
Dissolve 3 tablespoons salt in 6 cups warm water in a large bowl. When the water is cool, add the short ribs, cover, and refrigerate overnight.

Braising the short ribs.
Drain the ribs and blot them dry. Heat the oil in a large, deep, flameproof roasting pan over medium-high heat. Season the ribs with pepper. Working in batches, brown the ribs on all sides, 30 to 40 minutes per batch. Transfer the ribs to a large plate and pour off all but about 2 tablespoons of fat from the pan.

Add the onions, carrots, celery, turnips, shallots, and garlic. Cook, stirring occasionally, over medium heat until the vegetables soften, about 15 minutes.

Preheat the oven to 325°F.

Add the thyme, peppercorns, and bay leaves to the roasting pan and cook, stirring frequently, for about 5 minutes more. Return the meat to the pan, add the wine, and bring to a simmer. Reduce the wine mixture by half, about 15 minutes.

Add the beer, stock, and enough water just to cover the meat. Season with salt and bring the liquid to a simmer, cover the pan with aluminum foil, and transfer it to the oven. Gently simmer until the ribs are tender enough to cut with a fork, 2 to 3 hours. Allow the meat to cool to room temperature in the braising liquid.

Remove the ribs from the braising liquid. Strain the liquid through a fine sieve into a large skillet and bring it to a simmer. Skim the fat, then reduce by about one-third. Add the ribs to the pan and heat through. Serve warm.

Appetizer
Pickled Beet Salad
with Oranges and
Taleggio Cheese
(page 71)

Main Course
Beer-Braised
Short Ribs

Accompaniment
Horseradish
Dumplings
(page 43) or
Celery Root Mash
(page 39)

Wine
Ale—Belgian
Trappist ale

I have included two braised short rib recipes (see page 160) to show the difference that the choice of liquid can make in a recipe. The cooking liquid and meat are the two variables in a braise. The technique changes little: Brown seasoned meat, sweat or brown aromatic vegetables, then slowly simmer the two together in a flavorful broth until the meat is fork-tender. Choose the right cut of meat—tough, never tender—cook the mirepoix with care, and avoid boiling the liquid.

adding meat and poultry   169

chicken stock

*To make chicken soup:
Fill a sachet with
1 bay leaf, 1 bunch
thyme, 1 bunch parsley,
1 teaspoon black
peppercorns, and
1 tablespoon coriander
seeds and add it to the
strained chicken stock.
Simmer for 30 minutes,
then serve garnished
with Poached Chicken
(see page 174), diced
vegetables, and noodles.*

5 pounds chicken legs, wings,
   and backs
2 onions, peeled and quartered
2 carrots, peeled and chopped
2 stalks celery, peeled and
   chopped
1 leek, white part only, chopped

No herbs are added to this chicken stock because I want the flavor of the chicken to be very clear.

Rinse the chicken and place it in a large stockpot. Add water to cover (about 1½ gallons) and bring to a simmer over medium heat. Skim any foam as it rises to the top. Add the onions, carrots, celery, and leek and simmer until the stock is flavorful, about 1½ hours.

Strain, then refrigerate for up to 2 weeks or freeze for up to 2 months.

VARIATION

brown chicken stock

Brown 3 pounds chicken bones in 2 tablespoons vegetable oil in a roasting pan in a 400°F oven, turning occasionally, for about 1 hour. Add 1 peeled onion, 1 peeled and chopped carrot, and 1 stalk chopped celery. Brown, stirring once or twice, for about 20 minutes more. Combine the browned bones, 8 cups chicken stock, and 4 cups water in a large pot. Simmer until the stock darkens, about 2 hours; strain. (Makes about 6½ cups.)

baby lamb chops with roasted eggplant salad

SERVES 4
AS AN ENTRÉE

2 Italian eggplants, peeled
½ cup extra virgin olive oil
Kosher salt
2 tablespoons sugar
1 tablespoon umeboshi paste
   (see the sidebar)
2 tablespoons soy sauce
2 tablespoons sesame oil
1 tablespoon sesame seeds,
   lightly toasted
1 tablespoon grated fresh ginger
2 scallions, thinly sliced on the bias
8 double baby lamb chops
Freshly ground black pepper

In baby lamb chops the "eye" of the meat is a consistent size and is relatively lean. One double chop is approximately the same size as a single mature chop. Larger chops, because they are generally cut thinner, take a little less time to cook. New Zealand and Australia produce lovely lamb. Locally raised meat can be even more delicious, so look for it at butcher shops, gourmet stores, and farmers' markets.

Making the salad.
Preheat the oven to 375°F.

Cut the eggplants into quarters by splitting them in half crosswise and then lengthwise. Cut each quarter into thin lengths. Toss the eggplant with ¼ cup of the olive oil, season with salt, and place on a baking sheet.

Roast the eggplant, turning once, until soft and golden, about 45 minutes.

Combine the sugar, umeboshi paste, and soy sauce in a large bowl and mix until the sugar dissolves. Add the sesame oil, sesame seeds, ginger, and scallions and mix well. Add the eggplant and mix gently; set aside while you cook the chops.

Sautéing the lamb chops.
Heat two large skillets over medium-high heat. Season the lamb chops with salt and pepper. Add 2 tablespoons of the remaining oil to each skillet, then add the chops. Brown the lamb on all sides, turning every 2 to 3 minutes, about 7 minutes total cooking time for medium-rare. Transfer the chops to a platter and allow them to rest in a warm place for about 5 minutes.

Serve the lamb chops with the eggplant salad.

Appetizer
Mushroom Torte
(page 113)

Main Course
Baby Lamb Chops
with Roasted
Eggplant Salad

Accompaniment
Mixed Grain Pilaf
(page 42)

Wine
Châteauneuf-du-
Pape–Rhône

Umeboshi paste is a tart Japanese plum paste available at Asian markets.

roasted leg of venison

SERVES 8
AS AN ENTRÉE

Appetizer
Roasted Winter
Vegetable Stew
(page 91)

Main Course
Roasted Leg of
Venison

Accompaniment
Wild Rice "Soufflé"
(page 109)

Wine
Bandol Rouge—
Provence

FOR THE MARINADE

2 tablespoons extra virgin olive oil
2 carrots, peeled and chopped
2 onions, peeled and chopped
2 stalks celery, chopped
¼ cup juniper berries
2 star anise
4 cloves
4 allspice berries
1 bay leaf
1 bunch rosemary
½ bunch flat-leaf parsley
1 bottle dry red wine

FOR THE VENISON

4 pounds boneless venison leg
3 tablespoons extra virgin olive oil
Kosher salt and freshly ground
    black pepper
2 tablespoons butter (optional)

Older recipes typically call for marinating venison before cooking it, to eliminate the gamy taste of wild deer and elk. Most venison eaten today is farm-raised and consequently milder. I nevertheless like to marinate this meat in order to introduce additional flavor. Marinated or not, keep in mind that venison is very lean and must not be overcooked.

Marinating the venison.
Heat the oil in a large skillet over medium heat. Add the carrots, onions, and celery and cook, stirring occasionally, until the vegetables soften, about 15 minutes. Add the juniper berries, star anise, cloves, allspice, bay leaf, rosemary, and parsley. Cook until fragrant, about 2 minutes. Add the wine and bring to a boil, then remove the pan from the heat, cover, and allow the marinade to steep for 15 minutes. Uncover and cool completely.

Transfer the marinade to a bowl, add the venison, and refrigerate for 24 hours.

Roasting the venison.
Preheat the oven to 350°F.

Remove the meat from the marinade; reserve the marinade. Blot the meat dry with paper towels. Heat the oil in an ovenproof skillet or flameproof roasting pan over medium-high heat. Salt and pepper the venison, then add it to the skillet. Brown the meat on all sides, about 25 minutes. Transfer the pan to the oven and roast the venison, turning once, until the meat reaches an internal temperature of 130°F for medium-rare, about 1 hour. Transfer the meat to a plate and let rest in a warm place for about 10 minutes.

Making the sauce.
Meanwhile, strain the marinade, place it in a saucepan, and bring to a boil over medium-high heat. Allow the marinade to reduce by about two-thirds, until it coats the back of a spoon. Reduce the heat to low, stir in the butter, if using, and adjust the seasoning with salt and pepper.

Slice the venison and serve with the sauce.

chicken salad with roquefort dressing

SERVES 4
AS AN ENTRÉE

FOR THE CROUTONS

1 long loaf white country-style
    bread, crust removed and cut
    into 1½-inch cubes (about 4 cups)
¼ cup extra virgin olive oil
Kosher salt and freshly ground
    black pepper

FOR THE DRESSING

2 tablespoons Crème Fraîche
    (page 204)
¼ cup heavy cream
2 ounces Roquefort cheese,
    crumbled
1 cup Mayonnaise (page 73)
Cayenne pepper
Kosher salt and freshly ground
    black pepper

FOR THE SALAD

Shredded meat from Poached
    Chicken (page 174)
    (2 to 3 cups)
2 stalks celery, diced
½ fennel bulb, cored and diced
1 shallot, peeled and minced
¼ cup flat-leaf parsley leaves
¼ cup ½-inch chive lengths
¼ cup tarragon leaves
2 cups frisée (see the sidebar)
Kosher salt and freshly ground
    black pepper

Homemade mayonnaise is infinitely better than store-bought and makes all the difference in this recipe.

Making the croutons.
Preheat the oven to 350°F.

Combine the bread and oil in a bowl. Add salt and pepper and toss to coat the bread cubes. Spread the bread cubes in a single layer on a baking sheet. Bake the croutons for 10 minutes, then turn them and continue baking until they are crisp and golden all over, 5 to 10 minutes more.

Making the dressing.
Beat the crème fraîche with the cream in a medium bowl until smooth. Add the cheese, then the mayonnaise. Season to taste with cayenne, salt, and black pepper.

Making the salad.
Combine the chicken, celery, fennel, and shallot in a bowl. Add about two-thirds of the dressing and mix well.

In a second bowl, combine the parsley, chives, tarragon, and frisée. Dress with a little of the remaining dressing. Add the croutons and the chicken mixture and mix gently. Adjust the seasoning with salt, pepper, and/or more dressing if necessary, and serve.

Appetizer
Spinach and Ricotta
Dumplings in Broth
(page 95)

Main Course
Chicken Salad with
Roquefort Dressing

Wine
Gewürztraminer—
Alsace

To clean frisée, remove the core and any brown or tired-looking leaves. Pinch off and discard the dark green leaf-ends. Wash and spin-dry the remaining paler leaves as you would other lettuce.

poached chicken

Appetizer
Sweet Pea Soup
with Mint (page 86)

Main Course
Poached Chicken

Accompaniment
Biscuits (page 119)

Wine
Tavel (rosé)—Rhône

This makes a great Sunday supper, but the recipe is a starting place for others. The chicken is moist and delicious cold, as in Chicken Salad with Roquefort Dressing (page 173). I use the broth as a soup base. Add noodles, rice, or Spinach and Ricotta Dumplings (page 95).

One 3- to 3½-pound free-range chicken, the breast removed and skinned but left whole and on the bone, the legs separated from the thighs, the wings cut off, the back reserved
5 stalks celery, trimmed and cut into 2-inch lengths
3 medium carrots, peeled and cut into 2-inch lengths
1 fennel bulb, cored and cut into wedges
2 medium onions, peeled and cut into wedges
3 leeks, white parts only, cut into 2-inch lengths
Sachet filled with:
　6 sprigs marjoram
　1 bunch parsley
　1 bay leaf
　1 bunch tarragon
　1 tablespoon black peppercorns
　1 tablespoon coriander seeds
Kosher salt and freshly ground black pepper

Buy free-range, antibiotic-free chicken. Not only will it taste better, but, I am convinced, it is better for you. The chicken in this recipe is cut so all the pieces cook in about the same length of time. Have your butcher cut up the chicken if you prefer.

Place all the chicken pieces, including the back, in a large pot and add water to cover (about 10 cups). Bring the water to a boil, then reduce the heat to medium and skim thoroughly. Add the celery, carrots, fennel, onions, leeks, and sachet and simmer until the chicken is cooked through (you can test by cutting into a leg), about 45 minutes.

Discard the chicken back and the sachet. Strain the broth, reserving the chicken and vegetables. Taste the broth and return it to the pot to reduce if necessary to strengthen the flavor. Season to taste with salt and pepper.

Quarter the chicken breast, then divide the chicken and vegetables among four large bowls. Ladle some broth into each bowl and serve. (Freeze any remaining broth and use for soups or sauces.)

About Chicken
Chickens are categorized by age and size.

POUSSIN	6 to 10 weeks	1½ to 2 pounds
BROILER (fryer)	2½ months	3½ pounds
ROASTER	8 months	2½ to 5 pounds
STEWING CHICKEN	10 to 18 months	3 to 6 pounds
CAPON (castrated rooster)		4 to 10 pounds
CORNISH GAME HEN (miniature hybrid chicken)		2½ pounds

roasted chicken

One 2- to 3-pound free-range
chicken
Kosher salt and freshly ground
black pepper
1 bunch flat-leaf parsley
1 bay leaf
6 sprigs marjoram
1 lemon, cut into wedges
1 shallot, peeled and sliced

My secret to perfect roasted chicken: Quick-brine the bird, then cook it first at high heat, then moderate heat. Brining infuses the meat with flavor, rather than simply seasoning the skin, and varying the oven temperature crisps the skin without drying out the meat.

Brining the chicken.
Combine the chicken and 1 cup salt in a large bowl. Add water to cover and refrigerate for 1 hour.

Roasting the chicken.
Preheat the oven to 500°F.

Dry the chicken thoroughly, then season inside and out with salt and pepper. Place the parsley, bay leaf, marjoram, lemon, and shallot in the chicken's cavity. Truss the chicken (use string or skewers). Place the chicken on a rack set inside a roasting pan.

Roast the chicken until the skin begins to brown, about 20 minutes, then reduce the oven temperature to 350°F. Continue cooking the chicken until the thigh juices run clear, about 20 minutes more. Allow the chicken to rest for 10 minutes, then carve and serve.

Appetizer
Toasted Angel Hair
Pasta in
Shiitake Broth
(page 97)

Main Course
Roasted Chicken

Accompaniment
Mushroom Torte
(page 113)

Wine
Merlot–Bordeaux

quinoa-crusted chicken

Appetizer
Spicy Green Salad
with Strawberry
Vinaigrette
(page 62)

Main Course
Quinoa-Crusted
Chicken

Accompaniment
Spinach and
Herb Sauce
(page 54)

Wine
Sauvignon Blanc—
California

2 cups Quinoa (see page 53)
2 large scallions, chopped
2 tablespoons minced fresh ginger
Grated zest of 1 lemon
Kosher salt and freshly ground
   black pepper
½ cup all-purpose flour
2 eggs
4 boneless, skinless chicken
   breasts
¼ cup extra virgin olive oil

Using quinoa instead of bread crumbs as a coating for fried chicken gives a nice texture to the crisp crust. It is a healthier alternative too (see the sidebar on page 53).

Combine the quinoa, scallions, ginger, lemon zest, and salt and pepper to taste in a bowl. Spread the flour on a plate. Beat the eggs in a shallow bowl.

Dip each chicken breast first in the flour, then the egg, and then the quinoa"breading"; pat the breading so it adheres.

Heat one or two large nonstick skillets over medium heat. Add the oil, then the chicken breasts and cook until browned on the first side, 5 to 8 minutes. Flip the breasts, reduce the heat to medium-low, and continue cooking until the second sides are browned and the chicken is cooked through, 5 to 7 minutes more.

mushroom chart: a kingdom apart

Mushrooms are not part of the plant kingdom but rather the kingdom of fungi. Fungi are distinguished from plants by the fact that they reproduce by single-cell spores and cannot photosynthesize sugar. Most mushrooms—the fruiting body of fungi— grow wild in decayed forests on wood, logs, and dead tree trunks. The Agaricaceae is the family that contains fungi with gills. Common cultivated mushrooms and cremini, portobello, and oyster mushrooms belong to this group. The chart is in alphabetical order by botanical family.

MUSHROOM	FAMILY	GENUS/SPECIES	FLAVOR	TEXTURE
BUTTON	Agaricaceae	*Agaricus bisporus*	mild	tender
CREMINI	Agaricaceae	*Agaricus bisporus*	meaty	firm
ENOKI	Agaricaceae	*Flammulina velutipes*	mild	viscous
PORTOBELLO	Agaricaceae	*Agaricus bisporus*	meaty	spongy
BOLETUS/CÈPE/ PORCINI	Boletaceae	*Boletus edulis* spp.	aromatic	slightly viscous
BLACK TRUMPET	Cantharellaceae	*Craterellus fallax*	meaty	firm
CHANTERELLE	Cantharellaceae	*Cantharellus cibarius*	sweet	viscous
HEDGEHOG	Hydnaceae	*Hydnum repandum*	sweet	firm
MOREL	Morchellaceae	*Morchella* spp.	meaty	firm
HEN-OF-THE-WOODS/ MAITAKE	Polyporaceae	*Grifola frondosa*	meaty	firm
SHIITAKE	Polyporaceae	*Lentinus edodes*	aromatic	spongy
FAIRY RING/ MOUSSERON	Tricholomataceae	*Marasmius oreades*	sweet	delicate
OYSTER/PLEUROTTE	Tricholomataceae	*Pleurotus ostreotus* spp.	mild	tender

pan-roasted duck breast with pineapple chutney

*Pekin duck, like most
poultry and all duck,
benefits from dividing
and conquering:
The legs and breasts
cook at very different
rates. I generally
pan-roast or grill
breasts and braise or
confit legs (see page 163).*

FOR THE CHUTNEY

2 tablespoons extra virgin olive oil
1 red onion, peeled and sliced
½ fennel bulb, cored and sliced
½ cup dry red wine
½ cup sherry vinegar
2 tablespoons dark brown sugar
1 cinnamon stick
1 tablespoon mustard seeds
2 tablespoons grated fresh ginger
1 cup diced pineapple (about
   ¼ pineapple)
2 cups Chicken Stock (page 170)
1 tablespoon finely chopped
   tarragon
½ pound sugar snap peas, thinly
   sliced on the bias

FOR THE DUCK

4 boneless Pekin (Long Island)
   duck breasts
1 tablespoon duck fat or extra
   virgin olive oil
Kosher salt and freshly ground
   black pepper

All domestic ducks are descendants of either the mallard or Muscovy. I like Pekin (or Long Island) ducks, a type of mallard, for this dish. The breast meat is flavorful and best cooked to medium temperature. Moulard duck breasts (sometimes sold as magrets) would be a distant second choice. Moulard ducks are a cross between mallard and Muscovy, bred for their large livers (foie gras) and breasts. Their flesh is dark and meaty and best cooked to medium-rare.

Making the chutney.
Heat the oil in a medium saucepan over medium-high heat. Add the onion and cook, stirring frequently, until it begins to soften and brown, about 10 minutes. Add the fennel and continue to cook until the fennel is also soft and golden, about 10 minutes more.

Add the wine, vinegar, sugar, cinnamon, mustard seeds, ginger, pineapple, and stock and bring to a simmer. Reduce the heat and simmer gently until the pineapple is soft and the liquid slightly thickened, about 20 minutes. Add the tarragon and keep warm over low heat.

Cooking the duck.
Meanwhile, preheat the oven to 400°F.

Score the fat of each breast, cutting a crisscross through the skin but stopping short of the flesh. Melt the fat in a very large ovenproof skillet over medium heat. Salt and pepper the breasts, add to the pan, skin side down, and cook until the skin begins to crisp, about 7 minutes. Pour off most of the fat.

Transfer the skillet to the oven and roast until the meat is cooked through, about 15 minutes.

Return the skillet to the stovetop, turn the duck skin side up, and cook over medium heat until the second side is browned, about 1 minute. Allow the duck to rest off the heat for 5 minutes.

Add the sugar snaps to the chutney and heat through. Slice the duck and serve with the chutney.

potato galette
with duck confit

SERVES 4 TO 6
AS AN APPETIZER

FOR THE TOPPING

2 whole legs Duck Confit
(page 163)
2 tablespoons duck fat from the
confit
¼ teaspoon celery seeds
1 clove garlic, peeled and chopped
4 cups shredded Savoy cabbage
Kosher salt and freshly ground
black pepper
1 tablespoon thyme leaves

FOR THE GALETTE

1 Idaho or other russet potato
1 tablespoon extra virgin olive oil
1 tablespoon butter
Kosher salt and freshly ground
black pepper

In the restaurant, I serve individual galettes as a first course with the Leek and Apple Hash (page 46) and Sauteed Greens (page 43).

Making the topping.
Warm the confit in a small skillet over low heat. Remove the duck, and strain and reserve any rendered fat.

Shred the meat, discarding the skin and bones (you should have about 2 cups).

Heat the duck fat in a medium nonstick or well-seasoned skillet over medium heat. Add the celery seeds, garlic, cabbage, and a little salt and pepper. Cook, stirring frequently, until the cabbage is wilted, then add the thyme and duck and continue cooking until the cabbage is golden, about 15 minutes in all. Transfer the cabbage mixture to a bowl, leaving any fat in the skillet; set the skillet aside.

Making the galette.
Peel the potato and slice it as thin as possible (use a mandoline if you have one). Do not rinse the potato slices.

Heat the oil and butter in the skillet over medium heat. Arrange the potato slices in overlapping concentric circles, covering the bottom of the skillet in more or less a single layer. Season the potatoes with salt and pepper and cook until they begin to brown and crisp at the edges, about 10 minutes. Flip the potato galette (this is most easily done by inverting it onto a plate, then sliding it back into the skillet). Spoon the cabbage mixture over the galette, pressing to even it, then continue cooking until the second side is crisp, about 10 minutes more. Cut into wedges and serve warm.

Appetizer
Cod Poached in
Herbed Clam Broth
(page 148)

Main Course
Potato Galette
with Duck Confit

Wine
Pinot Noir—
California

This recipe can be altered in several ways: Try slicing the potatoes lengthwise into oblongs (to make slicing easier, cut off one end of the potato). This has a surprisingly marked effect on the texture of the galette. Or try replacing about a third of the potato slices with sliced parsnips (see Parsnip and Potato Galette, page 51).

adding meat and poultry

179

rolled roasted turkey with mushroom gravy

SERVES
IO TO 12

Appetizer
Oyster Stew
(page 137)

Main Course
Rolled Roasted
Turkey with
Mushroom Gravy

Accompaniments
Corn Bread Stuffing
(page 123) and
Parsnip Puree
(page 51)

Wine
Pinot Noir—
Burgundy or
California Zinfandel

2 tablespoons extra virgin olive oil
One 14-pound turkey—have the
   butcher remove the whole breast
   from the bone in a single piece,
   leaving the skin on, cut off the
   legs and thighs, and reserve the
   wings, neck, and carcass
1 onion, peeled and chopped
2 carrots, peeled and chopped
2 stalks celery, chopped
2 medium leeks, chopped
1 bay leaf
12 peppercorns
4 sprigs rosemary
1 bunch flat-leaf parsley
4 cups Chicken Stock (page 170)
Kosher salt and freshly ground
   black pepper
1/2 cup Crème Fraîche (page 204)
1 tablespoon chopped thyme
1 tablespoon chopped marjoram
3 tablespoons butter
3 tablespoons all-purpose flour
1/4 cup Mushroom Worcestershire
   Sauce (page 49)

Poultry breasts and legs do not cook at the same rate. This is the essential problem faced in virtually every American home the fourth Thursday in November. You can solve this conundrum by cooking the breast and legs separately. Season the boneless breast with salt, pepper, and crème fraîche, then roll it. The crème fraîche keeps the breast meat moist, and rolling it keeps it protected. Cook the rolled breast for about 45 minutes less than the legs. You lose the drama of carving a whole bird at the table but are more than compensated by perfectly cooked meat.

Making the brown turkey stock.
Heat the oil in a large stockpot over medium-high heat. Add the turkey wings, neck, and carcass and brown, stirring occasionally, for about 30 minutes.

Add the onion, carrots, celery, and leeks and cook, stirring occasionally, until the vegetables are soft and browned, about 30 minutes more.

Add the bay leaf, peppercorns, rosemary, parsley, chicken stock, and 4 cups water and bring to a boil, scraping up any browned bits that have stuck to the bottom of the pan. Skim the stock, reduce the heat to medium, and simmer until it is flavorful, about 1½ hours.

Strain the stock, then return it to the pot, bring it to a simmer, and skim off the fat. Reserve 4 cups of the stock; refrigerate or freeze the remainder for later use in soups or sauces.

Roasting the turkey.
Preheat the oven to 350°F.

Season the turkey legs with salt and pepper. Place them in a large roasting pan and roast for 45 minutes.

While the turkey legs are roasting, prepare the breast. Lay the breast flat, skin side down, on a work surface. Season the meat with salt and pepper. Spread the crème fraîche evenly over it and sprinkle with the thyme and marjoram. Fold the breast in half and tie it at regular intervals with kitchen string (tie it in the middle first, and tie it in about six places in all). Season the breast liberally with salt and pepper.

Add the breast to the legs, propping them against the breast so they continue to brown evenly. Roast the turkey until the breast registers an internal temperature of 145°F on an instant-read thermometer and the legs are browned and the meat is beginning to pull from the bone, about 1½ hours longer (a total of 2 hours and 15 minutes for the legs). Cover the turkey loosely with aluminum foil and allow it to rest for about 10 minutes.

Preparing the gravy.
Meanwhile, combine the butter and flour in a medium saucepan and heat over medium heat, stirring the butter as it melts and mixes with the flour, forming a roux. Cook the roux, stirring frequently, until it is golden, about 10 minutes. Stir in the mushroom Worcestershire and whisk until it has absorbed the roux. Whisk in the reserved 4 cups turkey stock. Continue to whisk the gravy as it comes to a simmer and thickens. Gently simmer for 3 to 5 minutes. Adjust the seasoning with salt and pepper and keep warm over very low heat.

Slice the turkey and serve with the gravy, and Corn Bread Stuffing (page 123), if desired.

concluding with a sweet

desserts

For many years, I divided the culinary world into savory and sweet. I no longer draw this distinction. Now, I raid the pastry kitchen for ideas and flavors, using fresh fruit—lemons, strawberries, quinces, apples—to add texture and sweet, tart, and fruity notes to salads, sauces, and stews. Raisins and currants lend chewy dense sugar to my cooking, and honey smooths rough edges in sauces and broths. I don't limit myself to stealing ingredients but borrow freely from the roster of the pâtissière's

This last section of the book focuses on desserts. Because the recipes are in part combinations of fruit and grain, I have found it easy to arrange them loosely by season.

techniques, inventing savory cakes, tarts, and breads.

I pillage the pastry kitchen, but I repay my debt by appropriating the attitudes and approaches of other culinary disciplines for my confectionery work. Thinking of desserts as an integrated part of the larger food world, necessitating the same balancing of flavor and texture, allows me to compose dessert plates in a different way. I pair simpler flavors with richer concoctions—caramelized nectarines with meringues and ginger sabayon—using the same analysis I employ when combining meat, sauce, and vegetables for an entrée. Presentation, though important, is not the major concern (in fact, I am increasingly drawn to a more natural look). Taste is the master. At home, where I am much more likely to make a single-element dessert—a tart,

for example—I still feel the reverberations of my new attitude. Thinking of dessert as an aspect of dinner rather than a culinary show allows me to make more delicious doughs, richer caramels, and more intense pastry creams.

The trick is that I now bake the way I cook, tasting as I go. I taste the berries and adjust the sugar if necessary; I taste the caramel and let it go another minute if need be, always experimenting and keeping notes. Sweets and savories follow the same rules, but the dramatic and instantaneous transformations that characterize the combination of flour and eggs (so essential to this branch of cooking) make careful written records essential to repeated success. Armed with these tools, I let the balance of flavor and texture be my guide. For me, the dessert no longer stands alone.

Two families
of fruit: Rutaceae
and Rosaceae—
orange, pear, grapes,
blackberry, quince

rhubarb crumble

2½ pounds rhubarb, trimmed and
  cut into 1-inch pieces
1 cup sugar
1 vanilla bean, split
½ pound (2 sticks) butter, softened
1¾ cups cake flour
3 cups oats
½ cup coarsely chopped almonds
1 teaspoon ground cinnamon

Rhubarb is a member of the Polygonaceae family, as is sorrel. It is a vegetable, not a fruit (fruits contain seeds). Oxalic acid gives the stalks their wonderful tart taste. This acid is so heavily concentrated in the leaves that they should not be eaten. Rhubarb can be used in both savory and sweet dishes. Here it is simply transformed into a classic American crumble. The cake flour makes for a more tender crust, but all-purpose flour is a fine substitute.

Preheat the oven to 375°F.

Combine the rhubarb and ¼ cup of the sugar in a 9- by 13-inch baking dish. Scrape the seeds from the vanilla bean into the mixture and mix gently.

Cream the butter with the remaining ¾ cup sugar in a large bowl. Add the flour, oats, almonds, and cinnamon and mix well. Spoon the crumb topping over the rhubarb.

Bake until the rhubarb is bubbly and the topping is brown and crisp, about 40 minutes. Serve warm, with vanilla ice cream or Crème Fraîche (page 204).

raspberry parfait

¾ cup sugar
Juice of 3 lemons
1 pint raspberries
One ¼-ounce packet powdered
  gelatin
½ cup Strained Honey Yogurt
  (below)

In this recipe I cook raspberries with sugar and lemon juice. I puree the raspberries and add gelatin to the liquid, then layer the gelée and pureed raspberries with sweetened thick yogurt to form a grown-up parfait.

Combine the sugar, lemon juice, and 1¼ cups water in a saucepan and bring to a boil. Add the raspberries, reduce the heat, and simmer until they are soft but not breaking apart, about 5 minutes. Strain the liquid, reserving the raspberries and the liquid separately.

Place the raspberries and ¼ cup of the liquid in a food processor or blender and puree. Strain the puree through a fine sieve, then chill thoroughly.

Warm the remaining poaching liquid in a small saucepan. Sprinkle the gelatin over ¼ cup water in a large bowl. Stir, then mix in the warm poaching liquid. Pour the "gelée" into four parfait glasses and chill until set, at least 2 hours.

To serve, top the gelée first with the yogurt, then with raspberry puree.

The components of this parfait deserve individual attention. The "gelée" can be served plain, topped with whipped cream. The puree is good spooned over fruit, ice cream, or cake or stirred into Crème Fraîche (page 204) or yogurt. The puree can also be used to fill a sweet soufflé (see the sidebar for Rolled Soufflé on page 108).

strained honey yogurt

2 cups plain yogurt
¼ cup honey
1 vanilla bean, split

A vanilla bean is a seed pod from a climbing orchid. The pods must be dried to produce their characteristic aroma. Here, the vanilla seeds perfume and flavor yogurt.

Mix the yogurt and honey in a bowl. Scrape the seeds from the vanilla bean into the yogurt mixture. Place the mixture in a strainer lined with a coffee filter set over a bowl. Refrigerate and allow the yogurt to drip for at least 2 hours. Discard the collected liquid.

Serve the yogurt, or cover and refrigerate for up to 1 week.

Serve the strained yogurt as a dessert topping, or mix it with ½ cup fruit puree (see Raspberry Parfait, above) and serve for breakfast or lunch.

caramelized nectarine and meringue tartlets

The elements of this dessert can be used separately. The meringues can be eaten on their own or used, whole or crushed, as a topping. The nectarines are good baked in a more conventional crust (see Pâte Sucrée, page 204), or they can replace the apples in Apple Upside-down Cake (page 196). The caramel can be used to poach other fruit or as a sauce, warm or at room temperature.

All the components of this dessert can be made ahead. The tarts can also be served topped with Chilled Ginger Sabayon (page 189).

FOR THE MERINGUE

1 cup hazelnuts
½ cup sugar
3 egg whites, at room temperature
Pinch of cream of tartar

FOR THE NECTARINES

½ cup sugar
1 tablespoon fresh lemon juice
4 tablespoons butter
3 nectarines

This is an impressive dessert. It is also a technique study. The caramel is a classic made by combining sugar and water, then cooking until nicely browned. Butter turns the caramel into a rich sauce in which to poach the nectarines. The caramel-cooked nectarines are spooned onto meringues, which serve as tart shells.

Making the meringues.
Preheat the oven to 275°F. Line a large baking sheet with parchment paper.

Coarsely grind the nuts in a food processor, then add ¼ cup of the sugar and grind the mixture to a powder.

Beat the egg whites in the bowl of an electric mixer on low speed until foamy. Add the cream of tartar and the remaining ¼ cup sugar, increase the mixer speed, and beat until the whites are shiny and hold soft peaks. Fold the ground nut mixture into the whites.

Transfer the meringue batter to a piping bag fitted with a 1-inch plain tip. Spiraling out from the center, pipe a meringue disk about 5 inches across onto the prepared baking sheet. Repeat, forming 6 meringues in all.

Dry the meringues in the oven until they are firm and light beige, about 1 hour. Remove the pan from the oven and allow the meringues to cool for about 5 minutes, then carefully lift them off the paper and onto a rack. Allow them to cool completely.

Making the caramel.
Combine the sugar, lemon juice, and ¼ cup water in a saucepan and heat over medium heat until the sugar dissolves. Allow the sugar syrup to simmer until it is dark amber, about 10 minutes. Add the butter and swirl to melt, then transfer the caramel to a medium skillet.

Caramelizing the nectarines.
Blanch the nectarines in boiling water just long enough to loosen their skins. Peel the nectarines, then cut each one into 8 wedges, and add them to the caramel. Bring the caramel to a gentle simmer over medium-low heat and cook the nectarines until they are very tender, 5 to 10 minutes. Remove the nectarines from the caramel and allow them to cool slightly. Set the caramel aside.

Finishing the tartlets.
Mound the nectarines on the meringues, drizzle with the caramel, and serve.

chilled ginger sabayon

MAKES ABOUT
2 CUPS

6 tablespoons Beaumes-de-Venise
  (or Lillet)
½ tablespoon finely grated fresh
  ginger
½ cup heavy cream
3 egg yolks
6 tablespoons sugar

A classic sabayon is flavored with Marsala and served warm. This variation is flavored with Beaumes-de-Venise, a subtly fruity dessert wine, and served cold. It is rich and refreshing and avoids the last-minute frenzy entailed by traditional sabayon.

Heat the Beaumes-de-Venise in a small saucepan over high heat. When the wine begins to simmer, add the ginger, remove from the heat, and set aside to steep.

Beat the cream in the bowl of a mixer, using the whisk attachment, until it holds soft peaks. Transfer the cream to a small bowl, cover, and refrigerate.

Whisk the egg yolks with the sugar in a metal bowl set over a pot of boiling water. Continue whisking until the yolks are pale and thickened sufficiently to coat the back of a spoon. Transfer the yolks to the mixer. Beat on high speed with the whisk until the yolks are the consistency of mayonnaise. With the mixer running, gradually add the warm alcohol mixture and beat the sabayon until it cools. Transfer to a bowl, cover, and chill thoroughly.

Fold the whipped cream into the cold sabayon and serve.

Serve the sabayon with Caramelized Nectarine and Meringue Tartlets (page 188) or over berries. Omit the whipped cream, and the sabayon can be served warm.

flavor chart for rosaceae

The Rosaceae family contains most of the dessert fruits grown in temperate climates. Within this family there are subcategories, each differentiated by seed or pit formation: plums, peaches, and apricots have stones; apples and pears have seedy cores; and raspberries and blackberries are seed clusters. The flavor range runs from quite sweet to tart.

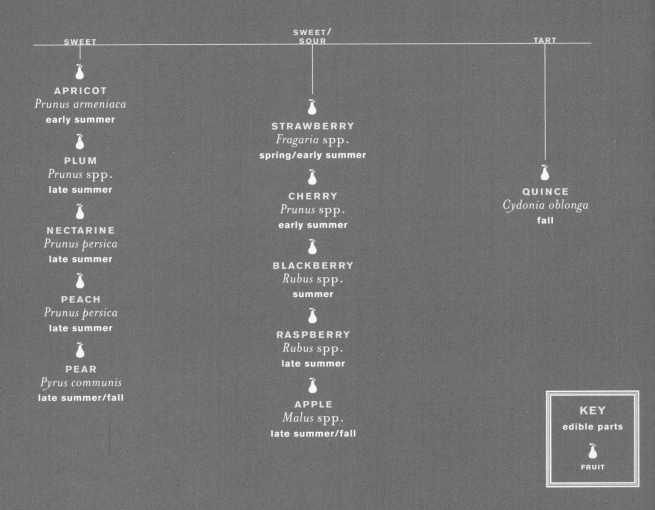

SWEET   SWEET/SOUR   TART

APRICOT
Prunus armeniaca
early summer

PLUM
Prunus spp.
late summer

NECTARINE
Prunus persica
late summer

PEACH
Prunus persica
late summer

PEAR
Pyrus communis
late summer/fall

STRAWBERRY
Fragaria spp.
spring/early summer

CHERRY
Prunus spp.
early summer

BLACKBERRY
Rubus spp.
summer

RASPBERRY
Rubus spp.
late summer

APPLE
Malus spp.
late summer/fall

QUINCE
Cydonia oblonga
fall

KEY
edible parts

FRUIT

leek and **APPLE** hash 46

spicy green salad with **STRAWBERRY** vinaigrette 62

bibb, endive, and blue cheese salad with **APPLE** vinaigrette 69

APPLE upside-down cake 196

carpaccio of **QUINCE** with endive salad and pecan vinaigrette 70

RASPBERRY parfait 187

caramelized **NECTARINE** and meringue tartlets 188

brown-butter **APRICOT** tart 192

flavor chart for rutaceae

The Rutaceae family includes all of the citrus fruits.
Its flavors range from sweet to sour to bitter.

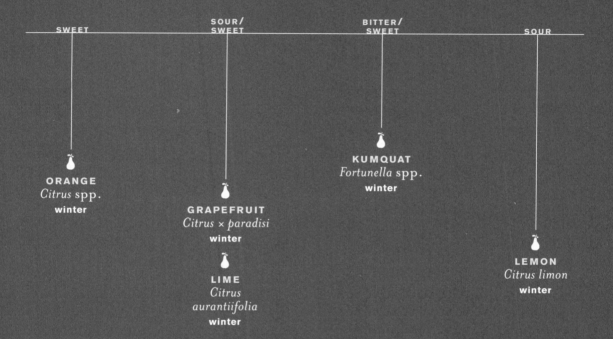

SWEET   SOUR/ SWEET   BITTER/ SWEET   SOUR

ORANGE
Citrus spp.
winter

GRAPEFRUIT
Citrus × paradisi
winter

LIME
*Citrus
aurantiifolia*
winter

KUMQUAT
Fortunella spp.
winter

LEMON
Citrus limon
winter

KEY
edible parts

FRUIT

candied **KUMQUATS** 45, roasted monkfish with curried **KUMQUATS** 154

quick preserved **LEMONS** 47

LEMON porridge with asparagus and basil 96, sea bass in **LEMON** nage 152

LEMON custard tart 199, **LEMON**-mustard vinaigrette 72

pickled beet salad with **ORANGES** and taleggio cheese 71

butternut squash ravioli with roasted **ORANGE** reduction 100

cinnamon toast with **GRAPEFRUIT** 198

brown-butter apricot tart

Pâte Sucrée (page 204)
8 tablespoons (1 stick) butter
1 vanilla bean, split
2 eggs
1 cup sugar
Chopped zest of 1 lemon
1/3 cup all-purpose flour
12 apricots, quartered and pitted
1/2 cup chopped pistachio nuts

Apricots are members of the Rosaceae family. They are, like plums, nectarines, peaches, and cherries, in the Prunus genus. Any of these fruits would be nice substituted in this tart.

Baking the crust.
Preheat the oven to 350°F.

On a floured surface, roll the dough out into a 14-inch round. Fit it into an 11-inch tart pan with a removable bottom. Trim the edges (use the trimmings to patch any holes in the crust).

Bake the crust (it is not necessary to weight it) until the edges brown, about 35 minutes. Leave the oven on.

Making the custard.
Combine the butter and vanilla bean in a saucepan. Melt the butter over medium heat, swirling it occasionally, until it browns. Remove the pan from the heat.

Beat the eggs with the sugar and lemon zest in a medium bowl until the mixture is pale. Whisk in the flour. Discard the vanilla bean and add the melted butter to the egg mixture.

Pour about one-third of the custard into the tart shell. Arrange the apricots skin side down in the custard. Sprinkle the chopped pistachios over the apricots, then top with the remaining custard.

Baking the tart.
Bake the tart until the custard is set and lightly browned, about 1 hour. Cool, and serve.

the anatomy of a dish

blueberry-lavender tart

MAKES ONE
9-INCH TART

FOR THE LAVENDER SYRUP

1 heaping teaspoon dried lavender or 2 teaspoons organic fresh lavender blossoms
½ cup sugar
2 tablespoons honey

FOR THE CRUST

½ pound puff pastry, defrosted if frozen
¼ cup heavy cream
3 tablespoons sugar

FOR THE FILLING

3 pints blueberries, picked over
2 tablespoons confectioners' sugar

Puff pastry should be baked at a high temperature to maximize its expansion and crispness. Prebaked puff pastry crusts, such as this one, are often weighted while they bake. To get the most control and the flakiest crust, depress the dough by hand. Glazing the crust each time it is pressed makes for a more complex taste and texture.

Making the syrup.
Combine the lavender, sugar, honey, and ½ cup water in a saucepan. Bring to a boil, then reduce the heat to medium-low and simmer gently until the syrup thickens slightly, about 10 minutes. Set the syrup aside.

Baking the crust.
On a floured surface, roll the puff pastry into a circle between ⅛ and ¼ inch thick (a rectangle will also work). Transfer the crust to a parchment-lined baking sheet and chill for at least 30 minutes.

Preheat the oven to 400°F.

Bake the crust (it is not necessary to weight it) until it begins to puff, about 7 minutes. Gently push it down with a spatula, brush with half the cream, and sprinkle with half the sugar. Bake the crust until it puffs again, about 7 minutes more, then push it down again. Brush it with the remaining cream and sprinkle with the remaining sugar. Bake until it is lightly browned, about 5 minutes more. Reduce the heat to 350°F and bake until the crust is well browned, 5 to 10 minutes longer. Remove the crust from the oven and allow it to cool slightly, then transfer to a rack and cool completely.

Finishing the tart.
Add the blueberries to the lavender syrup and heat over medium heat until they warm and soften, but not so long that they burst, about 2 minutes. Lift the berries out of the syrup with a slotted spoon and place them in a bowl.

Bring the syrup to a boil and reduce it until it is thick, about 5 minutes. Spoon the blueberries onto the crust. Strain the syrup over the berries, then dust the tart with the confectioners' sugar.

This tart could be made with raspberries, blackberries, strawberries, peaches, or apricots, adjusting cooking time as needed. The poaching syrup of sugar, honey, and water can be infused as it is here with dried flowers, or with tea, spices, or herbs. For a simpler fruit taste, poach the fruit in the syrup without adding flavor. Serve with vanilla ice cream or Crème Fraîche (page 204).

desserts

193

verbena madeleines

This batter can also be baked in small tea cake molds. The baking time will vary depending on the size of the molds. Both verbena madeleines and tea cakes are wonderful served warm, while the herbal aroma is still strong.

12 tablespoons (1½ sticks) butter
2 tablespoons crumbled dried lemon verbena
1 cup sliced almonds
1¾ cups confectioners' sugar
½ cup all-purpose flour
6 egg whites
1 tablespoon honey

Lemon verbena, thought by some to promote digestion, is the only member of the large Verbenaceae family used as a culinary herb. I was first drawn to this nonflowering plant by its intoxicating aroma.

Preheat the oven to 325°F. Butter and flour a madeleine pan.

Melt the butter in a small saucepan over medium heat. When the foam subsides, add the verbena and continue cooking until the butter begins to brown, about 2 minutes more. Remove the butter from the heat and set it aside to steep for 15 minutes, then strain through a fine sieve.

Coarsely grind the almonds in a food processor. Add 2 tablespoons of the confectioners' sugar and continue processing until the almonds are finely ground. Transfer to a bowl and add the remaining sugar and flour.

Whisk the egg whites in the bowl of an electric mixer until they are very frothy. With the mixer on low, add the dry ingredients, then the infused butter, and then the honey, mixing just until the batter is smooth.

Working in batches, fill each mold about three-fourths full and bake until the madeleines are golden brown, about 20 minutes. Serve warm or at room temperature.

florentine cookies

Pâte Sucrée (page 204)
1½ cups Crème Fraîche (page 204)
1¾ cups sugar
¼ cup honey
2 cups sliced almonds

These are my favorite cookies. They are topped with a caramel made from a combination of sugar and honey. This is a little less tricky than sugar-only caramel, as the honey prevents the sugar from crystallizing. It is nevertheless important to use a candy thermometer to check whether the sugar is properly cooked. Florentine cookies are often dipped in melted chocolate, but I like them plain.

Baking the crust.
Preheat the oven to 350°F. Line an 8- by 12-inch baking pan with 2- to 3-inch sides with parchment, leaving an overhang of several inches at either end.

On a floured surface, roll out the dough to a 12- by 16-inch rectangle. Fit the dough into the pan (don't worry about the tidiness of the edges—they are trimmed after baking). Save any scraps to patch the crust.

Bake the crust until the edges begin to brown, about 20 minutes. If there are any cracks in the crust, patch them with the reserved dough scraps.

Making the caramel filling.
While the crust is baking, combine the crème fraîche, sugar, and honey in a large deep pot (this mixture has a tendency to boil over). Attach a candy thermometer to the side of the pan. Heat over medium-high heat, stirring, until the sugar dissolves. Stop stirring, reduce the heat to medium, and allow the caramel to simmer until it is honey-brown and reaches a temperature of 240°F. Remove the caramel from the heat and add the almonds, then spoon the mixture evenly into the warm crust.

Finishing the cookies.
Place the baking pan on a larger baking sheet (in case of spills) and return it to the oven. Bake until the topping is darker and bubbly, 20 to 30 minutes. Turn off the oven and allow the filling to settle for about 10 minutes, then remove the pan from the oven. Let cool until the caramel is set but still warm, about 1 hour.

Use the parchment to lift the florentines out of the pan. Trim away and discard the pastry edges, then cut the florentines into 24 bars. Allow to cool completely before serving.

Heating sugar moves it from a granular solid to a liquid and then, through evaporation, to stages of solidity that range from syrupy to very hard. In this recipe, the sugar should be cooked to the "soft ball" stage (234° to 240°F), which in everyday language means the caramel will be solid but chewy when fully cooled.

All caramel can be difficult in the summer because heat and humidity prevent proper cooling. Storage can be a particular problem. If you do bake on a hot day, be sure to store the cookies in an airtight container between sheets of parchment paper. Add a desiccant (available in photo shops) to absorb moisture.

apple upside-down cake

The cake is also subject to variation: It is good plain, without the fruit topping (bake it in a 9-inch pan).

FOR THE APPLES

½ cup sugar
1 tablespoon fresh lemon juice
4 tablespoons butter
5 Granny Smith apples

FOR THE CAKE

½ cup sliced almonds
¾ cup sugar
1½ cups all-purpose flour
2 teaspoons baking powder
1 teaspoon kosher salt
8 tablespoons (1 stick) butter,
  softened
2 eggs
2 teaspoons vanilla extract
1 cup Crème Fraîche (page 204)

This recipe is a springboard for a range of other dessert possibilities. The same caramel can be used to poach pears, peaches, figs, or pineapple.

Making the caramel.
Combine the sugar, lemon juice, and ¼ cup water in a saucepan and heat over medium heat, stirring until the sugar is dissolved. Simmer, without stirring, until the syrup turns dark amber, about 15 minutes. Add the butter and swirl to melt it, then transfer the caramel to a medium skillet.

Caramelizing the apples.
Peel and core the apples. Cut each into 8 wedges and add them to the caramel. Add another ¼ cup water, bring the caramel to a gentle simmer over medium-low heat, and cook the apples until they are very tender, about 20 minutes. Remove from the heat.

Remove the apples from the caramel with a slotted spoon and arrange them in concentric circles in a 10-inch springform pan so they completely cover the bottom. Pour the remaining caramel over the apples.

Making the cake.
Preheat the oven to 350°F.

Pulse the almonds in a food processor until they are coarsely ground, then add ¼ cup of the sugar and continue pulsing until the mixture is finely ground. Combine the ground almonds with the flour, baking powder, and salt in a medium bowl.

Cream the butter with the remaining ½ cup sugar in the bowl of an electric mixer. Mix in the eggs one at a time, then add the vanilla extract. With the mixer on low, add one-third of the flour mixture, then one-third of the crème fraîche. Repeat until all the ingredients have been combined.

Spoon the batter over the apples and bake until the top of the cake springs back when lightly pressed and a toothpick inserted in the center comes out clean, about 40 minutes. Remove the cake from the oven, invert it onto a cake rack, remove the sides and bottom of the pan, and cool. Cut into wedges and serve.

the anatomy of a dish

chocolate pots de crème

1 cup milk
6 ounces hazelnut, bittersweet,
   or milk chocolate, chopped
6 egg yolks
¾ cup sugar
1½ cups heavy cream

The rich, smooth hazelnut (gianduja) chocolate is my preference in this recipe, but you can substitute any type of chocolate you favor. Whatever chocolate you use, take care never to let it overheat. The delicate balance chocolate strikes between fat, moisture, and sugar makes it subject to seizing, clumping, and scorching, so work carefully and over low heat.

Preheat the oven to 300°F.

Bring the milk to a simmer in a small saucepan over low heat. Add the chocolate and whisk it until it melts. Remove the pan from the heat.

Using a balloon whisk, beat the yolks with the sugar in a large bowl until they are pale, about 3 minutes. Gently stir in the chocolate mixture, then the cream (you want the custard to be smooth, not foamy, so stir only enough to combine the ingredients). Strain the custard through a fine sieve, then pour it into eight 4-ounce ramekins.

Place the ramekins in a large baking pan; fill the pan with hot water to come halfway up the sides of the ramekins. Cover with aluminum foil. Bake until the custard is just set (it should still have a little jiggle), about 1 hour and 15 minutes. Remove from the water bath and cool, then chill before serving.

VARIATION

earl grey tea pots de crème

Steep 1 tablespoon Earl Grey tea and 1 teaspoon orange flower water in the milk. Add the bittersweet chocolate. Strain the mixture, then add the eggs and cream and proceed as directed.

Chocolate is extracted from the beans of the cacao plant, a member of the Sterculiaceae family. The beans, which grow in pods, are harvested, fermented, dried, roasted, cracked, and ground. The ground beans, called chocolate liquor, are then mixed in a delicate series of steps with varying amounts of sugar, and sometimes milk and flavorings such as vanilla, to create different kinds of chocolate.

cinnamon toast with grapefruit

SERVES 4

To transform this traditional brunch dish into a dessert, make the toast with a sweet bread such as brioche and serve it with ice cream and perhaps raspberry puree (see page 187) or caramel sauce (see page 196).

2 tablespoons sugar
1 tablespoon ground cinnamon
½ teaspoon freshly grated nutmeg
8 tablespoons (1 stick) butter, melted
6 thick slices (about ¾ inch thick) white bread
2 grapefruit, peeled, pith removed, and separated into segments

Like many people, I grew up eating cinnamon toast. This is a grown-up version.

Preheat the oven to 400°F.

Combine the sugar, cinnamon, and nutmeg on a plate or in a shallow bowl. Pour the melted butter into another shallow bowl. Dip the bread slices in the butter, then coat them on both sides with the sugar and spice mix and arrange in a single layer on a baking sheet. Reserve the remaining spice mixture.

Bake the bread until the first side begins to crisp, about 20 minutes, then flip and bake for about 10 minutes longer. Remove the bread from the oven and preheat the broiler.

Place the grapefruit segments in a small baking dish, sprinkle with the reserved spice mixture, and broil just until they are warmed through, about 3 minutes.

To serve, cut each slice of bread into 4 strips. Arrange 6 strips of cinnamon toast and 3 or 4 grapefruit segments on each plate and serve.

lemon custard tart

FOR THE CRUST

12 tablespoons (1½ sticks)
  unsalted butter, softened
3 cups crushed graham crackers
1 cup all-purpose flour

FOR THE CUSTARD

3 tablespoons all-purpose flour
¾ teaspoon baking powder
3 eggs, lightly beaten
1½ cups sugar
6 tablespoons fresh lemon juice
2 tablespoons confectioners' sugar
  (optional)

This is a basic lemon tart recipe. It is lighter and simpler than a lemon curd tart because the custard contains no butter. There is a nice contrast between the slightly chewy golden surface and the creamy-gooey inside. A dusting of confectioners' sugar gives the tart a more finished appearance.

Making the crust.
Combine the butter, graham cracker crumbs, and flour in a large bowl and beat until creamy. Press the dough into an 11-inch tart pan with a removable bottom and chill for at least 30 minutes.

Preheat the oven to 375°F.

Trim the edges of the crust (save any scraps for use as patches if necessary) and bake until well browned, about 20 minutes. Remove the crust from the oven and lower the temperature to 325°F.

Making the custard.
Combine the flour and baking powder. Beat the eggs with the sugar in a mixer until pale. Remove the bowl from the mixer, add the lemon juice and flour mixture, and stir gently, just to combine (the mixture should be thick and smooth, not frothy). Skim off any surface foam, then pour the custard into the prepared crust.

Bake the tart until the filling is set and the top is lightly browned, about 30 minutes. Remove the tart from the oven and cool completely. Sprinkle with the confectioners' sugar, if desired, and serve.

Graham crackers are essentially sweet biscuits made with graham flour—a whole wheat flour that contains ground bran flakes. (Graham flour is named for Sylvester Graham, a nineteenth-century reformer who implored his followers to forsake their unhealthy habits and embrace whole-grain cooking and eating.)

I serve this tart with fresh fruit. I also sometimes bake fruit into the custard. Add about 1½ cups berries, but be aware that the juice will make for a slightly runnier filling.

verbena crème brûlée

This custard, my signature dessert, is served topped with Lace Cookies (page 201). I like the flavor and texture better than the traditional burnt sugar crust.

3 cups heavy cream
1 cup milk
1 vanilla bean, split
¼ cup dried lemon verbena
  (or 2 tea bags verbena tea)
½ cup sugar
8 egg yolks

When you are making crème brûlée or other custards, it is important to mix the eggs and cream together first with a whisk, then switch to a wooden spoon. Continued whisking can cause a layer of foam to develop that can mask thickening below the surface.

Combine the cream and milk in a saucepan. Scrape the seeds from the vanilla bean into the mixture and add the bean. Add the verbena and ¼ cup of the sugar and bring just to a simmer over medium heat. Remove the pan from the heat and set aside to steep for 1 hour.

Strain the cream mixture, then reheat in a large saucepan until it is warm but not hot.

Preheat the oven to 325°F.

Beat the egg yolks with the remaining ¼ cup sugar in a medium bowl until the mixture is pale. Very gradually whisk the warm cream into the yolks, then return the mixture to the saucepan. Mixing constantly, first with a whisk and then with a wooden spoon, cook the custard over low heat until it begins to thicken (the spoon will begin to leave a trail in the custard in the bottom of the pan as it is stirred), 5 to 10 minutes. Strain the custard through a fine sieve into a bowl and set over ice.

Divide the custard among six 4-ounce ramekins. Place the ramekins in a large baking pan and fill the pan with enough hot water to come halfway up the sides of the ramekins. Cover with aluminum foil and bake until the custard is just set (it should still have a little jiggle), about 1 hour. Remove from the water bath and cool to room temperature. Chill before serving.

lace cookies

½ pound (2 sticks) butter
1 cup sugar
¼ cup all-purpose flour
¼ cup heavy cream
½ teaspoon vanilla extract
¾ cup sliced almonds

A little advice: Don't be too eager to remove the cookies from the baking sheet. There is a particular point at which the cookies are malleable enough to mold but not so soft they will fall apart. The amount of time it takes to get to this point depends entirely on the temperature and the humidity. Like the Florentine Cookies (page 195), these cookies pose special problems on humid days. Work in as cool an area as possible, then store the cookies in an airtight container, separated by layers of parchment, with a desiccant if available.

Preheat the oven to 400°F. Butter two nonstick baking sheets, or, better yet, line them with nonstick pads.

Heat the butter with the sugar in a medium saucepan over medium heat, stirring occasionally until the butter melts and the sugar dissolves. Remove the pan from the heat. Whisk in the flour, then the cream and vanilla, then the almonds. Set the batter aside to cool until it solidifies slightly.

Working in small batches, drop teaspoonfuls of the batter onto one of the prepared baking sheets. Take care to allow at least 3 inches around each cookie so it can spread (you can bake 6 to 8 at a time on a standard baking sheet). Bake the cookies until they are well browned, about 7 minutes. Remove the pan from the oven and allow the cookies to cool until they are slightly firm, about 3 minutes. At this point, they can be cut into a neat shape with a cookie cutter, molded (see the sidebar), or simply transferred to a rack to cool completely.

To make tuiles, the classic French molded cookies, allow the cookies to cool enough so they can be picked up without ill effect, then lift each one from the baking sheet and drape over a rolling pin to finish cooling. The cookies can also be draped over small bowls to form cups. If the cookies get too stiff to mold, simply return them to the oven until they become pliable again.

I cut these cookies to fit the tops of Verbena Crème Brûlée (page 200). Molded, they make fancy berry bowls, and they are quite lovely as is, with a cup of tea.

frozen mocha roulade

FOR THE CAKE

6 eggs separated
¾ cup plus 3 tablespoons sugar
1 teaspoon vanilla extract
2 tablespoons brewed coffee
½ cup cocoa powder plus
   additional for dusting, sifted
¼ teaspoon cream of tartar

FOR THE FILLING AND GARNISH

1 cup sugar
2 tablespoons coffee liqueur, such
   as Kahlúa
2 tablespoons confectioners' sugar
2 pints coffee ice cream
2 tablespoons cocoa powder

If you are careful not to overbeat the cake, it will be wonderfully light and airy. Because this dessert is frozen, it should be made a day ahead.

Making the cake.
Preheat the oven to 325°F. Butter a 13- by 18-inch jelly roll pan or rimmed baking sheet, then line the pan with parchment.

Whisk the egg yolks in a mixer at medium speed. Gradually add the ¾ cup sugar. Reduce the speed to low and add the vanilla, coffee, and cocoa; mix until just combined. Transfer the mixture to a large bowl.

Whip the egg whites at low speed until frothy, then increase the speed to high and add the 3 tablespoons sugar and the cream of tartar. Beat the whites until they hold soft peaks.

Fold the egg whites into the yolk mixture a third at a time. Pour the batter into the prepared pan and spread evenly with an offset spatula or knife. Gently tap the pan on the table so the batter settles. Bake until the cake is springy and beginning to pull away from the sides of the pan, about 20 minutes. Remove from the oven and let cool slightly.

Making the filling.
While the cake is baking, combine the 1 cup sugar with 1 cup water in a small saucepan and bring to a boil over high heat. Once the sugar dissolves, reduce the heat to low and simmer for 5 minutes. Add the liqueur, bring to a boil, remove from the heat, and set aside to cool.

Rolling the cake.
Spread a clean dishtowel on a large work surface. Sprinkle it with the confectioners' sugar. Turn the cake out onto the towel. Peel away the parchment

paper (brush the paper with a little hot water if it sticks). Starting with either of the cake's long edges, and using the towel to help, roll the cake into a tight cylinder. Place the cake (now wrapped in the towel) seam side down on the baking pan and set aside to cool for 10 minutes.

Filling and finishing the cake.
Unroll the cake, leaving a slight curl at one end. Refrigerate for at least 15 minutes.

Allow the coffee ice cream to defrost enough so it is soft but not liquid, then spread an even ½-inch-thick layer over the cake. Starting with the curled edge, tightly reroll the cake. Transfer the cake to the baking pan. Wrap it in plastic wrap and freeze for at least 12 hours before serving.

To serve, slice the roulade using a warm knife. Dust each slice with cocoa powder, and top with sweetened whipped cream, if desired.

VARIATION

mocha-glazed frozen roulade

This cake is also good with a mocha glaze. Combine ½ cup heavy cream and 1 tablespoon corn syrup in a small saucepan and bring to a simmer over medium heat. Whisk in 5 ounces chopped bittersweet chocolate and cook just until the chocolate melts. Strain the glaze through a fine sieve and stir in 1 tablespoon coffee liqueur.

Omit the dusting of cocoa powder. Place the frozen roulade on a wire cake rack set over a sheet pan. Pour the tepid glaze evenly over the cake, then smooth it with an offset spatula or knife. (The top and sides will be glazed, but not the bottom.) Allow the glaze to harden for a few minutes before slicing to serve.

pâte sucrée

MAKES ENOUGH
FOR ONE 11-INCH
TART SHELL

2½ cups all-purpose flour
¼ cup sugar
Pinch of kosher salt
8 tablespoons (1 stick) butter,
  diced and chilled
1 egg yolk
¼ cup heavy cream

This sweet flaky pie crust is used to make the Brown-Butter Apricot Tart (page 192) and Florentine Cookies (page 195).

Combine the flour, sugar, and salt in a large bowl. Cut the butter into the flour mixture until it resembles coarse crumbs. Combine the egg yolk and cream and mix well. Add the yolk mixture to the flour mixture and mix until smooth. Form the dough into a ball, flatten into a disk, wrap in plastic, and chill until ready to use. (The dough can be made up to 2 days in advance.)

---

crème fraîche

MAKES
5 CUPS

4 cups heavy cream
1 cup buttermilk

Crème fraîche is easy to make at home, and it can be used in so many ways that I always have some on hand. In addition to serving it plain, I whip it with confectioners' sugar for a dessert topping and blend it with herbs or herb oils for a savory sauce.

Combine the cream and buttermilk in a bowl and mix well. Cover the bowl with a dish towel and set aside at room temperature overnight.

Cover and refrigerate the crème fraîche until ready to use. It will keep in the refrigerator for at least 2 weeks.

the anatomy of a dish

finding its family

When I started learning the relationship between fruits and vegetables through botanical reference, understanding their family groups taught me more about each food's characteristics. It's like learning a new language. This alphabetical chart of fruits and vegetables indicates the family, the Latin name, and, where a number of plants belong to a single species, the group name of each.

Note: Herbs and spices can be found on page 111.

INGREDIENT	FAMILY	GENUS AND SPECIES
ALMOND	Rosaceae	*Prunus dulcis*
AMARANTH	Amaranthaceae	*Amaranthus* spp.
APPLE	Rosaceae	*Malus* spp.
APRICOT	Rosaceae	*Prunus armeniaca*
ARTICHOKE	Compositae	*Cynara scolymus*
ARUGULA	Cruciferae	*Eruca vesicaria*
ASPARAGUS	Liliaceae	*Asparagus officinalis*
AVOCADO	Lauraceae	*Persea americana*
BARLEY	Gramineae	*Hordeum vulgare*
BEET	Chenopodiaceae	*Beta vulgaris* (Crassa)
BLACKBERRY	Rosaceae	*Rubus* spp.
BLUEBERRY/BILBERRY	Ericaceae	*Vaccinium* spp.
BROAD BEAN/FAVA	Leguminosae	*Vicia faba*
BROCCOLI	Cruciferae	*Brassica oleracea* (Italica)
BROCCOLI RABE	Cruciferae	*Brassica rapa* (Ruvo)
BRUSSELS SPROUT	Cruciferae	*Brassica oleracea* (Gemmifera)
BUCKWHEAT	Polygonaceae	*Polygonum fagopyrum*
BUTTERNUT SQUASH	Cucurbitaceae	*Cucurbita moschata*
CABBAGE	Cruciferae	*Brassica oleracea* (Capitata)
CAPE GOOSEBERRY	Solanaceae	*Physalis peruviana*
CARROT	Umbelliferae	*Daucus carota sativa*
CAULIFLOWER	Cruciferae	*Brassica oleracea* (Botrytis)
CELERY	Umbelliferae	*Apium graveolens* var. dulce

INGREDIENT	FAMILY	GENUS AND SPECIES
CELERY ROOT	Umbelliferae	*Apium graveolens* var. rapaceum
CHANTERELLE	Cantharellaceae	*Cantharellus cibarius*
CHERRY	Rosaceae	*Prunus* spp.
CHICKPEA	Leguminosae	*Cicer arietinum*
CHICORY	Compositae	*Cichorium intybus* (Foliosum)
CHILE PEPPER	Solanaceae	*Capsicum annuum* (Longum)
CHIVE	Liliaceae	*Allium schoenoprasum*
COLLARDS	Cruciferae	*Brassica oleracea* (Acephala)
CORN	Gramineae	*Zea mays*
CRANBERRY	Ericaceae	*Vaccinium macrocarpon*
CUCUMBER	Cucurbitaceae	*Cucumis sativus*
DANDELION	Compositae	*Taraxacum officinale*
EGGPLANT	Solanaceae	*Solanum melongena*
ENDIVE	Compositae	*Cichorium endivia*
ESCAROLE	Compositae	*Cichorium endivia* var. latifolia
FENNEL	Umbelliferae	*Foeniculum vulgare* spp.
FRENCH/KIDNEY/SNAP BEAN	Leguminosae	*Phaseolus vulgaris*
GARDEN CRESS	Cruciferae	*Lapidium sativum*
GARLIC	Liliaceae	*Allium sativum*
GRAPE	Vitaceae	*Vitis* spp.
GRAPEFRUIT	Rutaceae	*Citrus × paradisi*
HAZELNUT	Betulaceae	*Corylus* spp.
HORSERADISH	Cruciferae	*Armoracia rusticana*
JERUSALEM ARTICHOKE	*see* SUNCHOKE	
JICAMA	Leguminosae	*Pachyrhizus erosus*
KALE	Cruciferae	*Brassica oleracea* (Acephala)
KUMQUAT	Rutaceae	*Fortunella* spp.
LAMB'S LETTUCE/MÂCHE	Valerianaceae	*Valerianella locusta*
LEEK	Liliaceae	*Allium ampeloprasum* (Porrum)
LEMON	Rutaceae	*Citrus limon*
LENTIL	Leguminosae	*Lens culinaris*

INGREDIENT	FAMILY	GENUS AND SPECIES
LETTUCE	Compositae	*Lactuca sativa*
LIMA BEAN	Leguminosae	*Phaseolus lunatus*
LIME	Rutaceae	*Citrus aurantiifolia*
MELON	Cucurbitaceae	*Cucumis melo*
MILLET	Gramineae	*Panicum miliaceum*
MOREL	Morchellaceae	*Morchella* spp.
MUSHROOM (BUTTON)	Agaricaceae	*Agaricus bisporus*
NECTARINE	Rosaceae	*Prunus persica* var. *nucipersica*
OAT	Gramineae	*Avena sativa*
OLIVE	Oleaceae	*Olea europaea*
ONION	Liliaceae	*Allium cepa*
ORANGE	Rutaceae	*Citrus* spp.
PARSNIP	Umbelliferae	*Pastinaca sativa*
PEA	Leguminosae	*Pisum sativum*
PEACH	Rosaceae	*Prunus persica*
PEAR	Rosaceae	*Pyrus communis*
PINEAPPLE	Bromeliaceae	*Ananas comosus*
PINE NUT	Pinaceae	*Pinus* spp.
PISTACHIO	Anacardiaceae	*Pistacia vera*
PLEUROTTE/OYSTER	Tricholomataceae	*Pleurotus* spp.
PLUM	Rosaceae	*Prunus* spp.
PORCINI/BOLETUS/CÈPE	Boletaceae	*Boletus* spp.
POTATO	Solanaceae	*Solanum tuberosum*
PUMPKIN	Cucurbitaceae	*Cucurbita pepo*
PURSLANE	Portulacaceae	*Portulaca oleracea*
QUINCE	Rosaceae	*Cydonia oblonga*
QUINOA	Chenopodiaceae	*Chenopodium quinoa*
RADICCHIO	Compositae	*Cichorium intybus*
RADISH	Cruciferae	*Raphanus sativus*
RASPBERRY	Rosaceae	*Rubus* spp.
RHUBARB	Polygonaceae	*Rheum* × *culturum*

INGREDIENT	FAMILY	GENUS AND SPECIES
RICE	Gramineae	*Orzya Sativa*
RUTABAGA	Cruciferae	*Brassica napus* (Napobrassica)
RYE	Gramineae	*Secale cereale*
SALSIFY	Compositae	*Tragopogon porrifolius*
SCALLION	Liliaceae	*Allium fistulosum*
SCORZONERA (BLACK SALSIFY)	Compositae	*Scorzonera hispanica*
SESAME	Pedaliaceae	*Sesamum indicum*
SHALLOT	Liliaceae	*Allium cepa ascalonicum* (Aggregatum)
SHIITAKE	Polyporaceae	*Lentinus edodes*
SORREL	Polygonaceae	*Rumex* spp.
SPINACH	Chenopodiaceae	*Spinacia oleracea*
STRAWBERRY	Rosaceae	*Fragaria* spp.
SUNCHOKE	Compositae	*Helianthus tuberosus*
SUNFLOWER SEED	Compositae	*Helianthus annuus* spp.
SWEET POTATO	Convolvulaceae	*Ipomoea batatas*
SWISS CHARD	Chenopodiaceae	*Beta vulgaris* (Cicla)
TOMATILLO	Solanaceae	*Physalis ixocarpa*
TOMATO	Solanaceae	*Lycopersicon esculentum*
TURNIP	Cruciferae	*Brassica rapa* (Rapifera)
WALNUT	Juglandaceae	*Juglans* spp.
WATERCRESS	Cruciferae	*Nasturtium officinale*
WATERMELON	Cucurbitaceae	*Citrullus lanatus*
WHEAT	Gramineae	*Triticum* spp.
WILD RICE	Gramineae	*Zizania aquatica*
ZUCCHINI	Cucurbitaceae	*Cucurbita pepo melopepo*

finding its family

definitions

Plant Anatomy

STALK The above-ground portion of a plant that connects the leaves with the roots. Shoots are new stalk and leaf formations that grow from stalks.

LEAF The organ of photosynthesis that produces the high-energy food or sugars in a plant.

BULB An extension of a stem or stems enclosed in overlapping leaves. Edible bulbs include onions.

FRUIT The organ from a flower's ovary containing the seeds, characteristic of angiosperms. There are four distinct types of fruit: dry fruits, such as legumes, grains, and nuts; fleshy fruits, such as berries, grapes, and tomatoes; multiple fruits, such as pineapple (the eyes are all individual fruits); and accessory fruits, such as apples and pears.

SEED Contained in fruits of plants, seeds produce new plants once released from the fruit. Each seed contains three components: the germ, or embryo; the endosperm (stored food that the embryo consumes during early development); and the protective seed coat.

FLOWER The reproductive organ that produces the seed.

ROOT An organ that anchors the plant, absorbs and conducts moisture and nutrients, and stores food supplies. A taproot is a tapered primary root of a plant that reaches far into the soil for water and nutrients and stores them. Edible taproots include carrots, beets, and radishes.

TUBER An underground root that stores nutrients and water. Potatoes and sunchokes are edible tubers; the potato "eyes" are plant buds.

bibliography

Brezel, Kathleen, ed. *Sunset National Garden Book*. Menlo Park, CA: Sunset Books, Inc., 1997.

Brickell, Christopher, and Judith Zuk, eds. *The American Horticultural Society A–Z Encyclopedia of Garden Plants*. New York: D. K. Publishing, 1997.

Cronquist, Arthur. *Basic Botany*. New York: Harper & Row, 1961.

Fortin, François, ed. *The Visual Food Encyclopedia*. New York: Macmillan, 1996.

Glimn-Lacy, Janice, and Pete Kaufman. *Botany Illustrated: Introduction to Plants' Major Groups*. New York: Van Nostrand Reinhold Company, 1984.

Griffiths, Mark, ed. *The New Royal Horticultural Society Dictionary of Gardening*. New York: The Stockton Press, 1992.

L. H. Bailey Hortorium. *Hortus Third: A Concise Dictionary of Plants Cultivated in the United States and Canada*. New York: Barnes & Noble Books, 1976.

Margulis, Lynn, and Karlene Schwartz. *Five Kingdoms: An Illustrated Guide to the Phyla of Life on Earth*. New York: W. H. Freeman and Co., 2001.

McGee, Harold. *On Food and Cooking*. New York: Charles Scribner's Sons, 1984.

Merill, Richard, and Joe Ortiz. *The Gardener's Table*. Berkeley: Ten Speed Press, 2000.

Root, Waverly. *Food*. New York: Simon & Schuster, 1980.

acknowledgments

I want to express my gratitude to those who have been influential in both my career and my personal life. To be able to share my experience as a chef by writing a book is a great honor.

I feel fortunate to have had a strong kitchen staff at Verbena. Many have worked hard since our opening in 1994, distinguishing Verbena with a life force of strong, spirited people. It is partially because of their long hours and dedication to their craft that I have been able to attain my goals, one of which is to write a cookbook. Amanda Freitag, who has worked with me as executive sous-chef for many years, has helped me to carry through many of these recipes with her dedicated support and companionship. Amy Topel, who has worn many hats here—as sous-chef, kitchen manager, and publicist—has been an invaluable assistant who has made it possible for me to follow through on projects by keeping me organized with her insightful input and motivation. Many thanks to Meredith Kurtzman, Michelle Masiello, Amy Wilkins, Stacey Meyer, Tom Guttow, and Katsuya Fukushima, who are only some of the senior staff that have passed through the restaurant and contributed their time and their talents to Verbena's kitchen. Aaron von Rock, my sommelier, contributed his wine suggestions for food pairings not only in this book but at Verbena and Bar Demi, our wine bar. I am grateful to all the farmers of the Union Square Farmers' Market for bringing an awareness of the seasons to the public and supplying the restaurant with new ingredients to experiment with. Dean Riddle, Verbena's first plantsman, developed the restaurant's first garden and taught me the basic language of botany.

Although I have worked with many great chefs, it is Michel Fitoussi, of the Palace Restaurant in New York, whom I must thank. My first chef-mentor, he dared me to become a chef and gave me a chance to prove myself.

Without the initial belief in this book at its conceptual phase, it would never have come to fruition. I thank first my book agent, Liv Blumer, who believed in the idea from the beginning. Her guidance has been extremely valuable and helped lead me in the right direction. I thank Ann Bramson, Artisan's publisher, for respecting the creation of a book and actually making it happen. Thanks to Deborah Weiss Geline for organizing the different parts and stages of the book and seeing it to its completion. Thanks also to Judith Sutton and Judit Bodnar for excellent copyediting, Barbara Sturman for typesetting, Nancy Murray for production expertise, and Burgin Streetman and Amy Corely for publicity. Stephen Doyle, with Rosemarie Turk and Ariel Apte, wrapped his beautiful design around the words in the book. Victor Schrager composed sculptural still-life photographs.

Thank you to Larry Castoro, a very special friend who helped us with our recipe testing and whose knowledge of plants came in very handy. I am especially grateful to Cathy Young, not only co-writer but a friend, who tested and retested the recipes as well as reviewed the material with her great attention to detail. She became my interpreter, gathering my thoughts and putting them into writing. She has done an amazing job.

I thank my family, who has always loved to eat and has been extremely supportive. I thank my mother, who is an inspiring cook in her own right, always creating new ideas in the kitchen and sharing her ideas with me since a young age, instilling me with a confidence around food. My father has been a guiding force, continually encouraging me to do what I enjoy, to be my own boss, and helping me attain my dreams. My brother

Bryan has always been a willing participant as taster and an objective listener. I thank my brother Glenn for his great ability to envision space and to conceptualize ideas. He not only helped build and design Verbena with his partner, Natalie, but also assisted in this book, deciphering the graphs and charts and helping me put things into the right words.

Finally, my husband, Michael, who has patiently been at my side during this process. He has joined me not only as my partner in the restaurant but as my partner in life. His kindness and caring are immeasurable. Michael, I thank you dearly for being there. And thank you to our baby daughter, Olivia, for joining us in such a timely fashion as to be able to celebrate the book together as a family.

—*Diane Forley*

I join Diane in thanking all those who made this book possible. I would also like to thank Diane for inviting me to work with her on this project. My agent, Marion Young, husband, Jim Chudy, and daughter, Charlotte, also deserve my applause for their endless support and willingness to eat roasted turkey during a June heat wave.

—*Catherine Young*

212

acknowledgments

index

Page numbers in italics refer to charts and tables.

Worcestershire, seared
 sirloin with, 168
Worcestershire sauce, 49
see also specific
 mushrooms
mussels, 132
 in curried broth with
  coconut jasmine rice,
  135
 purging of, 135
 selection of, 131
mustard, *20, 111*
 honey sauce, 162
 -lemon vinaigrette, 72
mustard greens, *67*

N

naan, 124
nage, lemon, sea bass in, 152
nectarine, *24, 190, 207*
 and meringue tartlets,
  caramelized, 188–89
nightshade family, *see*
 Solanaceae
nutmeg, *111*

O

oak of Jerusalem, *20*
oats, *99, 207*
octopus, braised, 136
Oleaceae, *207*
olive, *207*
olive oil, 60
olive(s), black:
 in layered bread and tomato
  salad with tapenade
  vinaigrette, 65
 pasta, 102
onion(s), *17, 21, 133, 207*
 cooking, *23*
 pan gravy, sautéed scallops
  with, 140
 puree, smoked, 50
orange blossom, *21*
orange(s), *25, 191, 207*
 family of, *17, 21*
 pickled beet salad with
  Taleggio cheese and, 71
 reduction, roasted, butternut
  squash ravioli with,
  100–101

order, defined, *19*
oregano, *17*
oxalic acid, 186
oyster plant, *see* salsify
oyster (pleurotte)
  mushrooms, 97, *177,
  207*
 sautéed, 48
oyster(s), 132
 stew, 137

P

pancakes, *see* griddle cakes
panfried soft-shell crabs with
  jicama slaw, 141
pan-roasted duck breast with
  pineapple chutney, 178
pans, for baking popovers,
  118
pantry cook, 59
paprika, *111*
 sauce, mackerel with, 153
parfait, raspberry, 187
Parkerhouse rolls, 125
Parmesan (Parmigiano
  Reggiano):
 in asparagus crepes, 110
 broth with sautéed greens,
  82
 in corn bread, 122
 in kale pesto, 44
 in rolled soufflé, 108
parsley, *16, 22, 84, 111*
parsley root, *16*
parsnip, *16, 23, 84, 207*
 and potato galette, 51
 puree, 51
 in roasted winter vegetable
  stew, 91
parts of the plant and when we
  eat them, *22–25*
pasta(s), 15, 94, 100–103
 butternut squash ravioli with
  orange reduction,
  100–101
 couscous with artichokes
  and gigante beans, 89
 dough, semolina, 102
 farfalle and cauliflower with
  bread crumbs, 103
 flavorful broth for cooking
  of, 89

flavoring of, 102
 as food category, 93
 spaetzle, cabbage and lentil
  stew with, 88–89
 sunchoke ravioli with kale
  pesto, 105
 toasted angel hair, in
  shiitake broth, 97
pastries, savory, 15, 107–13
 asparagus crepes, 110
 braised greens tart, 112
 mushroom torte, 113
 rolled soufflé, 108
 wild rice "soufflé," 109
pastry flour, *121*
pâte sucrée, 204
peach, *16, 24, 190, 207*
peanut, *17*
pear, *16, 24, 190, 207*
pea(s), 9, *23, 25, 98, 207*
peas, split, with sausage, 37
pea, sweet
 family of, *17, 20*
 soup with mint, 86
pecan vinaigrette, carpaccio
  of quince with endive
  salad and, 70
pectin, 70
Pedaliaceae, *208*
pepper, hot, *see* chile
  (pepper)
pepper(corn), black, 77, *111*
 in puttanesca vinaigrette,
  56
peppercress salad with
  yellow pepper
  vinaigrette, 64
peppers, sweet (bell), *17, 24,
  75*
 flame-roasted, 52
 puree, 80
 yellow, vinaigrette,
  peppercress salad with,
  64
pesto:
 grilled vegetable, 44
 kale, 44
 kale, sunchoke ravioli with,
  105
petunia, *13, 21*